KV-510-062

European Accounting

John Blake

Professor of Accounting, University of Central Lancashire

Oriol Amat

Professor of Accounting, Pompea Fabra University, Barcelona

PITMAN
PUBLISHING

PITMAN PUBLISHING
128 Long Acre, London WC2E 9AN

A Division of Longman Group UK Limited

© Longman Group UK Limited 1993

First published in Great Britain 1993

ISBN 0 273 60113 X

British Library Cataloguing in Publication Data
A catalogue record for this book is available from the British Library

All rights reserved; no part of this publication may be
reproduced, stored in a retrieval system, or transmitted in any
form or by any means, electronic, mechanical, photocopying,
recording, or otherwise without either the prior written
permission of the Publishers or a licence permitting restricted
copying in the United Kingdom issued by the Copyright Licensing
Agency Ltd, 90 Tottenham Court Road, London W1P 9HE. This book
may not be lent, resold, hired out or otherwise disposed of by
way of trade in any form of binding or cover other than that in
which it is published without the prior consent of the Publishers.

Printed and bound in England by Clays Ltd, St Ives plc

CONTENTS

PREFACE

This book aims to describe and compare the accounting environment in each of the member states of the European Community. Sweden is also covered, in view of its distinct accounting tradition and prospective membership of the community. A brief look is also taken at the position in Eastern Europe.

To introduce the issues, the first three chapters explore the variations in accounting practices between nations. Chapter 1 identifies the importance of national variations in accounting practice, discusses the reasons for attempts to reduce such variations, and explains why such attempts are frequently frustrated. Chapter 2 explains the various national and international influences on accounting regulation, including both public and private sector bodies. Chapter 3 considers a range of specific issues of accounting practice, identifying the various areas where important national differences arise, with reference to the European Community Directives. Chapters on individual countries look both at the regulatory and professional environment and at specific accounting rules. Following an overview of Eastern Europe, a final chapter considers the problems of international variations in accounting practice from the point of view of the analyst.

The text is particularly appropriate for international accounting courses within accounting and business studies degree courses, drawing on a wide range of international accounting issues. The book is equally relevant to practitioners seeking to understand their discipline in a European context.

The authors met at the International Teachers' Programme at the Stockholm School of Economics in 1982, receiving financial support from the Foundation for Management Education and EADA respectively.

They would like to express their appreciation for advice on the chapter on Sweden by Jörgen Dahlgren of the University of Linköping and for research funding from EADA.

CHAPTER 1

Variations in International Accounting

R.T.C. LIBRARY, LETTERKENNY

INTRODUCTION   In this chapter we:

1. Identify the existence of material variation in accounting rules and practices between different nations.

2. Consider the factors leading to pressure for a reduction in these variations by 'standardization' or 'harmonization' of accounting internationally.

3. Discuss the range of factors that tend to promote differences in national accounting practices.

4. Briefly review some systems for classification of national accounting practices.

ILLUSTRATIONS OF NATIONAL ACCOUNTING DIFFERENCES

The significance of international differences in accounting practices can be measured in a number of ways. One is to see how profit measured for a single company varies under different national rules. D'Illiers (1990) cites the example of a European company that computes earnings per share on the basis of three different national accounting systems:

Germany	3 ECU
France	4 ECU
UK	6 ECU

Simmonds (1989) took the specific example of the UK company of Saatchi and Saatchi plc and considered the impact on profit of adjusting to common practice in three other countries for goodwill.

The common practices used were:

UK	Immediate write-off against reserves
Belgium	Amortization over 5 years
France	Amortization over 20 years
Netherlands	Amortization over 10 years

The 1987 accounts showed purchased goodwill of £151.5m, giving the following range of profit and earnings per share for each country:

	Belgium £m	France £m	Netherlands £m	UK £m
Profit attributable to ordinary shareholders – UK basis	69.6	69.6	69.6	69.6
Goodwill amortized	30.3	7.6	15.2	–
Adjusted	39.3	62.0	54.4	69.6
Earnings per share	25.9p	40.9p	35.9p	45.9p

(Simmonds 1989, p. 18)

Another approach is reported in Simmonds and Azières (1989). A single set of accounting data was assembled, and the accounts were prepared in each of seven European countries on the most likely basis, the lowest permitted basis, and the highest permitted basis:

	Most likely ECU m	Lowest permitted ECU m	Highest permitted ECU m
Belgium	135	90	193
Germany	133	27	140
Spain	131	121	192
France	149	121	160
Italy	174	167	193
Netherlands	140	76	156
UK	192	171	194

(Adapted from Simmonds and Azières 1989, p. 36)

Fitzgerald (1981) cites an example that was revealed when the UK government sold part of its holdings in British Petroleum:

> In prospectuses in the Securities and Exchange Commission (SEC), it is necessary to provide a reconciliation between operating results under the overseas company's regular method and US GAAP. The different results in this case were startling: the last two years' reported income of this enormous company was reduced by 67 per cent and 70 per cent, respectively, on the US basis (p. 25).

Adjustments made to company accounts by investment analysts also offer interesting insights into the range of international accounting practices. Gray (1980) looked at the adjustments made to accounts by European security analysts for investment decision making, and found that French and German accounts were regarded as very much more conservative than UK accounts in their measurement of income. One London research bureau, Smithers and Co, used national income accounts to estimate a 'true' income figure to compare with company accounts in each country. On this basis, a 'ratio of true to published profits' is computed for five countries as follows:

Japan	1.69
USA	0.77
Britain	0.75
France	0.84
Germany	1.00

This represents 'a factor by which company accounts should be adjusted to make them comparable from country to country. In Germany, no adjustment is needed. In Britain, by contrast, reported profits should be multiplied by a factor of 0.75 because of inventive accountants and a history of inflation' (reported in *The Economist*, 22 February 1992, p. 94).

Weetman and Gray (1991) considered major differences between accounting practices in the UK, the USA, the Netherlands and Sweden, and looked at the effects of these on a sample of companies. UK accounts were significantly less conservative than those in the USA, to a statistically significant extent. Swedish accounts appeared more conservative, and Dutch accounts less conservative, than those in the USA but the sample of companies was not large enough to be statistically significant.

Another form of study that has revealed national accounting differences has arisen from investigations into apparent national differences in financing. Thus White (1984) looked at gearing levels for France, Germany, Japan, the UK and the USA. It was found that after making adjustments for differences in national accounting practices 'effective differences in gearing ratios between the five countries which have been considered are much smaller than one is led to believe from looking at reported data'. Michel and Shaked (1985) identified a range of differences in accounting practices between the USA and Japan, which together tend to depress the reported equity in the accounts of Japanese companies. They found that if they measured equity on the basis of market capitalization then the apparent differences in gearing between Japanese and US companies were largely eliminated. On this basis they argued that the 'widely held belief among the Japanese business community, Japanese government officials, and academics worldwide that Japanese firms are more highly leveraged than their American counterparts' (p. 61) is 'more myth than reality' (p. 66).

Another approach is to consider specific examples of differences in national accounting requirements. To take two examples more or less at random from Spicer and Oppenheim (1989):

1. Dutch law favours the use of current values for fixed assets, Japanese law generally forbids revaluation and prescribes historical cost.
2. Research and development costs must be written off in the year incurred in the USA; in Norway capitalization is permitted but must be amortized within five years and rarely occurs because of tax law; in the UK capitalization is permitted, no maximum period of amortization is specified, and there is no tax effect in the choice of accounting policy.

Even where accounting regulations are similar in broad principle, their detailed application may involve substantial variations. In accounting for lease agreements (see Chapter 3 below for details) each of the USA, the UK, Spain and Sweden has provided that 'finance leases' should be capitalized. However, when we examine the detailed definition of a finance lease we find the following:

1. In the USA a definition of a finance lease in principle as one that transfers substantially all the risks and rewards of ownership from the lessor to the lessee is supported by a 200-page book on details of definition, making it difficult for companies to avoid finance lease capitalization.

2. In the UK a definition of a finance lease similar in principle to that in the USA has little supporting detail. Two UK surveys of management responses to this requirement found that a substantial number of managers expected to avoid this requirement by negotiating leases that technically fall outside the definition (Taylor and Turley 1985; Drury 1989) while an authoritative journal advised:

   in the current competitive market, many lessors may in future be prepared to accept the residual value risks themselves (*World Leasing Yearbook*, 1987, p. 253).

   This practice effectively allows lessees to claim these as operating leases.

3. In Spain only those leases where there is a provision for a purchase option at a bargain price are finance leases.

4. In Sweden only leases with a *requirement* to purchase are finance leases.

Thus there is a spectrum of finance lease capitalization requirements, from the broad based and rigorously defined in the USA, through the broad based and easily avoided in the UK, to the narrow definition in Spain and even narrower definition in Sweden.

THE PRESSURE TO REDUCE VARIATION

The terms 'harmonization' and 'standardization' both tend to be used in considering the question of processes to reduce international variations in financial reporting. Gray et al. (1981) distinguish between

1. *harmonization* of 'corporate reporting objectives and standards of disclosure', (p. 132), which they feel is best achieved by intergovernmental organizations, such as the UN, OECD and the EC.

   and

2. *standardization*, being provision of the detailed development and assistance with the practical implementation of the desired standards of disclosure and measurement. They see this as a role for the IASC (see Chapter 2 for the accounting regulatory activities of the bodies cited here).

Nobes (1991) observes a distinction between harmonization as an increase in comparability of accounting practices, and standardization as implying the imposition of more rigid and narrow rules. However, he adds:

> within accounting, these words have almost become technical terms, and one cannot rely upon the normal difference in their meanings (p. 70).

In practice, moves to achieve a reduction in international variations in accounting practice are commonly referred to either as 'harmonization' or 'standardization'. Such moves can be seen as attributable to four broad objectives, described below.

1. Meeting the Needs of Investors

A former Canadian Minister of Finance has observed:

> The greatest benefit that would flow from harmonization would be the comparability of international financial information. Such comparability would eliminate the current misunderstandings about the reliability of 'foreign' financial statements and would remove one of the most important impediments to the flow of international investment . . . (Turner 1983).

In a survey of 160 individuals with an interest in international accounting Mason (1978) found that 'investors and potential investors' ranked as the class of user to benefit most highly from international standardization of accounting practices (p. 53). An OECD survey found a concern amongst transnational corporations (TNCs) that international diversity in accounting practices may discourage international investment (OECD 1980). Views on the extent of the problem vary. On the one hand Carey (1970) offers the view:

> Private capital cannot flow freely over international boundaries unless the investors can receive reliable information about what is being done with their money – and this means financial statements audited by accountants in whom the investors have confidence (p. 54).

On the other hand, Samuels and Piper (1985) argue that:

> Private capital has flowed freely for a number of centuries. Investors are interested in balancing returns with risks. It is true that unreliable information adds to the risk, but if the returns are high enough the funds will still flow (p. 76).

Cook (1989) makes the point that global capital markets are likely to be more volatile than domestic capital markets because they are not attached to particular investments as a normal component of a national portfolio or by 'traditional loyalties'. Thus 'clarity of communication between management and the international investment community will be an essential element of support for the share price' (p. 40).

Thus failure to achieve international accounting harmonization is seen as creating 'an unlevel playing field for those international companies that are competing with one another for business opportunities. As a result, the free flow of capital and business is blocked' (Barthes de Ruyter 1990).

Drury (1979) offers some empirical evidence that US investors in Canadian listed companies found some difficulty in following accounts based on Canadian rather than US accounting rules:

> A large portion of the potential users of accounting information are not domestic Canadian investors. It is not always possible for interested readers to convert financial reports to a basis consistent with United States practices, and even when it is, the costs are not trivial (p. 85).

Choi and Levich (1990, 1991) report on a survey of International Capital Market participants and their attitudes to international accounting diversity. The question 'Does accounting diversity affect your capital market decisions?' produced the answer 'yes' from a majority of those (investors, issuers, and underwriters) directly linked with the provision of finance (see Table 1.1). This analysis understates the impact on company finance costs because some of those who replied 'no' did so on the basis that they benefited from the opportunities to increase charges. As one underwriter commented:

> As far as we're concerned, we regard accounting differences as working in our favour. The superior returns which we are able to get from international investing is related to the fact that the international markets are less perfect than the national markets. Therefore we believe you can improve your returns through management more in the international markets than you can within the national market (Choi and Levich 1990, p. 64).

and one investor:

> Sometimes the lack of disclosure provides you with investment opportunities (Choi and Levich 1990, p. 44).

Table 1.1 Summary Findings for Investors, Issuers, Underwriters, Regulators and Others

	Key question: Does accounting diversity affect your capital market decisions?			
	Yes	*No*	*N.A.*	*Total*
Investors	9	7	1	17
Issuers	6	9		15
Underwriters	7	1		8
Regulators		8		8
Raters and others	2	1		3
TOTAL	24	26	1	51*

*The International Accounting Standards Committee was interviewed but their answers are not included here.

(From Choi and Levich 1990, p. 127)

Thus, on balance it appears that international diversity of accounting practice does create problems for investors and therefore leads to higher finance costs.

Archer and McLeay (1989) point out that multinationals may also see their accounts as 'a valuable form of public relations' (p. 74). They cite the example of a number of multinationals that produce Spanish versions of their accounts without being listed in any Spanish-speaking country.

From the perspective of one of the world's major accountancy practices, Hanson (1989) sees the main demand for international harmonization coming from both stock exchange regulators and from 'sophisticated users in the capital markets of the world'.

2. Easing the Work of Transnational Corporations

International diversity of accounting regulation and practice creates a number of problems for transnational corporations. Mason (1978, p. 32) identifies three potential benefits of accounting harmonization for transnational corporations:

1. Costs of accounts preparation for the individual company would be reduced.
2. Costs would also be saved with a reduction in the number of adjustments required on consolidation.
3. The integration of internal and external reporting systems and the development of uniform measures of performance would be facilitated.

Cecchini (1988) reports that in a sample of European transnational firms

> The extra administrative burden imposed by different auditing and fiscal systems was estimated by the report at between 10 and 30 per cent of the costs of the company departments involved (p. 32).

Where a TNC reports in more than one country it may be impossible to meet the accounting rules of them all in a single set of accounts. Arpan and Radebaugh (1985, p. 344) cite the example of the 1980 Royal Dutch Shell accounts. Reporting in the USA, the UK, and the Netherlands, the company faced conflicting national standards on income tax allocation, making an audit qualification unavoidable. Although the change in the UK tax system in 1984 made the deferred tax position in the UK less material, so that an audit qualification ceased to be necessary, the enforced difference in accounting policy continues to apply.

3. Sharing Accounting Skills

One benefit of accounting harmonization is that it offers an opportunity to share skills. Turner (1983) observes:

> a third improvement from harmonization would be the tendency for accounting standards throughout the world to be raised to the highest possible level and to be consistent with local economic, legal and social conditions.

Mason (1978, p. 33) observes that small and developing nations lack a sufficiently large or well-developed accounting profession to produce a full set of domestic accounting standards, and benefit accordingly from the availability of international standards.

One response to this problem has been for some countries to seek advice from the USA. Enthoven (1983) cites US assistance to Zaire and Indonesia in developing accounting skills. Beresford (1990) reports that the Financial Accounting Standards Board has given advice to Hungarian government officials on how to establish accounting standards. Similarly a former chairman of the IASC has seen its early work as being 'largely for the benefit of third world countries' (Elliot 1983). The need for international cooperation in accounting to help underdeveloped countries is argued by Baccouche (1969):

> These countries cannot afford to duplicate research and, most importantly, repeat errors at a time when communication between nations is simple (p. 99).

Cairns (1990) quotes Malawi, Malaysia and Zimbabwe as examples of developing countries that use IASC standards to save the resources required to develop their own domestic standards.

Within Europe the inflation accounting debate offers an example of wasteful duplication of resources in researching the issues. The 'value to the owner' concept found its way into the English language debate derived from the works in Bonbright (1937) independently of the similar concept taught in the Netherlands by Limperg (see Tweedie and Whittington 1984, pp. 25, 32).

4. An Alternative to US Domination

One argument used in favour of international accounting harmonization is that it represents the only alternative to US domination. Mason (1978, p. 36) observes that:

> There are those who consider – and perhaps fear – that if international standards are not developed, US generally accepted accounting principles (GAAP) will fill the vacuum and become increasingly widely used in the international accounting language.

Reasons for this potential US domination suggested by Mason (1978) include:

1. The economic significance of US TNCs

2. The influence of US dominated international firms

3. The high technical quality of US produced standards

4. The quality of US accounting publications

5. The strength of the US academic accounting community.

Hopwood et al. (1990) argue that 'International trade and investment will increasingly require internationally acceptable and understandable financial statements. Standards will either need to provide for more harmonization than at present or, increasingly, one nation's system will come to predominate. That nation will be the United States' (p. 80).

One argument for seeking an alternative to US domination is that the distinctive cultural environment of the USA does not necessarily produce accounting regulations suitable to other countries. As an example Stamp (1980) argues that cultural differences lead to very different accounting requirements in Canada compared to the USA, and argues that countries sharing the Canadian tradition include the UK, Australia, New Zealand, and the Netherlands (p. 90).

There is also a less specific resistance to the general concept of US domination. As Zeff (1984) reports:

> Some Latin American countries would prefer not to follow the lead of the 'imperialist' US. Mexico acts as an important conduit in overcoming this reluctance. Mexico will adopt a given US standard, whereby it becomes a 'Mexican' standard. The others can then follow suit.

Resistance to US domination of accounting theory also plays a part in calls for a common European approach. To cite two examples:

1. Scheid and Standish (1989) argue against harmonization being a process whereby 'non-English-speaking countries give up whatever indigenous practices they may have developed in favour of Anglo-American accounting standards' (p. 163).
2. Le Fèvre (1990) adopts a somewhat emotive approach. 'Europe cannot adopt a subservient attitude towards countries in which it was the original civilizing influence. It should be an entirely separate partner and even, in some cases, play the leading role' (p. 104).

Similarly Baker (1986), in the context of International Accounting Standards (IAS) observes:

> For many countries, adopting an IAS is politically more acceptable than adopting, say, US or UK standards, as an IAS is not immediately associated with one particular country.

For those who manage the world's multinationals, on the other hand, the flexibility and pursuit of economic realism inherent in the Anglo-American model can be attractive. Slipkowsky (1988) reports comments made by the Financial Director of Volvo:

> I think that the harmonization to a large extent depends on the Anglo-Saxon countries. If these countries could harmonize their principles and standards, these rules could also serve as preliminary international standards which, I assume, would be gradually adopted by other countries (p. 23).

FACTORS THAT DETERMINE NATIONAL PRACTICE

A range of factors can be identified as helping to explain how distinctive accounting practices develop in a particular country.

The following are discussed here:

1. The influence of leading theorists and professional bodies
2. Economic consequences
3. The economic environment
4. Taxation
5. Nationalism
6. Users and objectives
7. Legal context
8. Sources of finance
9. Language
10. Other country influences
11. Scandal or calamity.

1. Theorists and Professional Bodies

In some countries, a particularly persuasive accounting theorist may have a significant influence. In the Netherlands, Theodore Limperg established a 'business economics' approach to accounting, and a consequent replacement cost system, that is reflected in the current practice of several large companies, notably Philips (see Chapter 12 below). In Finland, Marti Saario developed a distinctive approach to accounting, involving a particular focus on cash flows (see Näsi 1990). In some countries the accounting profession has been particularly influential. An example has been the success of the Institute of Chartered Accountants in England and Wales in promoting the 'true and fair view' approach (see Chapter 3 below).

2. Economic Consequences

Published accounts tend to be used – otherwise there would be little point in their preparation. They are used to establish contractual obligations – for example by the tax authorities and in establishing borrowing limits. They are also used by a range of users as a basis for decision making. A change in accounting rules may change these contractual obligations and decision makers, giving rise to 'economic consequences'. Because of these economic consequences of accounting rules, a range of interested parties, particularly company management, lobby for what they see as the most favourable outcome. In the USA the issue of economic consequences and the concomitant pressures from lobbyists have been seen as posing a fundamental challenge to the legitimacy of the role of professional accountants in the regulation of accounting. Some have seen it as essential for the survival of this role that accounting regulators should develop 'political' sensitivity in response to this challenge, seeing the demise of the APB as partly attributable to a failure to respond in this way. Such sensitivity is seen as legitimate in a democratic society (see for example Gerboth 1972, 1973, Horngren 1972, 1973, 1976 and Rappaport 1977).

An FASB chairman has appealed for moderation by the lobbyists if private sector regulation is to be saved (Armstrong 1977). On the other hand there are those who argue that accountants lose their credibility if they are seen to be influenced by non-technical considerations (e.g. Stamp 1980, Solomons 1978). Zeff (1978) argues for a middle course, basing accounting regulation primarily on technical reasons but being aware of economic consequences to ensure acceptability. Whichever view is taken, there is no doubt that there are well-documented cases in a number of countries of 'economic consequences' issues influencing accounting regulation. Since both the contractual and decision-making uses of published accounts vary between countries, the 'economic consequences' pressures also vary.

In the UK, discussion of economic consequences has been less widespread than in the USA, where the FASB has sponsored a number of studies on the subject. The UK ASC has referred to economic consequences issues in exposure drafts on several topics including leasing. An interesting example arose over the treatment of research and development expenditure. The ASC first proposed in ED 14 to require write-off of all research and development expenditure. Subsequently this proposal was amended so that SSAP 13 permits, subject to certain conditions, amortization of development costs. Both Eccles and Lifford (1979) and Hope and Gray (1982) identify, as a major factor in the ASC's decision to permit deferral, a linkage with Government regulations on the definition of capital employed for the purpose of computation of allowed profits on defence contracts. Hope and Gray further point out that one member of the ASC also served on the Government committee formulating these regulations, thereby having firsthand knowledge of this economic consequences issue. In the UK the ASC has been concerned not to be seen to be easily influenced by such issues. For example, the ASC made a material change in its stance when it withdrew SSAP 11 prescribing full provision for deferred taxation and replaced it with SSAP 15 prescribing only a partial provision. The then head of the UK government accounting service has referred to this as a case where the Government brought pressure to bear on the ASC in response to lobbying from industry (Sharp 1979). Nevertheless, the then chairman of the ASC persists in a denial that the change 'was for reasons of undue pressure' (Watts 1981, p. 33).

Sweden offers us an interesting example of a piece of creative accounting actually imposed by law in order to benefit one specific company. At the end of 1977, Uddeholm AB, a major Swedish manufacturer of steel and forest products, found that its loss for the year had depressed reported equity to a point where the company was in default of its agreed borrowing limits. The consequent requirement to repay outstanding loans would have destroyed the company. International agreements barring subsidies to steel producers prevented the Government from giving a grant to save the company. Instead the Government extended a line of credit to the company and passed a law requiring the company to treat this line of credit as part of the equity. Following the rescue of the company, the law was repealed in 1983. The case is fully described in Zeff and Johansson (1984).

3. Economic Environment

In Spain, an awareness that historic cost based depreciation gave inadequate tax relief lead to a system of *actualización*. This is a procedure whereby companies are allowed to revalue, tax-free, specified categories of fixed asset by specified indices; thereafter, depreciation of the revalued amounts is tax allowable. This practice has been permitted on some half dozen occasions between 1960 and 1983 (see Gonzalo and Tua Pereda 1988, pp. 148–9 for full details).

Special characteristics affecting the economy may influence a country's accounting system. A commonly cited example is that high levels of inflation may lead to development of an inflation accounting system, as in certain Latin American systems (see Tweedie and Whittington 1984, pp. 234–6).

In the UK, Westwick (1980) identifies a strong link between the degree of interest in inflation accounting, as evidenced by official proposals, and the level of inflation. In Spain an interesting example is that the *Plan General de Contabilidad* made special provision for deferral of translation gains by electricity companies (*Instituto de Planificación Contable* 1978, p. 137). There is no similar provision for any other industrial sector. The reason for this appears to be that several Spanish electricity companies borrowed substantial amounts in US dollars in the mid-1970s, shortly before the US dollar rose sharply against the peseta. It was felt unreasonable to require taking such substantial translation losses to the income statement in one year.

4. Taxation

In some countries the law requires accounts to be prepared in line with tax law. Germany, a country that leads this approach, uses the term *Massgeblichkeitsprinzip* (principle of bindingness), to express the principle. In other countries the law permits a choice of accounting policies but gives tax benefits that depend on the policy chosen. For example, Norway permits capitalization of development expenditure but this is rare in practice because tax allowances are only given when costs are written off in the accounts (Spicer and Oppenheim 1989, p. 244).

National peculiarities of tax law can give rise to accounting issues that do not arise in other countries. Cook (1989) cites the problem in the UK of 'daisy chain' transactions where a cargo of oil may change hands thirty or forty times between the producer and the ultimate buyer. An accounting problem arises when the same company appears more than once in the same chain and agrees with the intermediate parties to 'book out' the intervening contracts settling margins rather than full amounts. The question arises whether these transactions should be recorded at gross amounts or netted off. The 'book out' problem arises largely because of UK tax policies requiring evidence of market transactions.

5. Nationalism

As Doost and Ligon (1986) observe, in seeking international harmonization of accounting, 'Politics and nationalism is one major area of trouble. Everyone believes that his system is the best and is unwilling to change' (p. 41). Similarly, Cummings (1976) observed, accountants' calls for uniformity 'weren't sounded in Esperanto . . . . All thought *their* accounting standards were best, and should be applied universally'. An example of national pride in the formulation of accounting standards is the UK choice of associated companies as the first topic to be covered in an SSAP – seen as attributable to the wish of the UK profession to be seen tackling an area in advance of US accountants (Blake 1991, p. 10).

In some cases, national pride is particularly intense:

> The newly independent Third World countries highly value their sovereign status. Any infringement on the 'highly valued assets' (sovereignty) becomes a source of considerable concern to the leaders of such countries (Ndubizu 1984).

Even in countries as closely linked as the USA and Canada, there can be a strong feeling that a distinct accounting approach is desired:

> Simply adopting FASB standards on a wholesale basis in Canada is unequivocally not the course to take. Canada is a unique country, and it should have its own standard-setting body and its own standards (Bloom 1984, p. 56).

6. Users and Objectives

Accounts may vary from country to country because they aim to satisfy different objectives and different user groups. Gray, Owen and Maunders (1987) review international corporate social reporting and comment on the 'diversity of aims, target audiences and practices' (p. 37) that they find between different countries.

In the UK there is some uncertainty as to the range of users and objectives supposed to be served by published accounts. *The Corporate Report* identified as users of accounts equity investors, loan creditors, employees, analyst-advisers, business contacts, the Government and the public (Accounting Standards Steering Committee 1975, pp. 19–27). However, in commenting on the *Corporate Report*, the Law Society representing UK solicitors argued that the spirit of existing UK law confined company accountability to shareholders and creditors. Thus the idea of a broader range of users is controversial. By contrast, in Spain the accounting plan includes a specific statement that the users who ought to be served by accounts include 'shareholders, creditors, employees, the Government and also competitors' (*Plan General de Contabilidad* 1990, p. 31). Cañibano Calvo (1990, p. 31) cites a somewhat wider range of users for the accounts of a large company embracing shareholders, workers, lenders, financial analysts, potential investors, trade contacts such as suppliers and customers, the Government, particularly for taxation, consumers, political parties, and unions.

In an analysis of nine countries, Bloom and Naciri (1989) conclude:

> the United States is less concerned with social welfare than Britain, Canada, West Germany, Australia, New Zealand, and Sweden (p. 92).

7. Legal Context

Countries with a common law traditon, such as England, are likely to legislate on broad principles of accounting rules rather than on laying down detailed requirements. By contrast countries with a Roman law tradition, such as West Germany. are likely to have a codified set of accounting rules laying out required disclosures and practices in detail. Accounting practices may also vary depending on how strictly rules are applied in practice. Busse von Colbe (1983) cites Italy as a country where accounting rules are applied more flexibly than we might expect from the strict legal position (p. 125).

Similarly Treffers (1967) comments on 'differences in, for example, the moral attitude toward taxes; not everywhere is the payment of taxes in accordance with law considered to be a duty' (p. 45).

Experience in the USA shows that in a highly litigious environment accountants and auditors seek clear unambiguous accounting rules. Referring to a case where a firm of accountants had to defend in court 'an issue of disclosure for which no specific requirements could be found' a leading US practitioner commented:

> the more rules the profession has concerning matters of accounting and presentation, the less likely it will be that the auditor will become involved in this type of difficult judgment situation (Ferst 1973, pp. 313–14).

8. Sources of Finance

Where a company raises finance from the general public through the stock market, the quality of published accounting information required might be expected to be higher than where finance is raised by private arrangement, since in the latter case the provider of finance can obtain the required information by private agreement. A number of studies have found that companies with a stock exchange listing have a higher quality of accounting disclosure. For example:

1. In the USA, both Cerf (1961) and Singhvi and Desai (1971) found that the listed companies provided higher levels of disclosure.

2. In the UK, Firth (1979) found a higher level of disclosure amongst listed companies.

3. In Sweden, Cooke (1989) found that companies listed on a number of the world's stock exchanges showed a higher quality of disclosure than those listed only in Stockholm, while in turn locally listed companies showed a higher quality of disclosure than those with no listing.

Within the European Community a number of directives have been issued to harmonize stock exchange practices. Tondkar et al. (1990) observe that 'harmonized listing and filing requirements of EEC stock exchanges could induce EEC firms to list more frequently within the EEC capital market' (p. 128).

This emergence of a common European stock exchange system may, therefore, be a force in support of European accounting harmonization.

Other sources of finance may also lead to different types of disclosure. One example is in Israel, where a substantial number of industrial companies are directly owned, fully or partially, by the Government. For these companies accounting disclosure rules are more detailed than for other companies (Lev 1976).

9. Language

Confusion can arise where accounting regulations are translated into different languages. Hussein (1981, pp. 152–3) reports on an experiment in evaluating the official Spanish translation of IAS 3 on consolidated financial statements which identified a number of errors. Problems also arise when accounting concepts that derive from the culture of one country are translated into a language where the culture is different, a point illustrated by attempts to translate the term 'true and fair view' discussed in Chapter 3 below.

10. Other Country Influences

For a variety of reasons, one country may allow its accounting practices to be influenced by another country or group of countries. In some cases the influence seems totally accidental. For example, the French 'Plan' based system of accounting was first introduced by the occupying German forces in World War II, and was continued after the war by the French government as a useful tool for economic management (see Standish 1990 for a full discussion). Membership of the British Commonwealth has exposed a number of countries to UK accounting influence. Walton (1986) explores the influence of UK accounting legislation on four Commonwealth countries. He notes that each has felt free to choose those parts of the UK legislation that suit them best; for example Antigua has chosen not to update legislation based on the UK Companies Act of 1862. Cyprus has chosen not only to use UK company law but also to state that an auditor must be 'a member of a body of accountants established in the United Kingdom'. In Australia, the state of

Victoria departed from UK accounting practice in the Companies Act of 1896 but returned to a UK approach in the Companies Act of 1910, apparently to appeal to UK investors (Gibson 1971). Thus, the choice of what part of the UK example is followed appears to be made locally on a widely varying basis.

11. Scandal or Crisis

Accounting regulation may emerge in response to a scandal or crisis. This may be at a wide ranging level. For example, in the UK the Companies Act 1856 did not require company audits, on the grounds that market forces would be adequate to induce shareholders and creditors to require an audit where appropriate. However, the City of Glasgow Bank collapsed in 1878, revealing the publication of falsified accounts, and leading to the bankruptcy of four-fifths of the Bank's shareholders. As a response, a legal requirement for bank audits was introduced in 1879 (see Tyson 1974).

Response to a crisis can also influence the detail of accounting regulation. In the UK, when the ASC first formulated an exposure draft on research and development, a write-off approach was chosen. This appears to have been a response to the dramatic collapse of the Rolls Royce group which had shown large, and in the event unjustified, capitalized R&D costs in the balance sheet (see Underdown and Taylor 1985, p. 262). In fact, this particular proposal was changed in response to the economic consequences factors discussed above.

Cowan (1979) comments on how, following the Watergate scandal, US legislators became more prescriptive on accounting issues, observing:

> There may well have been an overreaction from the public to failures and 'scandals', a kind of backwash from Watergate (p. 381).

CLASSIFICATION SYSTEMS FOR NATIONAL ACCOUNTING PRACTICES

Nobes (1983b, pp. 26–30) reviews reasons for seeking to classify national accounting systems:

1. The activity encourages precision in examining the exact nature and importance of differences, and similarities, between countries.

2. Classification may help in the development of accounting, for example in helping a country understand the differences between available accounting systems and choosing an appropriate one.

3. Classification systems offer a valuable educational tool in enabling teachers to focus on 'key countries' each of which illustrates the broad characteristics of one group.

4. For accounting regulators a classification system gives guidance on which similar countries to watch, to predict problems that may have to be faced.

PIONEERING WORK

As early as 1911, Henry Rand Hatfield, in a paper presented to the American Association of Public Accountants, identified a distinctive French influence on one group of countries. Referring to legal requirements to record transactions in a journal he stated:

> Of the more than 25 countries having such a provision, almost all follow rather slavishly the provisions of the French Code, which, indeed, has set the standard for most of the continental regulation of accounting practice (Hatfield 1966, pp. 171–2).

Seidler (1967) argued the need to identify 'coherent patterns of international accounting variation' (p. 775) to facilitate the teaching of international accounting. One such concept he identified was that of 'spheres of influence', where traditional associations caused one 'mother country' to dominate the accounting practices of other countries. He cited three examples:

1. The British model; influencing Australian and Indian accounting.
2. The American model; influencing Mexico and large parts of South America, as well as Israel and Japan.
3. The French school; covering most of Southern Europe and the Mediterranean area, as well as those South American countries with commercial codes modelled on the Code Napoléon.

Previts (1975) in analysing Seidler's approach, played down the US influence in South America (referring to 'to some extent in South America' p. 3) and added to the British model the examples of Canada, New Zealand, South Africa, Nigeria, the British West Indies, Thailand, Greece, and 'certain South American countries' (p. 2).

Mueller (1967) argued that four patterns of accounting development could be identified and that 'this range of four is considered sufficient to embrace accounting as it is presently known and practised in various parts of the globe' (p. 2). The four were:

1. Accounting within a macroeconomic framework. Here accounting is seen 'as an instrument of national economic policies' (p. 6). Sweden is seen, 'probably more than any other country', as an example of this approach.
2. The microeconomic approach to accounting. Here accounting is seen as 'a branch of business economics' with a consequent tendency to use value based rather than cost based measures. The Netherlands is seen as an example.
3. Accounting as an independent discipline. Accounting develops from business practices, so that 'induction from existing business (accounting) practices is then the most important foundation in the erection of accounting concepts' (p. 60). The USA and the UK are cited as examples of this pragmatic approach.

4. Uniform accounting. Accounting is used by governments to monitor and control the economy based on standardized definitions, measurement and presentation. France is the cited example.

Mueller (1968) offers an alternative form of classification based on ten (then) business environments:

1. USA/Canada/The Netherlands
2. British Commonwealth (excluding Canada)
3. Germany/Japan
4. Continental Europe (excluding Germany, the Netherlands, and Scandinavia)
5. Scandinavia
6. Israel/Mexico
7. South America
8. Developing nations of the Near and Far East
9. Africa (excluding South Africa)
10. Communist nations.

Given this range of business environments, Mueller concluded 'United States generally-accepted accounting principles should not be enforced arbitrarily in other countries' (p. 102). The American Accounting Association Committee on International Accounting Operations and Education (1977) suggested a classification system based on a number of states of society. The Committee also suggested a 'subjective' classification scheme based on five zones of influence:

1. British
2. Franco-Spanish-Portuguese
3. Germanic/Dutch
4. US
5. Communistic.

SYSTEMATIC CLUSTER STUDIES

A number of studies have classified accounting systems into groups by using cluster analysis of the descriptions of accounting practices offered in international surveys, particularly those reported by Price Waterhouse in 1973, 1975, and 1979.

Da Costa et al. (1978) identified two cluster groups, one based on the UK with former colonies and one other. Two countries, Canada and the Netherlands, fell outside both clusters.

650 6265

Nair and Frank (1980) used two different Price Waterhouse surveys and distinguished between measurement practices and disclosure practices. The number of cluster groups identified was:

Measurement practices, 1973 study   4

Measurement practices, 1975 study   5

Disclosure practices, 1973 study   7

Disclosure practices, 1975 study   7

Nair (1982) used the same method with the 1979 Price Waterhouse survey, identifying seven measurement and ten disclosure clusters. The 1973 measurement study offered the most coherent set of characterizations with four models:

British Commonwealth

Latin American

Continental European

United States.

R.T.C. LIBRARY, LETTERKENNY 657

It is interesting to note how the countries covered in this book appear in these clusters (see Table 1.2). The UK and Ireland appear in one cluster, not surprisingly since they share a common system of accounting standard development, while the Netherlands appears either in the same cluster or independently of other European countries. Other 'continental European countries' tend, at least in some studies, to appear in one cluster.

A TESTED JUDGMENTAL APPROACH

Nobes (1983a,b) argues the case for a different approach to classification systems. He argues that the Price Waterhouse data were not designed for the identification of clusters of similar national accounting practices and were unsuitable for this purpose. Reasons for this include:

1. The Price Waterhouse data are based on returns by partners in different countries who appear, in some cases, to have addressed issues in different ways, e.g. in deciding whether to describe formal requirements or general practice.

2. Major issues, such as the extent to which consolidated accounts are required, are swamped by less detailed issues such as some 40 questions on the detail of consolidation practice.

3. Differences between the UK and the USA tended to be exaggerated because of the familiarity of the compilers of the survey questions with issues in those two countries.

Nobes identifies nine major areas of variations in accounting approach, and grades each of 14 countries on each area. For example, in relation to the

Table 1.2   European Countries in Systematic Cluster Studies

	Da Costa et al. 1978	Nair and Frank 1980				Nair 1982	
		1973 Measure-ment practices	1975 Measure-ment practices	1973 Disclosure practices	1975 Disclosure practices	1979 Measure-ment practices	1979 Disclosure practices
Continental European	France Belgium Germany Italy Spain Sweden	France Belgium Germany Italy Spain Sweden	France Belgium Germany Sweden Denmark	France Belgium Italy Spain	France Belgium Spain Greece	Belgium Germany Sweden Denmark	Belgium Italy Portugal
British Common-wealth	UK Ireland	UK Ireland Netherlands	UK Ireland Netherlands	UK Ireland	UK Ireland Netherlands	France UK Ireland Netherlands	UK Ireland Netherlands Denmark Sweden
Grouped together			Greece Italy Spain			Greece Italy Spain Portugal	
Grouped together					Sweden Denmark		
Appear in separate groups	Netherlands	—	—	Germany Netherlands Sweden	Germany Italy		Germany Greece France Spain

question of how far historic cost is a requirement, the countries were graded as follows:

0	(No exceptions)	Germany, Italy, Japan, Sweden
1		Belgium, Canada, France, Spain, USA
2		Australia, New Zealand
3	(Many exceptions)	Netherlands, Ireland, UK

The data was analysed in a variety of ways that tended to support the classification system in Table 1.3.

Table 1.3 Nobes' Judgmental Classification System

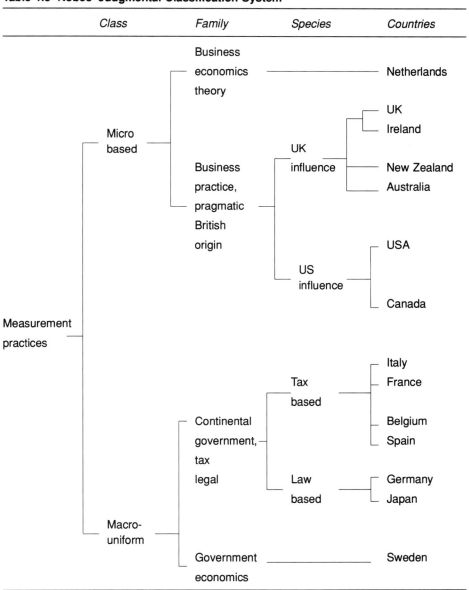

Class	Family	Species	Countries
	Business economics theory		Netherlands
		UK influence	UK / Ireland
Micro based			New Zealand / Australia
	Business practice, pragmatic British origin	US influence	USA / Canada
Measurement practices		Tax based	Italy / France
	Continental government, tax legal		Belgium / Spain
		Law based	Germany / Japan
Macro-uniform	Government economics		Sweden

SOME PROBLEMS WITH CLASSIFICATION SYSTEMS

One problem with attempting to identify 'clusters' of countries is in deciding whether to focus on accounting regulations or on actual accounting practices. The distinction can be particularly important for a country like Sweden with a legal set of accounting requirements based on tax requirements and a voluntary set of guidelines from the accounting profession, with a high level of support by large companies, designed to give high quality investor information. Tay and Parker (1990, p. 85) argue the case for comparing countries on the basis of surveys of practice in each country producing data on proportions of companies using different accounting methods. On the other hand, studies of the rules applied can be of interest in themselves. For example, Al Najjar (1986) in a review of eight countries from 1970 to 1985 found growing standardization as a common factor, concluding:

> national accounting practice has gradually come under more government legislation and control regardless of the particular existing national economic and political systems (p. 176).

Another problem in identifying clusters is that a country can move from one cluster to another. This can happen very rapidly, as in the case of Iran. Foroughi (1981) describes the major changes in the accounting environment that took place in the 1970s with the fall of the Shah. Many large privately owned companies were nationalized. Application of Islamic law meant the abolition of interest. Some business schools were abolished and others merged. Such a change can also occur slowly. Thus New Zealand has moved from a close relationship with the UK in the 1960s, when some accounting pronouncements were taken directly from the English Institute of Chartered Accountants (see Zeff 1979). In the 1990s New Zealand has its closest accounting links with Australia, each country having an observer at the other's accounting standards' board meetings.

CONCLUSION

So far we have identified that:

1. There are substantial differences between accounting regulations in different countries.
2. There is a demand for international accounting harmonization.
3. There are strong reasons for international diversity in accounting regulation, and consequently significant obstacles to international harmonization.
4. 'Clusters' of countries with similar cultural and economic environments and similar patterns of accounting regulation can be identified.

It is important to distinguish between finding disclosures of the same types of item in the accounts and variations in the underlying computation of those items. Most (1964) looked at the accounts of chemical companies from the USA, the UK,

Germany, France and Italy. He concluded that 'financial accounting statements published in Europe are comparable with those published in the USA'. However, Shillinglaw (1966) argued that while comparable disclosure for the five companies could be found, differences in areas such as depreciation and consolidation policy meant that 'Mr Most's optimistic conclusions seem somewhat overdrawn' (p. 83).

A number of observers have questioned both the practicality and desirability of international accounting harmonization, given the range of factors that lead to the present situation of diversity. Choi (1989) asks:

> Would it be reasonable to impose an accounting straitjacket on all reporting entities when studies have shown that accounting principles and practices are environmentally based? (p. 120).

Samuels and Oliga (1982) arrive at a similar conclusion based on an analysis of accounting requirements in Egypt at various stages in that country's development. They conclude:

> we need to consider the accounting needs within a country, particularly the developing countries, not just the needs of the international business community (p. 88).

This view, that there is a conflict between the accounting needs of the local and the international business, is echoed by Wilson (1991):

> it would seem to be counterproductive and injudicious to impose inappropriate financial reporting requirements on domestic companies to appease the multinational corporation which is attempting to attain international comparability or to facilitate mutual recognition on international stock exchanges (p. 82).

Wilson concludes that some form of two-tier reporting is the solution. Fantl (1971) came to a similar conclusion following an analysis of the difficulties in achieving accounting harmonization:

> Underlying the quest for uniformity is a need to understand and rely upon financial data from other countries. If instead of seeking uniformity, accountants were to develop reconciliation systems as a reliable means to translate unfamiliar data into familiar terms, that need would be met (p. 16).

By contrast, Aitken and Islam (1984) argue strongly that the obstacles to international accounting harmonization can be overcome. For example, they argue that in the case of restrictive domestic legislation:

> accountants have an obvious responsibility to report to the authorities concerning the probable undesirable consequences of, and inequities in, such legislation and, thus, attempt to amend the legislation (p. 42).

However, they do accept that the process of harmonization will take time and, as an interim measure, argue the case for disclosure by way of note that will make accounts comparable on an international basis.

REFERENCES

Accounting Standards Steering Committee (1975) *The Corporate Report*.

Al Najjar, F. (1986) 'Standardization in accounting practices: a comparative international study', *International Journal of Accounting*, Spring, pp. 161–76.

Aitken, M.J. and Islam, M.A. (1984) 'Dispelling arguments against international accounting standards', *International Journal of Accounting*, Spring, pp. 35–46.

American Accounting Association (1977) Committee on International Accounting Operations and Education – Report 1975–6, *Accounting Review* Supplement to Vol. 52.

Archer, S. and McLeay, S. (1989) 'Financial reporting by interlisted European companies: issues in transnational disclosure' in Hopwood, A.G. (ed.) *International Pressures for Accounting Change*, pp. 73–115, Prentice Hall.

Armstrong, M.S. (1977) 'The politics of establishing accounting standards', *Journal of Accountancy*, February, pp. 76–9.

Arpan, J. and Radebaugh, L.H. (1985) *International accounting and multinational enterprises*, Warren, Gorham and Lamont.

Baccouche, M. (1969) 'The need for international accountancy', *International Journal of Accounting*, Fall, pp. 97–9.

Baker, S. (1986) 'Growing prestige of the IAS setters', *Certified Accountant*, May, pp. 10–11.

Barthes de Ruyter, G. (1990) 'The harmonization of accounting standards within the EC in relation to third countries' in *The Future of Harmonization of Accounting Standards within the European Communities*, pp. 40–3, Commission of the European Communities.

Beresford, D. (1990) 'Internationalization of accounting standards', *Accounting Horizons*, March, pp. 99–107.

Blake, J. (1991) *Accounting Standards*, Pitman.

Bloom, R. (1984) 'American and Canadian accounting standard setting: a comparative analysis', *International Journal of Accounting*, Spring, pp. 47–57.

Bloom, R. and Naciri, M.A. (1989) 'Accounting standard setting and culture: a comparative analysis of the United States, Canada, England, West Germany, Australia, New Zealand, Sweden, Japan, and Switzerland', *International Journal of Accounting*, **24**, pp. 70–97.

Bonbright, J. (1937) *Valuation of Property*, McGraw-Hill.

Busse von Colbe, W. (1983) 'A discussion of international issues in accounting standard setting' in Bromwich, M. and Hopwood, A.G., *Accounting Standards Setting – An International Perspective*, pp. 121–6, Pitman.

Cairns, D. (1990) 'Aid for the developing world', *Accountancy*, March, pp. 82–5.

Cañibano Calvo, L. (1990) *Contabilidad: Analisis Contable de la Realidad Económica*, Ediciones Piramide.

Carey, J.L. (1970) 'How can barriers against international accounting practice be eliminated?', *International Journal of Accounting*, Fall, pp. 53–8.

Cecchini, P. (1988) *The European Challenge 1992*, Gower.

Cerf A.R. (1961) *Corporate Reporting and Investment Decisions*, University of California, Berkeley.

Choi, F.D.S. (1989) 'Economic effects of multinational accounting diversity', *Journal of International Financial Management and Accounting*, 1:2, pp. 105–29.

Choi, F.D.S. and Levich, R.M. (1990) *The Capital Market Effects of International Accounting Diversity*, Business One, Irwin, Illinois.

Choi, F.D.S. and Levich, R.M. (1991) 'International accounting diversity: does it affect market participation?', *Financial Analysts Journal*, July–August, pp. 73–82.

Cook, A. (1989) 'International business: a channel for change in the United Kingdom' in Hopwood A.G. (ed.) *International Pressures for Accounting Change*, pp. 33–42, Prentice Hall.

Cooke, T.E. (1989) 'Disclosure in the corporate annual reports of Swedish companies', *Accounting and Business Research*, Spring, pp. 113–24.

Cowan, T.K. (1979) 'The accounting backwash from Watergate', *Accountant's Journal*, November, pp. 379–81.

Cummings, J.P. (1976) 'Bringing the world together at IASC', *World*, Winter, pp. 6–8.

Da Costa, R.C., Bourgeois, J.C. and Lawson, W. (1978) 'A classification of international financial accounting practices', *International Journal of Accounting*, Spring, pp. 73–85.

D'Illiers, B. (1990) 'Mutual recognition of accounts between the EC and third countries' in *The Future of Harmonization of Accounting Standards with the European Communities*, pp. 44–5, Commission of the European Community, Luxembourg.

Doost, R.K. and Ligon, K.M. (1986) 'How the US and European accounting practices differ', *Management Accounting* (US), October, pp. 38–41.

Drury, C. (1989) 'A survey of UK leasing practice', *Management Accounting* (UK), April, pp. 40–3.

Drury, D.H. (1979) 'Effects of accounting practice divergence: Canada and the United States', *Journal of International Business Studies*, Fall, pp. 75–87.

Eccles, G. and Lifford, W. (1979) 'Accounting for research and development', *Accountants Digest* **74**, Institute of Chartered Accountants in England and Wales.

Elliott, S. (1983) 'Beware lion's mouth, warns head of IASC', *Accountant's Journal*, February, pp. 4–6.

Enthoven, A.J.H. (1983) 'US accounting and the Third World', *Journal of Accountancy*, June, pp. 110–18.

Fantl, I.L. (1971) 'The case against international uniformity', *Management Accounting* (US), May, pp. 13–16.

Ferst, S. (1973) 'The accountancy profession in transition', *Accountant's Journal*, April, pp. 313–20.

Firth, M.A. (1979) 'The impact of size, stock market listing and auditors on voluntary disclosure in corporate annual reports', *Accountancy and Business Research*, Autumn, pp. 273–80.

Fitzgerald, R.D. (1981) 'International harmonization of accounting and reporting', *International Journal of Accounting*, Fall, pp. 21–32.

Foroughi, T.K. (1981) 'Accounting in developing countries before and after social crisis: the case of Iran', *International Journal of Accounting*, Fall, pp. 181–223.

Gerboth, D. (1972) 'Muddling through with the APB', *Journal of Accountancy*, May, pp. 42–9.

Gerboth, D. (1973) 'Research intuition and politics in accounting inquiry', *Accounting Review*, July, pp. 475–82.

Gibson, R.W. (1971) *Disclosure by Australian Companies*, Melbourne University Press.

Gonzalo, J.A. and Tua Pereda, J. (1988) *Introducción a la contabilidad internacional*, Instituto de Planificación Contable, Ministerio de Economía y Hacienda.

Gray, R., Owen, D. and Maunders, K. (1987) *Corporate Social Accounting*, Prentice Hall.

Gray, S.J. (1980) 'The impact of international accounting differences from a security analysis perspective', *Journal of Accounting Research*, Spring, pp. 64–76.

Gray, S.J., Shaw, J.C. and McSweeney, L.B. (1981) 'Accounting standards and multinational corporations', *Journal of International Business Studies*, Spring/Summer, pp. 121–36.

Hanson, D. (1989) 'Internationalization of the accounting firm' in Hopwood, A.G. (ed.) *International Pressures for Accounting Change*, pp. 43–56, Prentice Hall.

Hatfield, H.R. (1966) 'Some variations in accounting practices in England, France, Germany and the United States', *Journal of Accounting Research*, Autumn, pp. 160–82.

Hope, A. and Gray, R. (1982) 'Power and policy making: the development of an R&D standard', *Journal of Business Finance and Accounting*, Winter, pp. 531–58.

Hopwood, A., Page, M. and Turley, S. (1990) *Understanding Accounting in a Changing Environment*, Prentice Hall.

Horngren, C.T. (1972) 'Accounting principles: private or public sector?', *Journal of Accountancy*, May, pp. 37–41.

Horngren, C.T. (1973) 'The marketing of accounting standards', *Journal of Accountancy*, October, pp. 61–6.

Horngren, C.T. (1976) 'Will the FASB be here in the 1980s?', *Journal of Accountancy*, November, pp. 90–6.

Hussein, M.E. (1981) 'Translation problems of international accounting standards', *International Journal of Accounting*, Fall, pp. 147–55.

Instituto de Planificación Contable (1978) *Empresas Eléctricas – Plan General de Contabilidad, Normas de Adaptación*, Ministerio de Hacienda.

Le Fèvre, A. (1990) 'Amendments to the 4th Directive' in *The Future of Harmonization of Accounting Standards within the European Communities*, pp. 104–5, Commission of the European Communities.

Lev, B. (1976) 'The formulation of accounting standards and rules: a comparison of efforts in Israel and the United States', *International Journal of Accounting*, pp. 121–31.

Mason, A.K. (1978) *The Development of International Financial Reporting Standards*, International Centre for Research in Accounting, University of Lancaster.

Michel, A. and Shaked, I. (1985) 'Japanese leverage: myth or reality?', *Financial Analysts Journal*, **41**, 4, pp. 61–7.

Most, K.S. (1964) 'How bad are European accounts?', *Accountancy*, January, pp. 9–15.

Mueller, G. (1967) *International Accounting*, Macmillan, New York.

Mueller, G. (1968) 'Accounting principles generally accepted in the United States versus those generally accepted elsewhere', *International Journal of Accounting*, Spring.

Nair, R.D. (1982) 'Empirical guidelines for comparing international accounting data', *Journal of International Business Studies*, Winter, pp. 85–98.

Nair, R.D. and Frank, W.G. (1980) 'The impact of disclosure and measurement practices on international accounting classifications', *Accounting Review*, July, pp. 426–50.

Näsi, S. (1990) 'The development of accounting thought from the middle of the last century to the present day in Finland', Paper to the EIASM Workshop on Accounting in Europe, Brussels, May 1990.

Ndubizu, G.A. (1984) 'Accounting standards and economic development: the Third World in perspective', *International Journal of Accounting*, Spring, pp. 181–96.

Nobes, C. (1983a) 'A judgmental international classification of financial reporting practices', *Journal of Business Finance and Accounting*, **10**, 1, pp. 1–19.

Nobes, C. (1983b) *International Classification of Financial Reporting*, Croom Helm.

Nobes, C. (1991) 'Harmonization of financial reporting' in Nobes, C. and Parker, R. (eds) *Comparative Financial Accounting*, pp. 70–91, Prentice Hall.

Plan General de Contabilidad (1990) Actualidad Editorial S.A., Madrid.

Previts, G.J. (1975) 'On the subject of methodology and models for international accountancy', *International Journal of Accounting*, Spring.

Price Waterhouse (1973) *Accounting Principles and Reporting Practices: A Survey in 38 Countries*, Institute of Chartered Accountants in England and Wales.

Price Waterhouse (1975) *Accounting Principles and Reporting Practices: A Survey in 46 Countries*, Institute of Chartered Accountants in England and Wales.

Price Waterhouse (1979) *International Survey of Accounting Principles and Reporting Practices*, Butterworths.

Rappaport, A. (1977) 'Economic impact of accounting standards – implications for the FASB', *Journal of Accountancy*, May, pp. 89–98.

Samuels, J.M. and Oliga, J.C. (1982) 'Accounting standards in developing countries', *International Journal of Accounting*, Fall, pp. 69–88.

Samuels, J.M. and Piper, A.L. (1985) *International Accounting: A Survey*, Croom Helm.

Scheid, J.C. and Standish, P. (1989) 'Accounting standardization in France and international accounting exchanges' in Hopwood, A.G. (ed.) *International Pressures for Accounting Change*, pp. 162–86.

Seidler, L.J. (1967) 'International accounting – the ultimate theory course', *Accounting Review*, pp. 775–81.

Sharp, K.J. (1979) 'The Whitehall perspective: Government and accounting standards; *The Accountant*, July 19, pp. 67–9.

Shillinglaw, G. (1966) 'International comparability of accounts', *Accountancy*, February, pp. 80–3.

Simmonds, A. (1989) '1992 – a force for change in corporate reporting?', *Accountant's Magazine*, January, pp. 16–18.

Simmonds, A. and Azières, O. (1989) *Accounting for Europe – Success by 2000 AD?*, Touche Ross.

Singhvi, S.S. and Desai, H. (1971) 'An empirical analysis of the quality of corporate financial disclosure', *Accounting Review*, January.

Slipkowsky, J.N. (1988) 'The Volvo way of financial reporting', *Management Accounting*, October, pp. 22–6.

Solomons, D. (1978) 'The politicization of accounting', *Journal of Accountancy*, November, pp. 65–72.

Spicer and Oppenheim (1989) *Financial Statements Around the World*, John Wiley and Sons.

Stamp, E. (1980) *Corporate Reporting: Its Future Evolution*, Canadian Institute of Chartered Accountants.

Standish, P.E.M. (1990) 'Origins of the *plan comptable général*: a study in cultural intrusion and reaction', *Accounting and Business Research*, Autumn, pp. 337–51.

Tay, J.S.W. and Parker, R.H. (1990) 'Measuring International Harmonization and Standardization', *Abacus* No. 1, pp. 71–88.

Taylor, P. and Turley, S. (1985) 'The views of management on accounting for leases', *Accounting and Business Research*, Winter, pp. 59–67.

Tondkar, R.H., Adhikari, A. and Coffman, E.N. (1990) 'An analysis of the impact of selected EEC directives on harmonizing listing and filing requirements of EEC stock exchanges', *International Journal of Accounting*, Vol 25, No. 2, pp. 127–43.

Treffers, H.C. (1967) 'The changing nature of the European accounting profession', *International Journal of Accounting*, Fall, pp. 43–54.

Turner, J. (1983) 'International harmonization: a professional goal', *Journal of Accountancy*, January, pp. 58–66.

Tweedie, D. and Whittington, G. (1984) *The Debate on Inflation Accounting*, Cambridge University Press.

Tyson, R.E. (1974) 'The failure of the City of Glasgow Bank and the rise of independent auditing', *Accountant's Magazine*, April, pp. 126–31.

Underdown, B. and Taylor, P.J. (1985) *Accounting Theory and Policy Making*, Heinemann.

Walton, P. (1986) 'The export of British accounting legislation to Commonwealth countries', *Accounting and Business Research*, Autumn, pp. 353–57.

Watts, T.R. (1981) 'Planning the next decade' in Leach, R. and Stamp, E. *British Accounting Standards – The Next 10 Years*, pp. 27–38, Woodhead-Faulkner.

Weetman, P. and Gray, S.J. (1991) 'A comparative international analysis of the impact of accounting principles on profits: the USA versus the UK, Sweden and the Netherlands', *Accounting and Business Research*, Autumn, pp. 363–79.

Westwick, C. (1980) 'The lessons to be learned from the development of inflation accounting in the UK', *Accounting and Business Research*, Autumn, pp. 353–72.

White, B. (1984) 'International differences in gearing: how important are they?', *National Westminster Bank Quarterly Review*, November, pp. 14–25.

Wilson, A. (1991) 'US and EC: harmonization through equivalence', *Accountancy*, April, pp. 81–2.

World Leasing Year Book (1987) Hawkins Publications.

Zeff, S.A. (1978) 'The rise of economic consequences', *Journal of Accountancy*, December, pp. 56–63.

Zeff, S.A. (1979) *Forging Accounting Principles in New Zealand*, Victoria University Press.

Zeff, S.A. (1984) 'Promoting international harmony', *Accountant's Journal*, August, p. 291.

Zeff, S.A. and Johansson, S.E. (1984) 'The curious accounting treatment of the Swedish government loan to Uddeholm', *Accounting Review*, April, pp. 342–50.

CHAPTER 2

National and International Sources of Authority

ABBREVIATIONS

AECA	Asociación Española de Contabilidad y Administración
AFA	Asian Federation of Accountants
APB	Accounting Principles Board (precursor of the FASB)
ASC	Accounting Standards Committee
ASEAN	Association of South East Asian Nations
CCA	Current Cost Accounting
CP	Contador Público
CPA	Certified Public Accountant
CPP	Current Purchasing Power
EC	European Community
ECU	European Currency Unit
ECFA	Evangelical Council for Financial Accountability
EEC	European Economic Community
FAR	Föreningen Auktoriserade Revisörer (Sweden)
FAS	Financial Accounting Standards
FASB	Financial Accounting Standards Board
FCPA	Foreign Corrupt Practices Act
FEE	Fédération des Experts Comptables Européens
FRS	Financial Reporting Standards
GAAP	Generally Accepted Accounting Principles
GEISAR	Group of Experts on International Standards of Accounting and Reporting
IAS	International Accounting Standards
IASC	International Accounting Standards Committee
ICAC	Instituto de Contabilidad y Auditoria de Cuentas
MNE	Multinational Enterprise
OECD	Organization for Economic Cooperation and Development
PGC	Plan General de Contabilidad
REA	Registro de Economistas Auditores (Spain)
ROAC	Registro Oficial de Auditores de Cuentas (Spain)
SEC	Securities and Exchange Commission (USA)
SFAC	International Federation of Accountants
SSAP	Statement of Standard Accounting Practice (UK)
TNC	Transnational Corporations
UEC	Union d'Experts Comptables
UK	United Kingdom
UN	United Nations
US	United States
USA	United States of America

INTRODUCTION   **In this chapter we:**

1. **Consider the sources of authority in the regulation of accountancy at the national level, and note the relative merits of public sector and private sector regulation.**

2. **Critically appraise a classification system for national modes of regulation.**

3. **Review the range of bodies engaged in promoting international accounting harmonization.**

4. **Discuss the audit role and some practical problems in the audit of multinational companies.**

5. **Analyse the nature and effect of the internationalization of professional accounting firms.**

NATIONAL SOURCES OF AUTHORITY

Sources of authority for accounting regulation in a country may include the following:

1. *Legislation* This may come under such headings as 'company law', 'accounting law', or, in those countries where tax practice dominates accounting practice, 'tax law'. In some countries, such as Sweden, a single 'accounting law' may apply to all reporting entities. In other countries, such as the UK, separate accounting legislation exists for different categories of reporting entity.

2. *Governmental bodies* In some countries bodies appointed by the Government have a role in formulating or interpreting accounting regulation. An example is Spain's *Instituto de Contabilidad y Auditoria de Cuentas* (ICAC) discussed below in Chapter 14. In the USA, Congress has delegated authority for accounting regulation of stock exchange listed corporations to the Securities Exchange Commission (SEC), a Government appointed body.

3. *Professional and private sector bodies* Professional accountancy bodies can produce statements which have the character of accounting regulations. In the English-speaking world these are commonly termed 'standards' e.g. Financial Accounting Standards (FASs) in the USA, Financial Reporting Standards (FRSs) in the UK since 1991, Statements of Standard Accounting Practice (SSAPs) in New Zealand and in the UK up to 1990. The authority of such statements can be of various kinds:

   (a) In some countries, such as Canada, the law may explicitly require companies to comply with accounting standards. This is now the case in the UK for large companies (see below Chapter 16).

   (b) A governmental regulatory body may, subject to review, require companies to comply with specific standards. This is the case of the SEC in the USA.

(c) The profession may use its influence with its own members to secure compliance. In 1959 in the USA an Accounting Principles Board was launched with the managing partners of the (then) 'big eight' accounting firms included in its membership; the hope was that, as participants in the formulation of the professions agreed collective view on best practice, they would then ensure its adoption by their firms (see Zeff 1972, p. 173). Another method is to require members, under threat of disciplinary action, to use their best endeavours to secure compliance. This is particularly effective where the professional body has a legal monopoly of appointment as auditors, who can use the audit report to identify non-compliance (see Blake 1991, pp. 5–6 for the UK example).

(d) Professional pronouncements may be influential despite lack of legal or professional disciplinary sanction simply because their technical quality commands respect. An example is in Spain where a private body of accountants, *Asociación Española de Contabilidad y Administración*, (AECA) produces recommendations which have, on occasion, later been adopted and issued as regulations by the government regulatory body ICAC.

Sometimes a private sector standard-setting body established by accountants may widen its range of sponsors to include representatives of users of accounts. For example, in the USA the Financial Accounting Foundation (FAF) that oversees the Financial Accounting Standards Board (FASB) is appointed by a range of representative bodies with an interest in accounting (see Miller and Redding 1988 for details).

4. *Industry specific initiatives* Sometimes a voluntary association of parties in one particular activity will agree on common reporting standards to enhance the credibility of their accounts. Two examples illustrate how this may arise:

(a) In 1979 the Evangelical Council for Financial Accountability (ECFA) was formed by US religious organizations. The organizations' objective is to establish standards for financial reporting and certify compliance with those standards so as to 'increase the public's confidence in the business affairs of evangelical organizations'. This voluntary association to enhance the credibility of financial reporting was particularly popular in 1987 when several leading evangelists were involved in scandal – that year saw some 160 new applications for membership (Harper and Harper 1988).

(b) Axelson (1975) reports that in the USA major retailers were believed to make excessive profits from their customer credit operations, and as a result a number of states legislated to reduce maximum service charges. One major retailer, J.C. Penney, responded with published information in the annual accounts showing that profit levels were in fact modest, and had the company's auditors cover these data. Axelson reports: 'when additional retailers and other credit granters adopted a similar disclosure practice and had their auditors attest to their operating results, the public began to recognize that the profitability of retail credit was, in fact, a myth' (p. 44).

In practice, virtually every country has some element of legislation on accounting requirements. The extent of private sector involvement in standard setting varies.

Zeff (1972) offers a justification for the role of the accounting profession in formulating accounting regulations in these terms:

> I cling to the belief that accounting principles should be established by agencies in the private sector, preferably professional accounting societies, not by government fiat, whether through legislation, Presidential or judicial decree, or administrative regulation. Surely the result would be more responsive to societal needs and less fettered by bureaucratic intrigue, political pressure, regulatory ossification, and the renowned capacity of the judiciary, at least in the US, to abide procedural obfuscation and delay (p. viii).

Internationally, a survey of 30 countries found that in 25 of them the professional accounting bodies set standards or guidelines relating to external financial reporting (Gray et al. 1984, p. 18). Thus at first sight the case argued by Zeff seems to have found favour across a wide range of countries. As we shall see below, the relationship between Government and accountants as sources of regulation is a complex one that varies widely between countries.

The role of the profession in formulating accounting regulations is subject to criticism from two sides. On the one hand are those who argue that accountants lack a broad social perspective. Tinker (1985) has articulated this view with particular vigour.

> The role of accounting in major social controversies is never articulated in accounting education because the intellectual apparatus necessary for conducting a comprehensive appraisal is withheld. Instead, every year some 50,000 new US students are overwhelmed with a welter of technical and legalistic material that has no apparent connection to the conflicts and complexities of social existence. The ultimate trivialization and degradation of accounting is the near obsession with rules and bookkeeping procedures. Today's students are trained to become greyhounds in bookkeeping and ignoramuses in social analysis (pp. xx–xxi).

On the other hand there is the argument that all regulation is unnecessary. This is because firms have an incentive to reduce 'agency costs', i.e. to convince those outside the firm that the managers can be trusted as agents to handle the resources entrusted to them. For example, Watts (1977) observes that 'in an unregulated economy, without legally required corporate financial statements, we could observe corporate financial statements fulfilling the function of reducing agency costs' (p. 58). It is argued that no set of accounting rules can adequately meet the very different needs that different firms will have with different users of accounts (Demski 1973). By contrast, the market mechanism means that firms will meet user demands. As an example of many studies that argue this point Chow (1982) looked back to 1926 to a time when a professional audit was not mandatory in the USA. He found that firms with high gearing were more likely to appoint an auditor, indicating responsiveness to the demands of providers of finance.

Thus accountants, in putting themselves forward to contribute to the process of accounting regulations, are open to two contrasting challenges:

1. On one side, it is argued that the traditional accounting framework is an inadequate basis to respond to social needs.
2. On the other side, the whole case for any form of accounting regulations is under challenge, with the argument that market forces are adequate to promote good practice.

A discussion by Al Hashim and Arpan (1988) on the accounting regulatory environment in 11 countries illustrates the variances in different countries' approaches to accounting regulation. Table 2.1 summarizes their discussion on three aspects:

1. The predominant sources of accounting regulations.
2. The broad tone of accounting regulations.
3. The role of the accounting profession in the development of accounting regulations.

In each country legislation has some role to play. There are, however, major variations in the influence of the accounting profession. In the USA, the UK, the Netherlands and the Philippines, the accounting profession has a direct role in formulating accounting regulations such as SSAPs.

In France, the profession also has a major role, but by the route of being consulted on legislation. In Switzerland, the accounting profession issues recommendations that are non-mandatory but are influential. In Germany, the accounting profession is concerned with legal compliance rather than developing new accounting procedures. In Taiwan, the accounting profession, founded as recently as 1945, had become more influential during the 1980s. In 1982 a committee to formulate statements of generally accepted accounting principles was established. In Brazil, Japan and Korea, the accounting profession has little influence.

The tone of accounting regulations varies significantly, even comparing European Community members which are supposed to have achieved a degree of harmonization following implementation of the Fourth Directive. Nobes (1980) discusses the contrasting accounting traditions of European Community members. Factors he identifies in a comparison of the UK, France, and Germany, include:

Table 2.1 A Comparison of Different Countries' Approaches to Developing Accounting Rules

Country	Predominant source of regulations	Tone of regulations	Role of profession
USA	Legislation and profession	Flexible	Substantial but under attack
UK	Legislation and profession	Becoming more subject to legislation	Substantial
Brazil	Legislation	*	Minor
France	Legislation	Dominated by conservatism consistency and tax law	Profession involved in preparing legislation and own, non-mandatory recommendations
Germany	Legislation	Tax-dominated extreme conservatism	Concerned with legal compliance rather than development of procedures
Japan	Legislation	Tax-dominated – very conservative	Under control of finance ministry
Korea	Legislation	Tax-dominated	Very limited
Netherlands	Legislation and profession	Flexible. Strong influence of business economics	Substantial
Philippines	Legislation, profession, stock exchange	Similar to USA	Major role
Switzerland	Little regulation – some basic disclosure legislation	Flexible, conservative, with minimum disclosure. German influence on voluntary disclosure	Influence through non-mandatory recommendations
Taiwan	Legislation	*	Traditionally minor but now growing

(Based on analysis in Al Hashim and Arpan (1988) pp. 20–42).

*No comment on general tone on these countries.

1. The contrast between the English common law system and the civil code systems that dominate continental legal systems, with their emphasis on detailed prescription.

2. The different financial systems, comparing the UK's 3,000 listed companies with the 900 in France and 500 in Germany and the tendency for control of French and German companies to be vested in banks, governments or families. This is seen as explaining the UK emphasis on 'fair' presentation.

3. France and Germany have an emphasis on tax law in the development of accounting practice.

A CLASSIFICATION SYSTEM FOR NATIONAL MODES OF REGULATION

Puxty et al. (1987) offer a framework for comparing national modes of accounting regulation. They identify three broad sources of regulation:

1. Market forces, guided by dispersed competition. They cite a range of literature that identifies accounting practices as emerging in response to market pressures.

2. The state, guided by hierarchical control. Legislation has some role to play in accounting regulation in all countries.

3. The community, guided by 'spontaneous solidarity'. Puxty et al. argue that while market forces clearly influence the actions of accountants 'it is important to acknowledge that accounting activities may also be defended and reproduced by practitioners because they offer a valued source of personal satisfaction, collective identity and social esteem, and not solely because they are of instrumental, material value' (p. 279).

On the basis of this analysis four strategies of regulation are identified, illustrated by the diagram reproduced in Fig. 2.1.

1. *Liberalism* provides regulation exclusively by the discipline of market principles.

2. *Legalism* involves the unreserved application of state principles.

3. *Associationism* where 'there is some dependence upon principles of community. However, such principles are routinely subordinated to those of the market. Membership is founded principally upon calculative rationality rather than a desire to share common values' (p. 284).

4. *Corporatism* arises where the state incorporates organized interest groups into its own system of regulation. 'In doing so, the state simultaneously recognizes its dependence on these associations and seeks to use them as an instrument in the pursuit and legitimation of its policies.'

Fig. 2.1 Puxty et al.'s view of accounting regulations

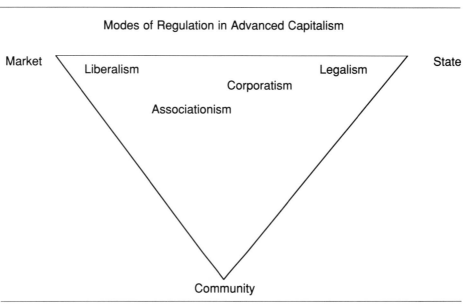

(*Source*: Puxty et al. (1987) p. 283)

Puxty et al. use their analysis to consider four countries' systems of accounting regulation. Three of these countries, 'Germany, Sweden, and the United Kingdom are considered below (see Chapters 7, 15 and 16). The fourth, the USA, offers some interesting contrasts.

In the USA, corporate legislation is a matter for individual states, which license certified public accountants (CPAs). However, the dominant influence is at the Federal level where the Securities and Exchange Commission (SEC), a Government-appointed body, prescribes rules for publicly held companies. In practice the SEC has generally been willing to entrust the process of accounting standard setting to the Financial Accounting Standards Board (FASB), a private sector body. The FASB consists of seven full-time members who are required to sever links with existing employers when appointed. The FASB is supported by a large staff.

The limitations of the authority of the private sector were dramatically illustrated by the investment tax credit case in 1971. The Accounting Principles Board (APB), precursor of the FASB, proposed an unpopular reporting requirement for the effects of the investment tax credit. Vigorous lobbying culminated in Congress enacting that 'no taxpayer shall be required, without his consent, to use . . . any particular method of accounting for the credit' (Horngren 1972, p. 40). Horngren (1976) observes that 'the FASB has limited power. The Board exercises authority primarily at the pleasure of the SEC and other governmental forces. Therefore, principles are set in close informal contact . . . responsibility does not now lie in the private sector. At best, it is a joint private-public undertaking' (p. 91).

The contrast between the UK and the USA is interesting. In the UK, Government influence has generally been exercised by informal, indeed rather secretive, channels. In the USA, Government influence through the SEC, and ultimately Congress, is open and clearly structured.

Some academics have raised the question whether the SEC's role in controlling accounting standards has been strictly within the law, arguing that an unconstitutional application of delegated legislation may be involved (see Johnson 1981, Committe 1990). By contrast, in the UK discussion of the legal standing of accounting standards has seen them as a useful source of technical guidance to the courts (Sherrard 1981).

Puxty et al. classify the four countries as follows:

1. Germany is seen as a clear example of legalism.

2. In view of the UK accountancy profession being 'nominally independent' of the state, the UK approach is seen as associationist.

3. The direct involvement of the Swedish state in accounting regulations is seen as an example of corporatism.

4. The USA 'cannot be typified quite so easily' (p. 286). In view of the dependence of the FASB on the support of the SEC the USA is said to 'contain elements of legalism and associationism, with the later subordinated to the former' (p. 286).

Cooke (1988), discussing this analysis in the context of Sweden, is critical: He expresses a broad distaste for the approach, criticizing the use of 'highfalutin terms'. A number of specific criticisms focus particularly on the importance of FAR's recommendations in Swedish practice (p. 7) which Cooke feels Puxty et al. grossly underestimate.

Puxty et al.'s distinction between the UK as associationist and the USA as predominantly legalist accepts at face value the apparent independence of the UK accounting profession. This may be justified by their emphasis on identifying 'the *formal* modes of accounting regulations' (p. 286). However, it can be argued that in the UK the state influences the accountancy profession through informal channels at least as strongly as the formal channels used in the USA. This can happen in several ways:

1. On occasion the Government may intervene directly. For example, in the mid-1970s the Government set up the Sandilands Committee on inflation accounting thereby disrupting the ASC's work on a CPP approach (see Westwick 1980 for a discussion of the Government's motives and Myddelton 1981 for an analysis of how the Government directed the Committee towards a CCA approach).

2. The Government may intervene behind the scenes to influence the ASC. Sharp (1979) cites the deferred tax debate as an example.

3. ASC members may also be members of Government-nominated committees and thereby be privy to, and influenced by, Government

thinking. Hope and Gray (1982) identify research and development as an issue where this has occurred.

Puxty et al. seek to identify and classify a single Swedish mode of regulation. The analysis of Swedish accounting in Chapter 15 suggests two parallel systems. One, based on law, applies to all companies and in Puxty et al.'s terms is firmly legalistic. The other, based on voluntary support for FAR recommendations, applies particularly to listed companies and, responding to market forces, might be seen as a form of liberalism.

To summarize, Puxty et al. offer an interesting framework for discussion of modes of accounting regulation but we would see three of their four examples as open to considerable debate.

INTERNATIONAL SOURCES OF AUTHORITY

A number of organizations are involved in the international promotion of accounting harmonization.

The *International Accounting Standards Committee* (IASC) was established in 1973 by the professional accounting bodies of nine countries, namely Australia, Canada, France, Germany, Japan, Mexico, the Netherlands, the UK with Ireland[*], and the USA. By 1991 it had grown to include 106 professional accounting bodies in 79 countries, and had issued 31 standards. National professional bodies are committed to promoting IASs in their own country. The ability of a national professional body to do this does, of course, depends on the role of accountants in the process of accounting regulation in that particular country. There are a number of ways in which IASs may be applied in a country:

1. An IAS may simply be adopted as a national requirement, normally with a foreword spelling out any conflicts with local law. Cairns (1990) claims that this is a particularly useful approach for developing countries, saving the technical costs of developing national standards. On the other hand there are those who argue that IASs do not serve developing countries well, being dominated by US requirements; Hove (1989) identifies the failure of IAS 24 on related party disclosures to require extensive disclosure on transfer pricing as an explicit example of this problem.

2. An IAS may be used as the basis of a national requirement but with material local adaptations.

3. National requirements may be developed from IASs but be adapted to conform to them.

[*]Having common professional accounting bodies the UK and Ireland count as one for this purpose.

Table 2.2 IAS 1, Disclosure of Accounting Policies

	IAS adopted as a national requirement	IAS used as the basis for a national requirement	National requirement developed separately and conforms in all material respects with IAS	No national requirements but national practice generally conforms with IAS	National requirement developed separately but does not conform with IAS	No national requirements and national practice does not generally conform with IAS
Abu Dhabi				■		
Australia			■			
Austria				■		
Bahrain				■		
Belgium			■			
Botswana	■					
Brazil			■			
Canada			■			
Cyprus	■					
Denmark			■			
Dubai				■		
Fiji		■				
Finland					■	
France			■			
Germany					■	
Ghana				■		
Greece						■
Hong Kong			■			
Iceland			■			
India			■			
Indonesia			■			
Ireland			■			
Italy			■			
Jamaica		■				
Japan			■			
Kenya		■				
Kuwait		■				
Lesotho		■				
Malawi	■					
Malaysia	■					
Malta				■		
Mexico			■			
Morocco				■		
Netherlands			■			
New Zealand			■			
Nigeria			■			
Norway			■			
Oman	■					
Pakistan	■					
Saudi Arabia				■		
Singapore		■				
South Africa					■	
Spain			■			
Sri Lanka		■				
Swaziland			■			
Sweden			■			
Switzerland						■
Taiwan						
Tanzania			■			
Trinidad and Tobago				■		
United Kingdom			■			
United States			■			
Yugoslavia			■			
Zimbabwe	■					
Totals	7	7	25	9	3	2

(Reproduced from IASC 1988, p. 21)

A survey by IASC in the 1980s examined compliance in a range of countries. Table 2.2 summarizes compliance with IAS 1, a keystone standard.

Schoenfeld (1981) identified three 'problems' with International Accounting Standards:

1. because they are based on consensus, at present, too much rigidity is avoided;

2. in some instances, standards are contrary to national regulations . . . and in such cases domestic laws take precedence;

3. divergence from IAS should be disclosed (in footnotes), however the extent of such disclosure is not well defined (p. 87).

The secretary-general of the IASC has referred to the problem that arises when the professional accounting bodies that subscribe to IASC do not have standard-setting authority, and he reports that IASC is seeking to involve 'all standard-setting bodies, whatever their form' in developing International Standards (Cairns 1989, p. 82).

Fleming (1991) reports on an interview with Arthur Wyatt, chairman of IASC, in which there was some discussion of the problem of how to reduce the range of accounting treatment presently permitted by IASs. This problem is attributed to the role that 75 per cent of the 14 voting members of the IASC board must agree before an IAS can be issued, and Wyatt is quoted:

> If you could get agreement on two alternatives you could capture the 11 required votes and eliminate some of the less-used practices

and

> it's not much of a standard if you have two alternatives, but it's better than having six (p. 101).

In 1988 the IASC embarked upon the 'comparability project', later renamed the 'improvements project', to reduce the number of alternative accounting approaches permitted in IASs. So far the alternatives permitted in IASs have almost invariably embraced existing US practice. Narrowing the range of permitted practices is likely to involve conflict with some existing US rules posing a challenge to the Financial Accounting Standards Board (FASB) in the USA.

In 1989 the IASC produced a 'framework for the preparation and presentation of financial statements'. This responded to the comments of those such as Violet (1983) who saw a need for a 'framework of universally accepted postulates' (p. 1) to underpin standard setting.

The IASC identifies seven purposes for the framework, which can be analysed under three broad headings:

1. To assist the work of accounting regulations, i.e. accounting policy choice at the 'macro' level.

R.T.C. LIBRARY, LETTERKENNY

Three aspects explicitly covered by the IASC are

(a) to assist IASC to develop new IASs

(b) to justify reductions in permitted alternatives

(c) to assist national standard setters.

2. To assist those connected with the production of accounts, i.e. accounting policy choice at the 'micro' level. Specifically the IASC see two types of use:

(a) To assist preparers of accounts

(b) To assist auditors.

3. To provide information on the IASC's approach, i.e. an educational role. Two specific groups are identified:

(a) Users of accounts interpreting the application of IASs

(b) Those interested in understanding the work of IASC.

The framework has detailed sections on:

1. Scope of accounts

2. Objectives of accounts

3. Underlying assumptions of accounts

4. Qualitative characteristics of accounts

5. Constraints on relevance and reliability

6. Elements of financial statements

7. Recognition of elements of financial statements

8. Concepts of capital maintenance.

The IASC's conceptual framework is, unavoidably, a compromise between various viewpoints. For example, in identifying the user groups whose needs must be considered there is range of national positions ranging from the FASB in the USA, where SFAC 1 identifies providers of capital as the focus, to the French accounting plan with its detailed analysis of a wide range of users and purposes of accounts. The IASC conceptual framework, having identified a range of users to be served, asserts that accounts that meet the needs of investors 'will also meet most of the needs of other users that financial statements can satisfy' (para. 10). It would be easy to challenge this assertion with a demonstration of a range of instances where this is not the case, and in the UK a discussion paper, the *Corporate Report*, identified a number of examples (Accounting Standards Steering Committee 1975). However, the IASC's position offers a convenient compromise, allowing those who prefer a shareholder orientation to cite the provision quoted above and those who prefer a broader view of users to be served to cite the full list provided in the framework.

It is doubtful whether one framework can actually serve the wide range of purposes to which the IASC aspires. As an example, Blake and Higson (1992) have examined the 'neutrality' concept, that accounting policy choice should be unbiased, that the IASC identifies as a 'qualitative characteristic'.

They argue that:

1. At the 'macro' level the achievement of neutrality is achievable at a substantial cost. It may have been achieved in some countries; equally, it has clearly not been achieved in others.

2. At the 'micro' level the achievement of neutrality is inherently unlikely since, within the range of choices they are permitted, companies are likely to make a choice based on the image they wish to present.

3. Since the extent to which neutrality applies is small at the 'micro' level and variable between nations at the 'macro' level then its assertion for 'educational' purposes is positively misleading.

In some cases, such as the UK, the IASC framework has been adopted in its entirety by a national standard-setting body. In some cases this leads to a need for a clarification of terms in a national context. Miller (1990) discusses, as one example, the problems of interpretation in South Africa.

Hines (1989) has reviewed a number of national 'conceptual framework' (CF) projects and concludes:

> the major rationale for undertaking CFs was not functional or technical, but was a *strategic manoeuvre* for producing legitimacy to standard-setting boards and the accounting profession during periods of competition or threatened government intervention (p. 89).

Similarly the IASC's conceptual framework appears as a bid for legitimacy in influencing national standard setters and in confronting alternative transnational sources of authority such as the European Community (see below).

One particular point of contrast with the European Community Fourth Directive has been observed by Agrawal et al. (1989):

> There is a definite shift from the concept of the true and fair view (or fair presentation) to decision usefulness of information. This is a significant change in the paradigm of accounting based on theoretical considerations (p. 246).

Although the IASC's conceptual framework may be open to criticism, this venture does respond to a need for a defensible base for the development of IASs. Bedford (1966) observes:

> unless an international body of accounting thought is developed, effective international transmission of accounting practice is not possible (p. 51).

Reviewing the early years of the IASC, McComb (1979) saw a need for developing an understanding of how international accounting differences arise in order to promote harmonization more effectively:

> emphasis should be upon investigation, analysis, and education rather than upon speeding the process of promulgating further international accounting standards (p. 15).

IASC is closely linked to the *International Federation of Accountants* IFAC, founded in 1977. The two bodies have a common membership, IFAC nominates up to 13 members of the IASC board, IFAC contributes 10 per cent of IASC's budget, and the IASC reports on its work annually to the IFAC council. IFAC has undertaken not to issue accounting standards in competition with IASC. IFAC has a number of committees dealing with other aspects of harmonization of the work of the accounting profession internationally, such as the International Auditing Practices Committee (IAPC). It also promotes regional professional accounting bodies such as FEE (see below) (Cummings and Chetkovich 1978). Chandler argues that

> the existence of IFAC makes it possible for the accountancy profession to be moving in the same direction on a worldwide scale (p. 42).

The *United Nations* first became involved in proposals for international accounting regulation in 1972 when the Secretary-General set up a group to examine the impact of multinational companies. This group identified a need for international accounting harmonization leading to the formation of the Group of Experts on International Standards of Accounting and Reporting (GEISAR) in 1976. In 1978 this group published its report which proposed detailed disclosure requirements, similar to those in the USA, together with:

1. Extensive requirements for disclosure by segments and individual companies within groups
2. Detailed disclosures on transfer pricing policies
3. A variety of non-financial information.

These proposals proved highly controversial. Lord Benson, a founder of IASC, commented on the heavy cost of publishing such detail:

> Two typical examples are given merely to indicate the amount of detail which is required. The individual member company is asked to include in its labour and employment report a statement of the 'number of woman employees by function' and, in its production report, a 'description of practices regarding acquisition of raw materials and components (indicating the percentage acquired from intercompany foreign sources and the percentage from all foreign sources)' (Benson 1978, p. 130).

and

> 'The Group states that it has not costed the burden which the additional information requirements will impose. This is an astonishing omission, because the cost will be significant' (Benson 1978, p. 131).

Despite some reservations within the UN about these detailed recommendations (see Pomeranz 1981, pp. 11–14 for analysis of these) an Intergovernmental Working Group (IWG) was set up in 1979 to pursue the development of International Standards on accounting. This group reported in 1982, but was unable to make unified recommendations in the accounting area. Fitzgerald (1981) identifies the basic problem of the UN as a forum for securing agreement on harmonization:

> The performance of the Working Group so far is notable largely for its political rhetoric and the serious basic conflict of views between representatives of the developed nations and the Group of 77. The latter group seems determined to use the UN effort for purposes of demanding detailed disclosures by transnational enterprises which hardly fit within anyone's definition of general-purpose reporting (p. 29).

Broadly speaking, the United Nations is split along geographical and economic lines on the question of how international accounting harmonization should progress. The developing nations regard the UN as an appropriate forum within which to develop wide-ranging compulsory accounting requirements. The Western industrial nations would prefer any UN involvement in accounting harmonization to be on a voluntary basis. As Arpan and Radebaugh (1985) summarize the issue:

> The UN's efforts have become polarized along north–south, developed–less developed political lines, with little chance for reconciliation or agreement (p. 348).

The *Organization for Economic Cooperation and Development (OECD)* produced a set of guidelines to promote greater comparability in company financial reports. The OECD draws its membership from the industrialized nations which are the homes of most of the world's multinational companies, so it is not surprising that its proposals are less demanding than those of the UN. The OECD has sponsored surveys on the needs of international users of accounts which have been cited in Chapter 1 above (p. 5).

For European countries the *European Community* is a major force for accounting harmonization. The European Community promotes the creation of a free internal market within its membership. In order to promote free movement of capital a common framework of company law is being promoted through a series of directives. Three of these, the Fourth Directive on company accounts, the Seventh Directive on consolidation, and the Eighth Directive on auditing, are particularly important for European accountants. The first two of these are referred to in detail in Chapter 3 below, while the Eighth Directive is considered in the next section of this chapter.

Since the implementation of the Single European Act the procedure for producing a directive has been:

1. The Commission consults with a range of national and European experts and interested parties, offering a series of draft proposals, before formulating an official proposal. Vangermeersch (1985) reports that the department handling the Fourth and Seventh Directives was led by two lawyers and had only between two and four staff.

2. The official proposal is considered by the Economic and Social Committee and by the European Parliament. The Commission may modify its proposal in the light of comments and then submit it to the Council of Ministers.

3. The Council of Ministers considers the proposal, normally through a working party, and having reached a common position by qualified majority voting submits its revised version to the European Parliament for a second reading.

4. Following review, and possible amendments by the European Parliament the Council of Ministers reconsiders the proposal for adoption.

Once a directive is adopted it is then for each of the member states to incorporate the directive into national legislation by the prescribed date. In practice this objective is not always achieved – every single member state was late in enacting the Fourth Directive. In national legislation, there is normally some scope for variation in the form and method of implementation.

The evolution of the Fourth Directive offers an interesting illustration of the problems of harmonizing the very different accounting traditions. The first draft was produced in 1971 and reflected the accounting traditions of France and Germany in being based on rigid prescription. On 1 January 1973 the UK joined the Community. One of the UK's leading academic accountants commented:

> The most important fear of British accountants seems to be that the Directive, if implemented in its present form, would discount the importance which we in Britain attach to 'the true and fair view' provision of the British legislation, which leaves room for the necessary flexibility in preparing and reporting upon company accounts (Stamp 1973, p. 14).

Under pressure from the UK government, the second draft was amended to incorporate the 'true and fair view' concept. As a partner in the UK firm of Price Waterhouse commented:

> This is a most important change in emphasis weakening as it does the original prescriptive approach of the first draft (Burnett 1976, p. 29).

In practice, the Fourth Directive has left a number of major areas, such as that of foreign currency translation, with no guidance at all. Where choice is allowed this often tends to differ by country. Simmonds (1989) gives the example of the four types of permitted profit and loss format and the common practice in each of the UK, France, the Netherlands, and Belgium:

Type of format	Commonly used in
Vertical, costs analysed by function	UK
Vertical, costs analysed by type	France, Netherlands
Horizontal, costs analysed by type	Belgium
Horizontal, costs analysed by function	

Turley (1983) comments upon the wide range of options and alternatives allowed in the Fourth Directive. He sees the main harmonization as relating to disclosure items rather than to the underlying basis of computation, so that there is a danger that the appearance rather than the substance of harmonization will result. He concludes that further work on EC harmonization will be needed:

> On the positive side, the Fourth Directive could be defended on the grounds that it represents a pragmatic attempt to move toward the ultimate goal of achieving harmonization of accounting and socioeconomic systems. It may represent the best that is currently attainable and its implementation should promote more fundamental harmonization in the future (p. 27).

Macharzina (1988) raises the interesting point that other directives on company law may have an influence contrary to the spirit of the accounting directives. He cites the case of the proposed Fifth Directive and a suggestion that company shareholders throughout the EC be entitled to vote increases in the dividends proposed by directors up to the amount of realized profit. He argues that this would encourage directors who wish to retain profits to create 'secret reserves', contrary to the Fourth Directive.

There is an interesting debate over the question of whether the EC or the IASC is the most appropriate source of harmonization of accounting in Europe. In favour of EC involvement it is argued that IASC does not have the same power to promote compliance, Benson (1976) argued that:

> I am sure that no accountancy body anywhere in the world has yet done enough to ensure that either its own local standards or international standards are, in fact, being applied by its members in the conduct of their professional practice or in their capacity as directors of business enterprises (p. 39).

Similarly Walker (1978) argues that:

> It would seem that the IASC has little authority. The status of its pronouncements is determined by local rule-making bodies. The major significance of the IASC's operations seems to lie in their influence upon the agendas of the standard-setting committees of several professional associations (p. 98).

In addition to some lack of commitment to implement IASCs by national professional bodies, in some countries the accounting profession has little influence. As McComb (1982) observes:

> In many countries the accountancy profession is not in a position to exercise a direct influence upon the promulgation of standards of accounting. The acceptance of international standards by the profession in those countries is therefore a symbolic act at best, since the power to implement such standards lies elsewhere (p. 48).

Nobes (1980) relates this problem explicitly to the European Community:

> harmonization in the EEC will not be due to the IASC's work, because company and revenue law in such countries as France and Germany is sufficiently weak that accounting standards can have little power in those countries (p. 6).

Choi (1981) argues that harmonization of accounting standards may be easier within a group of countries, a 'cluster', that have similar socio-economic environments and consequently similar accounting approaches. As an example he cites the Association of South East Asian Nations (ASEAN), being Indonesia, Malaysia, the Philippines, Singapore, and Thailand. Professional accounting bodies in these countries formed the ASEAN Federation of Accountants (AFA). Choi appears to envisage AFA having a role in modifying IASC standards. Indeed in an earlier paper he observes:

> Coordination of harmonization efforts in ASEAN and active participation in the formulation of international accounting standards will enable AFA to help buffer the mammoth IASC influence on its member countries. In so doing, AFA will foster a greater sense of confidence within ASEAN and a sense of not being dominated by what is often perceived as an extension of the former 'mother countries' (Choi 1979, p. 65).

The European Community does not have the same coherence as a 'cluster group', and indeed a number of the examples illustrating reasons for differences in accounting styles in Chapter 1 above were drawn from comparisons of EC members.

However, the very existence of the European Community is increasing the need for, and lowering the obstacles to, accounting harmonization (see Blake 1992). Van Hulle (1989) puts forward the interesting argument that the very diversity of accounting traditions in the EC makes it a useful testing ground for harmonization.

> Considering the variety of cultures and traditions in the 12 member states, there is no doubt that the Community's experience with accounting harmonization makes for interesting research material. If the Community can achieve harmonization it must be possible to do so at a broader international level (Van Hulle 1989, p. 97).

Gray et al. (1981) argue that setting international standards is essentially a political process which can only be achieved at the intergovernmental level. They see a benefit in a 'gradualist' approach whereby standards are 'implemented initially on a regional basis' (p. 132).

On the other hand, there are those who argue that the EC can actually disrupt true international harmonization. Thus a President of a major European multinational has argued:

> More disturbing, however, is the concern that by concentrating on harmonization within the member states, the EEC may overlook practices in other countries of the world (such as the US) and thereby further create disharmony in the wider international scene (De Bruyne 1980, p. 36).

Similarly Simmonds (1989) argues:

> I question the wisdom of a 'go it alone' policy whereby we expend time and effort in drawing together the peaks and troughs of European accounting, if the result is unacceptable to our main trading partners elsewhere in the world (p. 29).

An interesting issue that arises in a European Community committed to harmonization is the question whether international discussions should be conducted by the European Commission or by individual nations. *Accountancy* (1991) reports a comment by a senior EC official, Karel Van Hulle, on talks between the US, the UK, and Japan on accounting:

> The issue of harmonization cannot be dealt with in trilateral deals. We are in it together and any negotiations will have to be conducted by the Commission. That is a fact of life.

This assertion drew 'angry responses' from both the Government and the accountancy profession in the UK, asserting the right of the UK to deal directly with these issues.

In addition to the EC, Europe also has a regional grouping of professional accountants, the *Fédération des Experts Comptables Européens* (FEE). This was formed by a merger in 1987 of the UEC (founded 1951) and the *Groupe d'Études* (founded 1961). FEE has professional bodies from 22 countries as members, including all 12 EC countries. One of the roles of FEE is to represent the European accounting profession to the European Commission.

The European Commission has itself set up an advisory body, the Accounting Advisory Forum, composed of representatives from the national standard-setting bodies, European organizations of the main users and preparers of accounts, and the accounting profession. Established in 1991, it will be interesting to observe how influential this body becomes.

While international and regional organizations, both governmental and professional, strive with difficulty to harmonize accounting *regulations* there is an argument that market forces may promote harmonization of accounting *practices* more rapidly. Meek (1984) observes that:

> The competition for investment funds should propel the harmonization movement. This development, indeed, appears to be occurring as multinational corporations increasingly adopt a variant of multiple reporting. One set of financial statements meets local, statutory requirements while another set is prepared for the worldwide user group, based on accounting principles compatible with a decision usefulness orientation (and consistent with IASC standards as well) (p. 49).

In practice the 'second set' is often based on US rather than IASC standards.

THE AUDIT ROLE

Company accounts in all countries are normally supported by an audit report from an independent professionally qualified auditor. The European Community Fourth Directive requires an audit for all large companies, while allowing member states to decide whether or not to impose an audit requirement for small and medium-sized companies. The Eighth Directive requires member states to ensure that all auditors are qualified, achieving at least a university degree level qualification. Each state must also ensure that auditors are independent and carry out audits with due care. Table 2.3 summarizes the character of professional audit qualifications in the EC (Ireland is excluded, being similar to the UK).

A study of European audit reports by Archer et al. (1989) throws some interesting light on how auditing approaches vary between European countries.

Table 2.3 Characteristics of Largest Professional Audit/Accountancy Bodies

	Date founded	Qualification				
		Degree only	Special exam only	Degree or special exam	Degree plus special exam	Experience required
Belgium	1953			x		3 years
Denmark	1912		x (N1)			3 years
France	1942		x (N2)			3 years
Germany	1931				x	5 years
Greece	1955				x	11 years
Italy	(Note 3)			x		2 years
Luxembourg					x	3 years
Netherlands	1895			x		No formal requirement
Portugal	1977				x	3 years
Spain	1944				x	Adequate
UK	1880		x (N2)			3 years

Notes
1. A relevant degree may carry substantial exam exemptions
2. A relevant degree may carry some exam exemptions
3. Description here refers to procedures for achieving state qualification

In most countries a standard form of audit report has emerged. The IAPC have produced International Auditing Guideline (IAG) 13 'The Auditors' report on financial statements'. IAG 13 offers a framework for identifying the key features that should be included in an audit report.

Archer et al. (1989) have made a study of European practices in this area.

IAG13 identifies the following key elements in the audit report:

The Title

In some countries, legal requirements may provide for more than one 'audit report'. For example, Spanish accounts may include both an independent audit report and a report by the 'stockholder auditors' (*accionistas censores de cuentas*). Archer et al. found that in most countries the audit report is identified by a clear title.

The Addressee

National laws vary in their identification of the party to whom the audit report is addressed. Generally this will be either the shareholders or the directors. Identification of the addressee gives the reader of the report some idea of the nature of the audit engagement. However Archer et al. found that less than half of their sample of European companies provided this information.

Identification of the Financial Statements Audited

In different countries the parts of the annual reports covered by the audit process vary. For example, in some countries the funds flow statement may not be covered by the audit report. Archer et al. found that only a minority of companies clearly identified the parts of the annual report covered by the audit.

Reference to Auditing Standards

The Guideline calls for the audit report to indicate what auditing standards have governed the conduct of the audit. Unless otherwise indicated, these will be assumed to be those of the home country. Archer et al. found that just under 60 per cent of their sample mentioned auditing standards used, with no mention by any companies in Austria or Germany.

The Audit Opinion

The form of the audit opinion varies substantially between countries. Matters to consider include:

1. Reference to the 'true and fair view' or 'fair presentation', found by Archer et al. to be covered in some 75 per cent of their sample.
2. Reference to compliance with legal requirements, found in some 60 per cent of the Archer et al. sample.
3. Reference to compliance with accounting standards (national or international), or specific accounting principles. Such reference only occurred in a minority of the Archer et al. sample.

Auditors' Details

Different countries vary as to whether they give the name of an individual auditor or an audit firm. The latter information may be more useful to the international analyst, while naming the individual may be more useful to the domestic analyst who is more likely to know of the reputation of the individual concerned.

AUDITING IN THE MULTINATIONAL ENTERPRISE

The multinational enterprise (MNE) faces a number of issues in running an internal audit system and in the conduct of either an internal or external audit. To give some examples:

Home Country Legislation – the US Case

One issue the MNE may have to face is the need to apply legislation laid down in the holding company's country throughout the world. In the USA the Foreign Corrupt Practices Act (FCPA) of 1977 offers an interesting example of such legislation.

The legislation was formulated in the mid-1970s in response to a number of corrupt practices found by the SEC in the investigations following Watergate in 1972 and the suicide of Eli Black, Chairman of United Brands, in 1975.

Miller (1979) offers two interesting examples:

(a) In the US, it is illegal for corporations to use company funds to make political contributions in federal elections. MNEs were found to be using transfers between foreign subsidiaries to 'launder' illegal contributions. One company admitted such contributions totalling some $27 million – an amount found on investigation to be more than doubled (pp. 62–3).

(b) Corrupt payments by Lockheed aircraft were claimed to exceed $250 million dollars. Implication in these payments forced the resignation of Prince Bernhard of the Netherlands and rocked the Government of Japan. Other affected countries include Saudi Arabia, Italy, Germany, South Africa, Nigeria, Spain and Greece. US taxpayers felt particularly involved because Lockheed had been rescued by a $250 million federally guaranteed loan in 1971 (pp. 64–5).

In total, hundreds of MNEs were considered to have engaged in questionable payments.

The FCPA outlaws bribes to foreign government officials. Penalties are stiff – a fine up to $1 million for the company and a fine up to $10,000 plus five years in prison for the individual. To make these provisions effective, the Act requires US-based MNEs to ensure that all their subsidiaries keep detailed accounting records and operate a tight internal central system to ensure their accuracy. These requirements effectively make an internal audit system essential for the US-based MNE, and affect the work of both the internal and external auditor. Despite these elaborate, and expensive, procedures a survey by Kim and Barone (1981) of members of the Academy of International Business found a widespread view that the FCPA had failed to achieve its goal.

Personnel Issues

In administering the audit function of the MNE, a balance has to be struck between the use of a 'travelling team' covering several countries and employing local auditors. Each approach carries its own costs and problems.

Using local auditors involves:

(a) Training costs to bring local staff to employ the standards required by the MNE.

(b) Loss of 'economies of scale' unless the MNE has a substantial presence in the relevant country.

(c) A loss of comparability between audits in different countries covered by the MNE.

(d) Local auditors may identify with the interests of the local management, their compatriots, rather than the overall interests of the MNE.

(e) Local auditors may not be fully aware of the MNE's policies as laid down at headquarters.

Using headquarters staff involves:

(a) High costs of travelling and, in many cases, language training. Depending on the country where headquarters are based, salary levels may also be higher.

(b) Staff do not have the same knowledge of local business and cultural practices as indigenous auditors. Where headquarters staff are used, some training in sensitivity to variations in cultural norms is desirable.

(c) Time spent on travelling is expensive, while a 'discomfort' factor may reduce levels of performance through the wear and tear of travel and the strain of coping with an unfamiliar environment.

In practice a combination of approaches is common, with local audit staff at larger locations supported by a small headquarters team that also covers smaller locations. Another compromise is to set up regional audit teams covering several countries.

Other problems arise in some countries where local prejudices can diminish the authority of the auditor. In certain cultures, a female auditor may find local employees reluctant to acknowledge her authority. Similarly traditional antipathies between nationalities may create difficulties for an auditor from one country working in another.

Organizational Structure

By and large, the more senior the level of management to which the internal audit team reports the more effective will be their role. In the MNE, a question arises whether the internal auditor should report to the headquarters management or to the local management of the subsidiary being reported upon. Arguments for reporting direct to headquarters include:

(a) The credibility of the internal auditor with local management is enhanced. The internal audit team becomes a channel for communicating headquarters policy.

(b) Local managers know that their financial representations are subject to testing by a team that reports direct to headquarters.

(c) If all internal audit reports go direct to headquarters, greater uniformity of procedures is likely to be achieved.

Arguments for reporting direct to local management include:

(a) The internal auditor is seen as part of the local management team. This can create a more harmonious atmosphere with improved communications.

(b) Issues that arise in the internal audit can be reported directly to local managers and settled quickly.

In practice, internal audit systems will normally include provision for reporting both locally and direct to headquarters.

Operational Problems

The process of auditing across national boundaries raises a number of practical problems in the operation of normal audit procedures.

Some types of audit procedure may not be in common use in certain countries, and may create problems in securing the cooperation of third parties. Harding (1977) reports on problems in obtaining audit confirmation from German banks. In many countries, suppliers and customers commonly do not reply to requests for confirmation of balances because they are not used to this practice. Conversely, auditors who see these procedures in action for the first time may overrule their value. Hatherly (1980) cites a survey in the USA that involved circularizing customers with false balances. Fifty-four per cent proceeded to certify the false balance as correct! Table 2.4 shows the breakdown of responses in more detail. Sikka (1991) reports on a number of similar US studies. The moral is that an auditor who meets a new form of audit evidence in another country should think carefully about its reliability.

Local legislation may also make third parties reluctant to confirm balances. For example, a commodity broking firm in London with clients in a country with strict exchange controls might find that those clients are very hostile to details of their accounts passing through the post. Finally, in some cultures, such as Japan, it is considered most impolite to ask for proof of a statement or assertion. Since audit procedures are based on seeking exactly such proof the very basis of auditing is likely to give offence. As Choi (1989) reports:

> A US audit is based on an attitude of healthy skepticism. Owing his primary allegiance to the shareholders, the US auditor assumes more of an adversarial posture with respect to the client. In Japan, such an adversarial attitude is downplayed owing to cultural influences such as filial piety (p. 122).

Table 2.4 Responses to a debtor's circularization in the USA

Response		Small understatement of true figure	Large understatement	Small overstatement	Large overstatement	Total
(1) Incorrect balance confirmed	No	50	47	40	34	171
	%	68	62	51	39	54
(2) Error detected	No	23	29	39	54	145
	%	32	38	49	61	46
Total	No	73	76	79	88	316

(Cited in Hatherly 1980, p. 127)

The audit approach may also vary. Deering (1965) identifies a contrast between countries where the audit focuses on a broad review of clients' activities and countries where the audit focuses on a detailed examination of supporting documents.

THE INTERNATIONAL ACCOUNTING FIRMS AND THE ACCOUNTING PROFESSION

An important element in the move towards international harmonization of accounting practice has been the growth of the international accounting firms. Briston (1989) discusses three main factors that have promoted this growth:

1. 'The need for a firm to grow as its clients grow in order to be able to provide the increasing range of services that clients demand and to provide them in the locations they are needed.' In some cases a particularly large multinational client has drawn a firm into major international expansion – examples include Mars for Arthur Anderson and Unilever for Coopers and Lybrand.

2. 'Economies of scale and of scope': Briston questions whether most large accounting firms are sufficiently integrated internationally to achieve major economies but observes that such potential economies 'have been adduced by larger accounting firms as arguments for taking over the audit of all group subsidiaries'.

3. 'The third influence is reputation, which gives large accounting firms an enormous competitive advantage over smaller local firms.'

A fourth incentive for US firms has been the pressure that arises from the intensely litigious environment in the USA. Tipgos (1981) refers to:

> The difficulty of ensuring that foreign firms, particularly foreign correspondents, have adequate quality control and measures to monitor compliance through the peer review mechanism may pose serious legal problems for US accounting firms (p. 28).

Broadly speaking, three levels of internationalization can be identified:

1. The 'big six' tend to have a high degree of integration, with global harmonization of technical development, quality control, and public relations.

2. A further group of some 10 firms operate worldwide under a common name as a federation of national firms. One of the leading firms of this kind describes its international connection thus:

> BDO Binder is made up of leading indigenous national firms in 58 countries linked by common working standards and practices.

3. A large number of firms operate a number of international links, with various degrees of formality, often developed to cover specific needs rather than as a general international connection.

One of the 'big six', Arthur Anderson, has offered an interesting insight into how they organize internationally. Their US chief executive officer has claimed:

> The fact that our firm is a true worldwide partnership makes us unique among public accounting firms (Kullberg 1981, p. 1).

Worldwide coordination is achieved through a partnership in Geneva, Arthur Anderson and Co Société Coopérative (S.C.). Every partner in the worldwide organisation is a partner in the S.C. as well as being a partner in a national partnership. There is no gradation of voting partners – the rule is one partner one vote. The UK managing partner of Arthur Anderson cites some statistics on the worldwide size of the practice in 1986:

Worldwide fees	$1.8 billion
Source of fees:	
Accounting and audit	45%
Tax	23%
Management information consulting	32%
Countries with offices	49
Number of offices	215
Total personnel	30,000
Total partners	2,000
Number of clients	110,000

(Derived from Hanson 1989 pp. 46–7 and 48).

Costs shared on a worldwide basis include training, methodology, research and development, and professional indemnity insurance.

A feature of the Arthur Anderson international approach is a matrix structure with three dimensions:

1. Geographical, with offices in various countries, areas, or regions.

2. Practice, divided into three areas of accountancy/audit, tax, and management information consulting.

3. Functional, such as finance/administration, personnel, professional education.

It is claimed that 'an audit performed in Houston, Paris, or Tokyo, or a tax return, or consultancy assignment performed in one of those offices will have been conducted using essentially the same methodology, principles, skills and discipline applied by people of similar background, training and experience' (Hanson, 1989 p. 51).

The practice has sought to cultivate links at the national level with a policy of promoting local nationals to partnership.

Within this structure, the firm's international leadership needs to be sensitive to the feelings of the 2,000 partners. An example in 1979 illustrated this:

> As other firms expanded in 1979 with a rush to merge with accountants overseas to catch up in the international stakes, AA partners saw their leadership position slip away . . . In a major policy reversal AA went out looking for merger partners and with its customary efficiency it picked up Schwartz Fine, the largest firm in South Africa and then part of Tansley Witt in the UK. Dissent found a ready expression in the 1979 annual partners' meeting. The one firm concept meant every partner had a vote and a voice, and in an astonishing discovery of democracy the younger overseas partners voted against the seniors (*Multinational Business* 1980, pp. 6–7).

Clearly the international leadership of Arthur Anderson have learnt from this experience. Hanson (1989) offers this illustration of how agreement is reached internationally:

We recently had some new firms join us in the Far East and their association with us required virtually the unanimous support of our partners in the various partnerships we operate around the world. We got this on a virtually unanimous basis, not because it wasn't something that was questioned, it was severely questioned, but rather because by a great deal of information, a great deal of dialogue, documentation, and discussion, we thrashed out all the advantages and disadvantages so that every partner in each of our partnerships was absolutely sure of the facts of the circumstances and the benefits that would be derived from the association (p. 50).

By promoting international standards within the firm, an international practice can directly help to create international harmonization. The point is made by a partner in Arthur Anderson's Chicago office:

My firm, Arthur Anderson and Co, believes that the need for worldwide accounting standards is so great that progress in developing them should not be delayed by waiting for the creating of some authoritative international organization. Accordingly, we intend to formulate and articulate what we believe to be proper worldwide accounting standards consistent with our views on the objectives of financial statements and our understanding of the basic economic facts underlying business transactions . . . we will not be able at this time to apply our worldwide standards in all respects in all our reporting on financial statements. However, we will apply them to the extent possible and our personnel will use them as a platform to work from in assisting local accounting professions in developing standards (Hauworth 1973, pp. 33–4).

Standards of auditing and accountancy developed internationally by the 'big six' have formed the basis for standards lobbied for by their partners in their capacity as members of committees of professional accountants involved in developing pronouncements at the national and international levels. A former chairman of the American Institute of Certified Public Accountants has identified another way in which the standards set within the large international firms influence the rest of the accounting profession:

These firm engendered standards, in my opinion, are high and serve the public well. In addition, as national firms are established, particularly in developing nations, they are staffed at least in part by personnel, trained by international firms, who bring with them a knowledge and appreciation of these standards (Kanaga 1980, p. 59).

Training materials developed in the USA have also been influential when used by international firms in other countries. Thus Wasley (1966) reports that in New Zealand:

The larger firms are beginning to realize that international programmes offered the best method to train the newly employed young person to be proficient.

Several of the public accounting firms visited by the author were quite delighted with the materials they had received from their American affiliates (pp. 76–7).

A study by Soeters and Schreuder (1988) compared the organizational culture of the Dutch offices of three of the large international firms with that of three large national Dutch firms. They found significant differences in management policies:

> A particular case in point are the personnel policies with respect to career development. The Big Eight firms tend to operate an 'up or out' policy, whereas in the Dutch firms many more employees are traditionally maintained in sub-partner level ranks without prospects of further promotion and without any 'pressure' to leave the organization. All six firms work virtually entirely with Dutch employees (p. 77).

A questionnaire to employees of the six firms identified different patterns of work values between the international and national firms. This may be a result of 'self-selection' in that:

> Our findings suggest that the work values of these employees are already mainly oriented towards US culture upon entry (p. 83).

One problem that the international firms face is that of employing staff and partners with qualifications from one country in another country. Williams (1990) discusses the process whereby the European Community has sought to apply the 'Mutual Recognition Directive' to facilitate free movement of professionally qualified persons between member states. Migrant professionals must 'adapt' to the new country in which they wish to practice either by a period of supervised practical experience or by passing an 'aptitude test' which covers areas of difference between the original qualification they acquired and that applicable in the country where they seek to practice. An interesting, and as yet unresolved problem, is that of an auditor who originally acquired a lower tier qualification in a country where different levels of qualification are prescribed for different sizes or types of company. The problem is that if such auditors move to a country where only one level of qualification is prescribed then should those persons have a right to audit all types of company in the country to which they have migrated?

Curiously, within the USA a similar problem applies. The qualification of 'Certified Public Accountant' is obtained by registration with one of the 54 state boards of accountancy, covering each of the 50 states and four territories of the USA. By agreement each of the state boards accepts a common exam set by the American Institute of Certified Public Accountants. However, a number of areas of diversity in licensing requirements include:

1. Education. Requirements range from a high school diploma to 150 hours of education.

2. Experience. The range goes from none to six years and from experience in public accounting only to a mix of public and non-public.

3. General qualifications. Age, citizenship and residency or employment all vary widely.

4. Exam. There are various requirements for how many parts can be taken at any sitting, minimum grades in parts failed and the timing for passing the remaining subjects.

5. CPE. The variations cover reporting dates and frequency, number of credit hours and types of courses (Rimerman and Solomon 1991, p. 70).

With such a wide variety of professional qualification requirements within the world's leading nation on accounting practice the prospects for international harmonization of accounting qualifications seems remote.

The status of the professional accountant in different countries varies. Seidler (1969) explores the relative status of accountants in the UK and the USA. On the basis of a variety of indicators such as press coverage, numbers of accountants relative to population, relations with Government and institutions, representation on public bodies and in the legislative, and relative income levels, he concludes:

> a reasonable demonstration has been made that the profession of accountancy has a somewhat higher relative socioeconomic position in the United Kingdom than in the USA (p. 499).

This study took place in the late 1960s and is not necessarily applicable today. It remains of interest as an illustration of how the relative status of professions in different countries can be compared.

Briston (1989) argues that 'all in all the internationalization of accounting firms has been a very mixed blessing' on the grounds that, while the quality of accounting services has been improved, this has been:

> at the price of distorting the local accounting system by moulding it to the UK/US model rather than allowing the evolution of a model based on local needs (p. 17).

Linowes (1969) similarly saw a demand in the developing nations for 'a more extensive role for accounting than exists in the United States'. They feel that accounting should be an 'integral part of the central planning process which they regard as essential to the desired growth'. Reporting on visits to Pakistan, Iran, and Turkey he reports 'each of these governments has realized that through accounting legislation a profession will develop which will assume responsibility for promulgation of adequate accounting information to meet the needs of a developing nation' (p. 18).

Lelievre and Lelievre (1978) cite a Nigerian study of the accountancy profession that argues that the spread of the international firms has had a detrimental effect on service to local business:

> Successful local firms tend to merge with international firms who primarily serve the needs of the larger organizations. Small business has scant access to the services of public accounting . . . (p. 73).

The debate as to whether the influence of the international accounting firms is or is not beneficial to the developing world extends to the question of whether or not the Anglo-American accounting education tradition is useful to developing countries. Jagetia and Nwadike (1983) see many managerial problems in Nigeria as being 'primarily due to the critical shortage of qualified staff and the lack of good accounting systems' (p. 71). Hove (1986) reports a Nigerian study that identified a high failure rate in local professional examinations as a consequence of heavy reliance on the British exam model without comparable instruction being available to students. Moreover, Hove argues that in Zimbabwe a similar background means that 'the more technical aspects of accounting have been emphasized almost to the exclusion of the more intellectual aspects of the subject' (p. 97). Similarly Perera (1975) argues that the traditional technical training of accountants has been too narrow and detailed for a developing country like Sri Lanka, and calls for a broader educational approach. It is interesting to note that this dissatisfaction with a narrow technical basis for accounting education, articulated in a range of developing countries, is now also being observed by leading educators in the USA:

> Future accountants are not receiving the preparation they need to meet the increased demands of the expansive more complex profession that is emerging

and

> This requires a switch in focus from simply learning a body of knowledge to developing a process of continual learning (Sundem 1991, pp. 52, 53).

In summary, the major international accounting firms have successfully expanded in response to a market demand and in doing so have promoted international accounting harmonization. However, there is controversy as to whether this expansion has been beneficial to all the countries, particularly developing countries, in which they operate.

CONCLUSION

There is a range of processes by which accounting practice can be regulated, and a corresponding range of international and regional bodies trying to promote harmonization. Consequently there is a lively debate on how to make this range of effort complementary rather than conflicting. The audit role is prone to vary nation to nation in the same way as the accounting role. The large accountancy firms have developed into international organizations in the same way as their multinational clients, adding impetus to the move for international accounting harmonization.

REFERENCES   *Accountancy* (1991) 'UK "cannot agree standards on its own"' April, p. 11.
Accounting Standards Steering Committee (1975) *The Corporate Report.*

Agrawal, S.P., Jensen, P.H., Meadar, A.L. and Sellers, K. (1989) 'An international comparison of conceptual frameworks of accounting', *International Journal of Accounting*, **3**, pp. 237–49.

Al Hashim, D. and Arpan, J. (1988) *International Dimensions of Accounting*, PWS Kent.

Archer, S., Dufour, J.B., and McLeay, S. (1989) *Audit Reports on The Financial Statements of European Multinational Companies: A Comparative Study*, Institute of Chartered Accountants in England and Wales.

Arpan, J. and Radebaugh, L.H. (1985) *International Accounting and Multinational Enterprises*, Warren, Gorham and Lamont.

Axelson, K.S. (1975) 'A businessman's views on disclosure', *Journal of Accountancy*, July, pp. 42–6.

Bedford, N.M. (1966) 'The international flow of accounting thought', *International Journal of Accounting*, Spring, pp. 1–7.

Benson, H. (1976) 'The study of international accounting standards', *Accountancy*, July, pp. 34–9.

Benson, H. (1978) 'Danger! A corporate report from the UN', *Accountancy*, May, pp. 130–1.

Blake, J.D. (1991) *Accounting Standards*, Pitman.

Blake, J.D. (1992) 'Why Europe needs common accounting regulation', *European Research*, January, pp. 15–18.

Blake, J.D. and Higson, A. (1992) 'A consideration of the significance and value of the neutrality concept in financial accounting', *Accounting Forum*, September, pp. 5–35.

Briston, R. (1989) 'Wider still and wider – the international expansion of the accounting profession', *Accountant's Magazine*, August, pp. 16–17.

Burnett, R.A. (1976) 'The harmonization of accounting principles in the member states of the European Economic Community', *International Journal of Accounting*, Fall, pp. 23–30.

Cairns, D. (1989) 'IASCs blueprint for the future', *Accountancy*, December, pp. 80–2.

Cairns, D. (1990) 'Aid for the developing world', *Accounting*, March, pp. 82–5.

Chandler, R. (1988) 'International harmonies: the role of IFAC', *Accountants' Journal*, October, pp. 40–2.

Choi, F.D.S. (1979) 'ASEAN Federation of Accountants: a new international accounting force', *International Journal of Accounting*, Fall, pp. 53–75.

Choi, F.D.S. (1981) 'A cluster approach to accounting harmonization', *Management Accounting* (US), August.

Choi, F.D.S. (1989) 'Economic effects of multinational accounting diversity', *Journal of International Financial Management and Accounting*, 1:2, pp. 105–29.

Chow, C.W. (1982) 'The demand for external auditing: size, debt, and ownership influences', *Accounting Review*, April, pp. 272–91.

Committe, B.E. (1990) 'The delegation and privatization of financial accounting rule making authority in the United States of America', *Critical Perspectives in Accounting*, June, pp. 145–66.

Cooke, T.E. (1988) *European Financial Reporting: Sweden*, Institute of Chartered Accountants in England and Wales.

Cummings, J.P. and Chetkovich, M.N. (1978) 'World accounting enters a new era', *Journal of Accountancy*, April.

De Bruyne, D. (1980) 'Global standards: a tower of Babel?', *Financial Executive*, February, pp. 30–7.

Deering, J.J. (1965) 'The need for developing international terminology and uniform accounting practices', *Proceedings of the Fourth Conference of Asian and Pacific Accountants*, New Delhi.

Demski, J.S. (1973) 'The general impossibility of normative accounting standards', *Accounting Review*, October, pp. 718–23.

Fitzgerald, R.D. (1981) 'International harmonization of accounting and reporting', *International Journal of Accounting*, Fall, pp. 21–32.

Fleming, P.D. (1991) 'The growing importance of international accounting standards', *Journal of Accountancy*, April, pp. 100–106.

Gray, S.J., McSweeney, L.B. and Shaw, J.C. (1984) *Information Disclosure and the Multinational Corporation*, Wiley.

Gray, S.J., Shaw, J.C., and McSweeney, L.B. (1981) 'Accounting standards and multinational companies', *Journal of International Business Studies*, Spring/Summer, pp. 121–36.

Hanson, D. (1989) 'Internationalization of the accounting firm' in *International Pressures for Accounting Change*, Hopwood A.G. (ed.), pp. 43–56, Prentice Hall.

Harding, M. (1977) 'Problems of obtaining bank confirmations in Germany', *Accountancy*, August, pp. 88–9.

Harper, B.S. and Harper, P. (1988) 'Religious reporting: is it the Gospel truth?', *Management Accounting*, February, pp. 34–9.

Hatherly, D.J. (1980) *The Audit Evidence Process*, Anderson Keenan Publishing.

Hauworth, W.P. (1973) 'Problems in the development of worldwide accounting standards', *International Journal of Accounting*, Fall, pp. 23–34.

Hines, R.D. (1989) 'Financial accounting knowledge, conceptual framework projects and the social construction of the accounting profession', *Accounting Auditing and Accountability*, **2**, pp. 72–92.

Hope, A. and Gray, R. (1982) 'Power and policy making: the development of an R and D standard', *Journal of Business Finance and Accounting*, Winter, pp. 531–58.

Horngren, C.T. (1972) 'Accounting principles: private or public sector?', *Journal of Accountancy*, May, pp. 37–41.

Horngren, C.T. (1976) 'Will the FASB be here in the 1980s?', *Journal of Accountancy*, November, pp. 90–6.

Hove, M. (1986) 'Accounting practices in developing countries: colonialism's legacy of inapprorpriate technologies', *International Journal of Accountancy*, Fall, pp. 81–100.

Hove, M. (1989) 'The inappropriateness of International Accounting Standards in less developed countries: the case of Interntional Accounting Standard Number 24 – Related Party Disclosures – concerning transfer prices', *International Journal of Accounting*, Vol. 24, No. 2, pp. 165–79.

International Accounting Standards Committee (1989) 'Framework for the preparation and presentation of financial statements', July, reprinted in *Accountancy*, September 1989, pp. 141–8.

Jagetia, L.C. and Nwadike, E.C. (1983) 'Accounting systems in developing nations: the Nigerian experience', *International Journal of Accounting*, Spring, pp. 69–81.

Johnson, O. (1981) 'Some implications of the United States constitution for accounting institution alternatives', *Journal of Accounting Research*, pp. 89–119.

Kanaga, W.S. (1980) 'International accounting – the challenge and the chances', *Journal of Accountancy*, November, pp. 55–60.

Kim, S.K. and Barone, S. (1981) 'Is the foreign corrupt practices act of 1977 a success or failure?', *Journal of International Business Studies*, Winter, pp. 123–6.

Kullberg, D.R. (1981) 'Management of a multinational public accounting firm', *International Journal of Accounting*, Fall, pp. 1–5.

Lelievre, T. and Lelievre, C. (1978) 'Accounting in the third world', *Journal of Accountancy*, January, pp. 72–5.

Linowes, D.F. (1969) 'The role of accounting in emerging nations', *Journal of Accountancy*, January, p. 18.

McComb, D. (1979) 'The international harmonization of accounting: a cultural dimension', *International Journal of Accounting*, Spring, pp. 1–16.

McComb, D. (1982) 'International Accounting Standards and the EEC harmonization program: a conflict of disparate objectives', *International Journal of Accounting*, Spring, pp. 35–48.

Macharzina, K. (1988) 'Recent advances in European accounting: an assessment by use of the accounting culture concept', *Advances in International Accounting*, pp. 131–47.

Meek, G. (1984) 'Competition spurs worldwide harmonization', *Management Accounting*, August, pp. 47–9.

Miller, E.L. (1979) *Accounting Problems of Multinational Enterprises*, Lexington Books.

Miller, J. (1990) 'The IASC framework', *South African Chartered Accountant*, October, pp. 253–5.

Miller, P.B.W. and Redding, R. (1988) *The FASB: The People, The Process, and the Politics*, Irwin.

Multinational Business (1980) 'International accounting firms consolidate worldwide', pp. 1–13.

Myddelton, D.R. (1981) 'The neglected merits of CPP' in Leach, R. and Stamp, E. (eds), *British Accounting Standards, The First Ten Years*, pp. 85–101, Woodhead Faulkner.

Nobes, C.W. (1980) 'Harmonization of accounting within the European Communities: the Fourth Directive on company law', *International Journal of Accounting*, Spring, pp. 1–16.

Perera, M.H.B. (1975) 'Accounting and its environment in Sri Lanka', *Abacus*, June, pp. 86–96.

Pomeranz, F. (1981) 'Prospects for international accounting and auditing standards – the transnationals in government regulations', *International Journal of Accounting*, Fall, pp. 7–19.

Puxty, A.G., Willmott, H.C., Cooper, D.J. and Lowe, T. (1987) 'Modes of regulation in advanced capitalism: locating accountancy in four countries', *Accounting Organizations and Society*, Vol. 12, No. 3, pp. 273–91.

Rimerman, T.W. and Solomon, J.P. (1991) 'Uniformity of regulation – the time is now', *Journal of Accountancy*, April, pp. 69–72.

Schoenfeld, H.M.W. (1981) 'International accounting: development, issues, and future directions', *Journal of International Business Studies*, Fall, pp. 83–100.

Seidler, L.J. (1969) 'A comparison of the economic and social status of the accountancy profession in Great Britain and the United States of America', *Accountant's Magazine*, September, pp. 489–500.

Sharp, K.J. (1979) 'The Whitehall perspective: government and accounting standards', *The Accountant*, July 19, pp. 67–9.

Sherrard, M. (1981) 'Accounting standardization – a lawyer's view' in Leach, R. and Stamp, E. *British Accounting Standards the First Ten Years*, pp. 119–35, Woodhead Faulkner.

Sikka, P. (1991) 'Getting results', *Certified Accountant*, July, pp. 34–5.

Simmonds, A. (1989) 'Bridging the European GAAP', *Accountancy*, August, p. 29.

Soeters, J. and Schreuder, H. (1988) 'The interaction between national and organizational cultures in accounting firms', *Accounting Organizations and Society*, Spring, pp. 75–85.

Stamp, E. (1973) 'The EEC and European accounting standards: a straightjacket or a spur?', *Accountancy*, May, pp. 9–18.

Sundem, G. (1991) 'Accounting education – drastic changes needed', *Accountant's Journal*, September, pp. 52–3.

Tinker, T. (1985) *Paper Prophets*, Holt Rinehart and Winston.

Tipgos, M.A. (1981) 'Potential liabilities in international accounting practices', *Journal of Accountancy*, April, pp. 24–30.

Turley, W.S. (1983) 'International harmonization of accounting: the contribution of the EEC Fourth Directive on company law', *International Journal of Accounting*, Spring, pp. 13–27.

Vangermeersch R. (1985) 'The route of the Seventh Directive of the EEC on consolidated accounts – slow, steady, studied, and successful', *International Journal of Accounting*, Spring, pp. 103–18.

Van Hulle, K. (1989) 'The EC experience of harmonization', *Accountancy*, October, pp. 96–8.

Violet, W.J. (1983) 'A philosophical perspective on the development of international accounting standards', *International Journal of Accounting*, Fall, pp. 1–13.

Walker, R.G. (1978) 'International accounting compromises: the case of consolidation 'accounting', *Abacus*, December, pp. 99–111.

Wasley, R.S. (1968) 'The status of accountancy and of accounting practices in New Zealand', *International Journal of Accounting*, Spring, pp. 67–89.

Watts, R.L. (1977) 'Corporate financial statements, a product of the market and political process', *Australian Journal of Management*, April, pp. 53–75.

Westwick, C. (1980) 'The lessons to be learned from the development of inflation accounting in the UK', *Accounting and Business Research*, Autumn, pp. 353–72.

Williams, J. (1990) 'The first step to harmonization', *Accountancy*, December, pp. 21–2.

Zeff, S.A. (1972) *Forging Accounting Principles in Five Countries*, Shipes.

CHAPTER 3

An Overview of Areas of Difference in International Accounting Practice

INTRODUCTION In this chapter we consider some of the accounting issues where there are differences between countries in the accounting practices that are required or commonly used. For each issue we also consider the provisions laid down by European Community directives and the IASC.

ACCOUNTING CONVENTIONS

We have seen in Chapter 1 above that, in the negotiations leading up to the European Community's Fourth Directive, the United Kingdom was successful in introducing the concept of the 'true and fair view' as the basic objective of a set of accounts.

The Fourth Directive provides:

2.3 Annual accounts shall give a true and fair view of assets, liabilities, financial position and profit or loss.

2.4 Where the application of the provisions of this Directive would not be sufficient to give a true and fair view within the meaning of paragraph 3, additional information must be given.

2.5 Where in exceptional cases the application of a provision of this Directive is incompatible with the obligation laid down in paragraph 3, that provision must be departed from in order to give a true and fair view within the meaning of paragraph 3. Any such departure must be disclosed in the notes on the accounts together with an explanation of the reasons for it and a statement of its effect on the assets, liabilities, financial position and profit or loss. The member states may define the exceptional cases in question and lay down the relevant special rules.

These provisions are quite remarkable. They introduce an overriding condition, the 'true and fair view', that takes priority over all specific accounting regulation. At no point is this term 'true and fair view' defined. It has its origin in the UK Companies Act of 1947. However, the UK legislation also fails to define the term. Amongst UK practitioners there is a range of opinion as to the meaning of 'true and fair view'.

Some ambiguity in the expression arises because while the word 'true' has a range of compatible meanings such as 'consistent with fact', 'free from deceit', and 'exact, accurate, precise', the word 'fair' has a range of distinct meanings including:

1. 'Tolerable; passable; average.'

2. 'Clear, distinct, plainly to be seen.'

3. 'Free from bias, fraud, or injustice.'

Four distinct interpretations can be identified, the first two emerging by contrast with the earlier UK requirement that accounts should give a 'true and correct view':

1. The 'true and fair view' requirement was advocated, successfully, by the Institute of Chartered Accountants in England and Wales (ICAEW). The argument in favour was put by *The Accountant* on 1st July 1944:

   The word 'correct' has always been too strong because it implies that there is one view which is 'correct' as against all others which are incorrect. In published accounts there is no standard of absolute truth and the Institute's suggested amendment would recognize that the presentation of the figures can only be that which is, in the personal view of the auditor, a fair view (p. 2.).

   Similarly McMonnies (1967) observed

   'Fair' is possible in a way that the 'correct' of the 1929 audit report never was.

   Thus the 'true and fair view' is seen as acknowledging that accounts are based on 'reasonable' estimates and subject to the consequent limitations. This is in line with the first concept of 'fair' above.

2. One of the UK's leading accountants has observed that the 1947 Act:

   Changed the whole situation. It required that the accounts should be 'true and fair'. This meant that the doctrine of 'correctness' or 'is it on the right side' went out of the window. In effect substance took precedence over form (Benson 1989, p. 45).

   Lord Benson speaks with particular authority on this issue, having been considered for the chairmanship of the committee which drafted the 1947 Act (Bircher 1988, p. 118). This approach sees the term 'fair', in the light of the second definition identified above, as enhancing rather than moderating the 'true' requirement. Cowan (1965) illustrates this point with a story. The captain of a tramp steamer was annoyed by the mate's drinking habits. One day he was irritated to the point of writing in the ship's log the words 'The mate was drunk today'. This statement was both true and fair. On the following day the mate, now sober and on watch, entered in the log the words 'The captain was sober today'. The mate's observation was true but, because it implied that the event was so unusual as to warrant comment, was not fair.

3. A third view draws on the third definition of 'fair' above, 'free from bias', to mean that accounts should not attempt to manipulate users to a conclusion and should serve all user groups equally.

4. The UK's largest professional accounting body has argued that: 'A true and fair view also implies the constant application of generally accepted

principles'. Similarly Irish (1966) argues that 'true and fair' implies that 'the accounts follow the rules appropriate to this case'. In the one decided civil case on the issue, *Re* Press Caps Ltd (1949, ch. 434) a shareholder claimed that a balance sheet showing a freehold property at historic cost of £30,000 failed to show a true and fair view because the current value was £90,000. The Court of Appeal rejected the challenge. In doing so Lord Justice Somervell observed that the accounting treatment gave a true and fair view by virtue of being 'in accordance with what is very common practice'. The judgment is frequently cited as an indication that a true and fair view can be achieved by following normal accounting principles. However, Williams (1985) points out that the other two judges in the Court of Appeal decided the case on other grounds.

Given that the expression 'true and fair' has a range of meaning in the UK, the country of origin, it is not surprising that the term is incapable of consistent application across the European Community. In so far as the concept represents our fourth meaning above, as the normal practice of accountants, this implies different accounting approaches in each country, depending on the national accounting profession:

> You might not be able to satisfy a British court that your accounts are true and fair even if you can show that they satisfy the reasonable expectations of say Italian accountants! So there is no assurance that an EEC directive will produce harmonization even if its meaning is genuinely agreed (Bird 1984).

Moreover, each EC country tends to interpret the 'true and fair view' in the light of its own experience. A survey of 475 European companies' financial statements found that 10 used the true and fair override. The same survey pointed out that:

> The concept of a true and fair view has a different meaning in various countries (*Fédération des Experts Comptables Européens* 1991, p. 27).

By contrast the USA developed, in the 1930s, a form of audit report to the effect that accounts are fairly presented in accordance with 'Generally Accepted Accounting Principles' (GAAP) (Felt 1968, p. 21).

The Securities and Exchange Commission (SEC) requires accounts to be drawn up in accordance with GAAP, while the American Institute of Certified Public Accountants (AICPA) has published a 'hierarchy' of sources of GAAP, headed by statements by the US Financial Accounting Standards Board (see Sauter 1991 for details). This US formulation is unambiguous; not surprisingly a recent survey of US accountants, academics, and analysts found a high degree of satisfaction with the term (McEnroe 1991).

The EC Fourth Directive also identifies, in Article 31, six principles that should apply in accounts:

1. the company must be presumed to be carrying on its business as a going concern;

2. the methods of valuation must be applied consistently from one financial year to another;

3. valuation must be made on a prudent basis, and in particular:

   (a) only profits made at the balance sheet date may be included,

   (b) account must be taken of all foreseeable liabilities and potential losses arising in the course of the financial year concerned or of a previous one, even if such liabilities or losses become apparent only between the date of the balance sheet and the date on which it is drawn up,

   (c) account must be taken of all depreciation, whether the result of the financial year is a loss or a profit;

4. account must be taken of income and charges relating to the financial year, irrespective of the date of receipt or payment of such income or charges;

5. the components of asset and liability items must be valued separately;

6. the opening balance sheet for each financial year must correspond to the closing balance sheet for the preceding financial year.

IAS 1, 'Disclosure of Accounting Policies', identifies three 'fundamental accounting assumptions', namely Going Concern, Consistency, and Accruals, all in similar terms to the EC Fourth Directive. IAS 1 also lists three considerations that should apply in choosing accounting policies, namely prudence, substance over form, and materiality. The last two can be defined:

1. Substance over form means that the substance and financial reality of transactions should govern their treatment in the accounts rather than legal form.

2. Materiality, means that all items which are sufficiently material to affect evaluations or decisions should be disclosed.

PRESENTATION

The EC Fourth Directive prescribes layouts for the balance sheet and the profit and loss sheet. There is a choice of vertical or horizontal layout for both. There are also two types of profit and loss account layout:

1. A 'type of expenditure' basis analyses costs by type of expense

2. An 'operational' basis analyses costs by their purpose.

Table 3.1 shows a vertical profit and loss account on an 'operational' basis.

A horizontal profit and loss account would show much the same items but with expense items on one side, income items on the other, with profit or loss as a balancing figure.

A 'type of expenditure' basis replaces lines 1–6 of the operational basis as shown in Table 3.1 with eight lines as shown in Table 3.2. The remainder of this format continues with the same headings as 7 to 19 in Table 3.1.

Table 3.1 Profit and Loss Account Format – Operational Basis

1	Net turnover	X
2	Cost of sales (including value adjustments)	(X)
3	Gross profit or loss	X
4	Distribution costs (including value adjustments)	(X)
5	Administrative expenses (including value adjustments)	(X)
6	Other operating income	X
7	Income from participating interests, with a separate indication of that derived from affiliated undertakings	X
8	Income from other investments and loans forming part of the fixed assets, with a separate indication of that derived from affiliated undertakings	X
9	Other interest receivable and similar income, with a separate indication of that derived from affiliated undertakings	X
10	Value adjustments in respect of financial assets and of investments held as current assets	(X)
11	Interest payable and similar charges, with a separate indication of those concerning affiliated undertakings	(X)
12	Tax on profit and loss on ordinary activities	(X)
13	Profit or loss on ordinary activities after taxation	X
14	Extraordinary income	X
15	Extraordinary charges	(X)
16	Extraordinary profit or loss	X
17	Tax on extraordinary profit or loss	(X)
18	Other taxes not shown under the above items	(X)
19	Profit or loss for the financial year	X

Table 3.2 Profit and Loss Account Format – Type of Expenditure Basis

1	Net turnover		X
2	Variation in stocks of finished goods and work in progress		X
3	Work performed by the undertaking for its own use and capitalized		X
4	Other operating income		X
5	(a) Raw material and consumables	(X)	
	(b) Other external charges	(X)	
			(X)
6	Staff costs:		
	(a) wages and salaries	(X)	
	(b) social security cost, with a separate indication of those relating to pensions	(X)	
			(X)
7	(a) Value adjustments in respect of formation expenses and of tangible and intangible fixed assets	X	
	(b) Value adjustments in respect of current assets, to the extent that they exceed the amount of value adjustment which are normal in the undertaking concerned	X	
			X
8	Other operating charges		X

Table 3.3 shows the vertical balance sheet as provided for in Article 10 of the Fourth Directive. Further subheadings giving more detail are required to be shown either on the face of the balance sheet or by way of note. As an example, item D II, 'Debtors', is further analysed:

1. Trade debtors

2. Amounts owed by affiliated undertakings

3. Amounts owed by undertakings with which the company is linked by virtue of participating interests

4. Other debtors

5. Subscribed capital called but not paid

6. Prepayments and accrued income.

National law may provide for some variation in this format:

1. Item A may be shown at D II 5

2. Item E may be shown at D II 6

3. Item K may be shown at F9 or I9.

Table 3.3 Vertical Balance Sheet, Assuming Further Detail Shown by Way of Note

A.	Subscribed capital unpaid			X
B.	Formation expenses			X
C.	Fixed assets			
	i Intangible assets		X	
	ii Tangible assets		X	
	iii Financial assets		X̲	X
D.	Current assets			
	i Stocks	X		
	ii Debtors	X		
	iii Investment	X		
	iv Cash at bank and in hand	X̲		
E.	Prepayments and accrued income		X	
F.	Creditors: amounts becoming due and payable within one year		(X̲)	
G.	Net current assets			X̲
H.	Total assets less current liabilities			X̳
I.	Creditors due and payable after more than one year			X
J.	Provisions for liabilities and charges			X
K.	Accruals and deferred income			X
L.	Capital and reserves:			
	I Subscribed capital		X	
	II Share premium account		X	
	III Revaluation reserve		X	
	IV Reserves		X	
	V Profit or loss brought forward		X	
	VI Profit or loss for the financial year		X̲	
				X
				X̳

Individual national legislatives may choose which formats to apply or may give companies a choice. A survey by the European Commission shows that national laws on balance sheet layout are:

Horizontal	*Choice*
France	Luxembourg
Germany	Netherlands
Belgium	United Kingdom
Italy	Ireland
Greece	Denmark
Spain	
Portugal	

(p. 8)

National laws on profit and loss account layouts are:

Type of expenditure
France (Horizontal and vertical)
Germany (Vertical)
Belgium (Horizontal and vertical)
Spain (Horizontal)
Portugal (Horizontal)

Type of operation
Germany (Vertical)
Greece (Vertical)

All of the above
Luxembourg
Netherlands
United Kingdom
Ireland
Denmark
(*Commission of the European Communities 1987, p. 12*).

CONSOLIDATED ACCOUNTS

Group accounts are accounts which aim to show the financial position and results of a group of companies which are linked together. The simplest form of linkage is when one company, the holding company, owns a majority of shares in another company, the subsidiary company. The most common form of group accounting is to present consolidated accounts whereby, in addition to the preparation of individual company accounts, a set of 'consolidated accounts' is prepared; the consolidated accounts aim to show the holding company and its subsidiaries together as though they were one entity.

The European Community Seventh Directive addresses the issue of group accounts.

There are two broad approaches to the problem of identifying the situation where one company is a 'subsidiary' of another, so that the preparation of consolidated accounts will be appropriate:

1. By considering the ownership of shares in the investee company

2. By considering who controls the management of the company.

Both elements are involved in the Seventh Directive definition that consolidation is required in any of the following situations:

1. Where there is a majority of the share voting rights.

2. There is a shareholding plus the right to appoint or remove a majority of the directors.

3. There is a dominant influence under a control contract, even if there is no shareholding.

4. There is a shareholding plus a majority of the voting rights.

In addition, the Seventh Directive allows member states to require consolidation where there is a participating interest plus an actual dominant influence or unified management. An important exemption is that a parent company does not have to present consolidated accounts provided that it is not a listed company and is a wholly owned subsidiary of a company in another member state; the same exemption may apply with a minority interest of up to 10 per cent provided that the minority approves the exemption.

Member states may extend this exemption to subsidiaries of non-member state countries provided that the holding company presents consolidated accounts in line with the Seventh Directive. This provision has the interesting consequence that ultimate holding companies in non-member states, such as Switzerland and Sweden, have an incentive to follow the European Community's lead on accounting practice in order to avoid the costs of preparing consolidated accounts for intermediate holding companies within the European Community.

Exemptions may also be granted to financial holding companies and to small groups. Individual subsidiaries may be excluded from consolidation on the following grounds:

1. Materiality

2. Severe long-term restrictions on control

3. To obtain information would involve undue expense or delay

4. Shares are held exclusively for resale

5. Different activities.

There is a wide range of complications that can arise in the preparation of a set of consolidated accounts, and the detail of these falls outside the scope of this text. The four main ways in which a holding company might include the accounts of an investee in the consolidated accounts are:

1. Where a subsidiary company is to be included in the consolidation, this would normally be done by the purchase accounting method, also known as acquisition accounting. This treats the acquisition of a subsidiary as the acquisition of its assets and liabilities. The difference between the holding company's share of these and the purchase consideration is termed 'goodwill' (see below).

2. The European Community Seventh Directive also permits member states to allow the 'pooling of interests' method, otherwise known as 'merger' accounting. This is permitted, in the case of public companies, where acquisition is by a share for share exchange which results in at least 90 per cent of all equity shares being held by the acquirer.

   Table 3.4 (overleaf) shows an example of the two methods and their effects. It should be noted that

   (a) In acquisition accounting shares issued are recorded at their 'fair value', with any excess over nominal value shown as a non-distributable capital reserve, the share premium. In merger accounting, shares issued are shown at nominal value.

   (b) In merger accounting, the distributable reserves of both the acquirer and the acquiree are regarded as fully distributable reserves of the group. In acquisition accounting, the distributable reserves of the acquiree after the acquisition date are regarded as distributable by the group. In our example, the only reduction in group distributable reserves arises because the nominal value of the shares issued by the acquirer slightly exceeds (by £5,000) those taken over in the acquiree.

   (c) Merger accounting does not involve the creation of a goodwill balance, with the consequent obligation to write off the balance to profit and loss.

   Thus merger accounting is less prudent than acquisition accounting, creating higher distributable reserves and avoiding a goodwill write-off against profit. For this reason some countries do not permit merger accounting while others impose restrictions on its use.

3. Equity accounting is a partial method of consolidation. It involves showing the investment in the investee as a separate item in the group balance sheet and adjusting the amount shown each year for the group's share of the investee's profit or loss. This method is most commonly used when the investor has significant influence but not control over the investee.

4. The 'proportional method' means that the group accounts only include a proportion of items from the investee's accounts, being the proportion of the investor's holding in the investee. It is most commonly used for joint ventures.

Table 3.4

The summarized balance sheet of Sid Limited at 31 December 19X0 was as follows:

	£		£
Share capital issued and fully paid			
245,000 shares	245,000	Fixed assets	180,000
Retained profits	300,000	Current assets	565,000
Current liabilities	200,000		
	745,000		745,000

At that date the company acquired the whole issued share capital of Toad Limited by the issue of 75,000 new ordinary shares, at the day's market price of £3.20.

The balance sheet of Toad Limited immediately prior to acquisition was:

	£		£
Share capital 70,000 shares of £1	70,000	Fixed assets	90,000
Retained profits	50,000	Current assets	55,000
Current liabilities	25,000		
	145,000		145,000

Sid Ltd
Consolidated balance sheet 31 December 19X0

	Acquisition	Merger
	£	£
Share capital	320,000	320,000
Share premium	165,000	–
Retained profits	300,000	345,000
	785,000	665,000
Fixed assets	270,000	270,000
Goodwill	120,000	–
Current assets	620,000	620,000
	1,010,000	890,000
Current liabilities	225,000	225,000
	785,000	665,000

Workings
Share premium – acquisition method

	£
Market value 75,000 @ 3.20	240,000
Nominal value @ 1.00	75,000
	165,000

Merger retained profits

	£'000s
Sid Ltd	300
Toad Ltd	50
Nominal value shares issued	
Nominal value shares acquired	
(70 – 75)	(5)
	345

Nobes (1990) identifies a range of issues on which the European Community Seventh Directive permits a variety of approaches, and discusses ways in which member states have varied in their detailed rules. He concludes:

There is still scope for confusion and still a need for care and expertise when making European accounting comparisons (p. 85).

GOODWILL

'Goodwill' is a term used by accountants to describe the difference between the value of a business as a whole and the total of the values of the individual identifiable assets of the business. It arises because of a whole range of important but unquantifiable factors such as the trading connections of the business, the accumulated skills and experience of employees, relations with suppliers, and general standing with business contacts. A business may also have 'negative goodwill', where the value of the business as a whole is less than the total value of the identifiable assets of the business. The question then arises, if a business has 'negative goodwill', why do the owners not sell the individual identifiable assets and realize the surplus? There may be good reasons for the continuation of the business, such as high liquidation costs or some form of social obligation to continue trading. However, if a computation of the effects of a business acquisition shows a 'negative goodwill' figure, then it is wise to check the related tangible asset valuations and consider whether they might be too high. IAS 22 (Accounting for Business Combinations) defines goodwill as the difference between the acquisition cost of a business and the 'fair value' of the net identifiable assets acquired. Therefore the assets of the business have to be reported in the accounts of the acquirer at their fair value at the date of acquisition, not at their historic cost to the acquired company. This accounting objective can be achieved in group accounts either by revaluation in the books of the subsidiary or by a consolidation adjustment.

At first sight this may seem like a departure from the historic cost principle. However, on closer examination this is not true. Valuation in this case is a process for allocating the purchase consideration, which is the historic cost of the collection of assets acquired when a business is purchased, between the individual assets. To show assets in the accounts of the acquirer at their historic cost to the acquiree would be grossly misleading. Table 3.5 (overleaf) illustrates why this is so.

Table 3.5

Toro Inc, a Ruritanian company, buys the entire share capital of Almeida Inc for 5,000,000 crowns on 1 January 19X6. Almeida Inc runs a popular ferry service across Ruritania's largest river. The accounts of Almeida Inc at 1 January 19X6 show:

	Crowns '000
Boat	2,800
Share capital	2,000
Reserves	800
	2,800

The only asset of the company is one ferry boat. A valuer reports that at 1 January 19X6 the boat has a value of 4,000,000 crowns, an estimated useful life of ten years, and that in ten years' time the boat is expected to have a negligible value.

Toro Inc, in purchasing Almeida Inc might compute goodwill as follows:

	Revalue boat	Boat at historic cost to Almeida Inc
	Cr '000	Cr '000
Purchase consideration	5,000	5,000
Identifiable asset	4,000	2,800
Goodwill	1,000	2,200

For the next 10 years annual depreciation will be:

Boat revalued	$\dfrac{4,000}{10}$	=	400
Boat not revalued	$\dfrac{2,800}{10}$	=	280

The effect of a failure to revalue at the acquisition date will, therefore, be a material distortion in the accounts for 10 years to come.

Having ascertained the goodwill figure, the next question is how it should be treated in the accounts. There are two broad approaches to this question:

1. Purchased goodwill might be regarded as a 'freak' thrown up by the accounting system, to be excluded from the accounts as smoothly as possible. In line with this approach IAS 22 permits immediate write-off of goodwill against shareholders' equity.

   Another approach, not permitted in IAS 22, has been to carry goodwill in the balance sheet indefinitely either as an asset, or, by the 'dangling debit', as a deduction from the total shareholders' equity.

2. Alternatively goodwill might be regarded as a purchased asset, to be recorded in the balance sheet and amortized over its estimated useful life. IAS 22 permits this approach, subject to a requirement that each year

goodwill should be reviewed and written down to the extent that it is no longer of value to the company. Some countries that adopt this approach prescribe a maximum write-off period.

The choice between these two approaches can have a material effect on the accounts. To take our example of the goodwill on acquisition of Almeida Inc:

1. A write-off policy reduces the reported equity by 1,000,000 crowns at the time of acquisition, but has no effect on reported profits.
2. A policy of amortizing goodwill has no immediate effect on the reported equity, but will have an impact on profit in each year of amortization.

For negative goodwill, IAS 22 provides different rules. Clearly it would not be prudent to credit such a balance to equity immediately. Therefore such goodwill can be treated in one of two ways:

1. Treat it as deferred income and amortize it on a systematic basis.
2. Allocate it to depreciable non-monetary assets acquired in proportion to their fair values. The effect of this approach is to reduce depreciation charges in subsequent years and consequently credit the negative goodwill to income gradually.

The European Community Seventh Directive requires that goodwill be amortized over a period not exceeding its useful life, and suggests a maximum of five years. Member states are also allowed the option that goodwill be deducted from the equity on acquisition.

FOREIGN CURRENCY TRANSLATION

There is no guidance from the European Community on foreign currency translation, apart from a requirement in the Seventh Directive to disclose the basis used. The main accounting problems that arise are:

1. Which exchange rate to use in translation. The two most commonly used rates are the 'historic rate' applying at the time when a transaction originally occurred and the 'closing rate' applying at the balance sheet date. Various translation methods draw either on the closing rate or on a mixture of the two.
2. How to account for gains and losses on foreign exchange. 'Exposure' to such gains and losses is of two kinds:

   (a) *Transaction Exposure* Transaction exposure arises when there is a difference between the exchange rate at the time when a transaction is entered into and the time when it is completed. These realized gains or losses are quantified by the circumstances of the transaction, and there is general agreement that they should be taken through the profit and loss account.

(b) *Translation Exposure* Translation exposure arises when there is a difference between the exchange rate at the time when an item is brought into the accounts and the exchange rate used to translate that item at the balance sheet date. Thus it arises primarily where the 'closing rate' is used for translation. Rules on how such differences should be treated tend to be linked to the translation method used.

3. As we will see below, in many countries translation differences in a company's own accounts are reflected in the profit and loss account while differences arising from translation of a foreign subsidiary are often taken direct to reserves. However, often the economic reality is that such differences are linked. A common example is that foreign currency borrowing by a parent company may finance equity investment in a subsidiary. Where such 'hedging' occurs, some form of provision to treat the linked translation differences in the same way may be appropriate.

4. There is a particular problem that arises in translating accounts of companies operating in countries with high inflation rates. This arises because of two important economic relationships:

(a) The 'Fisher' effect, whereby it is argued that there is a link between interest rates and expectations as to future exchange rate movements, so that the weaker the currency the higher the interest rate.

(b) The purchasing power parity effect, whereby it is argued that there is a link between the rate of inflation and the strength of currency, so that the higher the rate of inflation the weaker the currency and vice versa.

It is not claimed that either of these relationships is cast iron, but research has shown that over a number of years, both these effects tend to operate in practice. For example, Giddy (1977) looked at the correlation between exchange rate changes and relative inflation and interest rates. Over the short run (i.e. three-month periods) correlation was poor, but over longer periods (e.g. three years) correlation was much closer. The specific problems that arise from this are considered below.

There are four major translation methods, the first three being based on a mixture of historical and closing rates.

1. *Current/Non-current* With this method, current items, e.g. stock, debtors, bank overdrafts, would be translated at the closing rate while long-term items, e.g. plant, debentures, would be translated at the historical rate.

2. *Monetary/Non monetary* Monetary items, being assets and obligations fixed in monetary amount, e.g. cash, loans, debtors, and creditors, are translated at the closing rate while non-monetary items, e.g. plant, stock, are translated at the historical rate.

3. *The Temporal Method* This method is based on the view that items should be translated by reference to the exchange rate ruling at the date when their

value has been established in the accounts. For monetary items this will be the closing rate, since the monetary amount expresses their value at the balance sheet date. In the case of unmodified historical cost accounts, non-monetary items will be translated at the historical rate, so that the temporal method will operate in the same way as the monetary/non-monetary method. However, where asset revaluations have been introduced into the accounts the exchange rate at the date of valuation will be used. Revaluation in the context of historic cost accounts is common in respect of fixed assets in a number of European countries.

Inventories are also normally shown at a valuation where this is lower than cost. Where replacement cost accounting is used, all items are expressed at value at the balance sheet date, so that under the temporal method the closing rate will apply to all items.

Where historical rate methods are used, often the average rate for a year is accepted as an acceptable approximation to be applied to all transactions in that year. The average rate will not necessarily reflect a simple average of the exchange rates reported during a year, but may be weighted in line with the flow of transactions in the year.

4. *Closing Rate Method* applies the closing rate to all balance sheet items and either the average rate or the closing rate to all profit and loss items. Since all items in the balance sheet are subject to translation exposure, it is the net investment in each foreign enterprise that is exposed and accordingly this is often referred to as the closing rate/net investment method.

Table 3.6 shows a simple example of a company with a foreign subsidiary. Table 3.7 shows how the balance sheets would translate under each of our four methods. Table 3.8 shows how the profit and loss accounts would translate under the temporal and closing rate methods.

Table 3.6

On 1st January 1991 Dolphin SA, a company registered in Lilliput where the unit of currency is the Gull (G), set up a subsidiary Panda Inc in the Miranda Islands where the unit of currency is the Bun (B). The initial investment of B 2600 million was partly financed by a B 1000 million loan. Plant was purchased on 1st January 1991 on the same date as the local loan of B 2000 million was raised. Exchange rates for the Gull were:

	Buns
1st January 1991	4
Average for 1991	3
Date closing stock acquired	2.5
31st December 1991	2

PANDA INC

Balance sheet as at 31 December 1991

	B.m	B.m
Plant – cost		5400
– depreciation		1080
		4320
Current assets:		
Stock note 1	660	
Debtors	680	
Cash	20	
	1360	
Current liabilities:		
Creditors	320	
Taxation	360	
	680	
Net current assets		680
		5000
Long-term loan		2000
		3000
Share capital		2600
Retained profit		400
		3000

PANDA INC

Profit and Loss account for the year ended 31 December 1991

	B.m	B.m
Sales		6000
Purchases	4260	
less Closing stock	660	
		3600
Gross Profit		2400
less:		
Depreciation	1080	
Other expenses	600	
		1680
Net profit		720
Taxation		320
		400

Note 1:

Stock is shown at the lower of cost and market value:

	Cost	360
	Market value	300
		660

Table 3.7 Balance Sheets

	Current Non-current	Monetary Non-monetary	Temporal	Closing rate
	G.	G.	G.	G.
Plant	1080	1080	1080	2160
Stock	330	264	144	330
			150	
Debtors	340	340	340	340
Cash	10	10	10	10
Current assets	680	614	644	680
Creditors	160	160	160	160
Taxation	180	180	180	180
Current liabilities	340	340	340	340
Net current assets	340	274	304	340
	1420	1354	1384	2500
Loan	500	1000	1000	1000
	920	354	384	1500
Share capital	650	650	650	650
Other equity	270	(296)	(266)	850
	920	354	384	1500

Table 3.8 Profit and Loss Accounts

	Temporal method		Closing rate	
	G.	G.	G.	G.
Sales		2000		3000
Purchases	1420		2130	
Closing stock	294		330	
		1126		1800
Gross profit		874		1200
less:				
Depreciation	270		540	
Other expenses	200		300	
		470		840
Net profit		404		360
Taxation		160		160
		244		200
Exchange gain/loss		(510)		650
Change in equity		(266)		850

Nobes (1980) reviews the history of the various translation methods. He finds that:

1. The closing rate method was used by British accountants in the nineteenth century.
2. The current/non-current method was advocated in the USA by Dicksee in 1911 and officially recommended by the Certified Public Accountants in 1931. It was common at a time when exchange rates tended to fluctuate reasonably gently. The underlying logic is that current items, by definition, turn into cash in the short term, so should be translated at the closing rate. By contrast, non-current items take some time to create related cash flows, by which time the exchange rate may have moved back towards the historic rate; in view of the unpredictability of this process, departure from a simple historic cost basis cannot be justified. This process lost its attractions with freely floating exchange rates. It is interesting to reflect, however, that similar arguments might still be justified when translating between currencies within a stabilization system such as the European Monetary System.
3. The monetary/non-monetary method is traced back to 1956.
4. The temporal method was first recommended by Lorenson (1972).

The temporal method is effectively a development of the monetary/non-monetary method, updating it to reflect increased use of revaluations in accounts. Thus currently the two methods in common use internationally are the closing rate method and the temporal method. The closing rate method has the merits of using the most recent data, it is applied to all items, so preserving the ratios of the subsidiary intact, and it is simple to apply. The temporal method is more consistent with historic cost accounting, and is more realistic when applied to subsidiaries in areas of high inflation.

An important difference between the two methods is that they tend to produce different types of result, arising from different elements of exposure. An investment in a foreign subsidiary normally has the following characteristics:

1. The assets less liabilities, i.e. the net investment, will tend to be positive. It is this net asset that will be 'exposed' under the closing rate method.
2. Monetary borrowings will normally exceed monetary assets, so that under the temporal method a net liability will be exposed.

When the foreign currency gets weaker the temporal method shows a gain, because the liability can be repaid with a smaller cash outflow in terms of the parent currency. The closing rate method shows a loss because the net investment in the subsidiary is an asset. The converse applies when the foreign currency gets stronger, as in our example in Table 3.9.

Table 3.9 Impact on Profit of Translation by Different Methods When Net Investment in Subsidiary is an Asset and the Subsidiary Has Net Monetary Liabilities

	Temporal method	Closing rate method
Strong foreign currency	LOSS	GAIN
Weak foreign currency	GAIN	LOSS

Many countries have followed the rules laid down in the USA in SFAS 52.

SFAS 52 states that its basic objective is to achieve *compatibility with expected effects*. This means that if a change in the exchange rate is expected to have a beneficial effect on the parent company cash flows and equity then the translation should reflect that. Conversely, if a change is expected to have an adverse effect on the parent company, that should also be reflected.

Two other major objectives are stressed in SFAS 52:

1. Translation should produce results conforming with Generally Accepted Accounting Principles.

2. The results and relationships in the foreign currency accounts should be retained on translation, so that the original accounting ratios are not distorted.

SFAS 52 then identifies two different types of foreign operation:

1. Self-contained and integrated foreign operations. It is argued that each such operation should be viewed as representing one net investment to which the closing rate should be applied. Changes in the exchange rate do not affect the cash flows of the parent company, because the foreign operation is regarded as self-contained, so that on consolidation gains or losses on translation of the net investment should not be taken through the income statement but should be taken directly to the equity.

2. Components or extensions of parent company domestic operations, where a foreign operation is an integral part or extension of the parent company's domestic operations, such as in the case of an import or export business, then it is argued that changes in the exchange rate directly affect individual assets and liabilities employed on behalf of the parent company. Accordingly the temporal method is used. Gains or losses on translation are reflected in the consolidated income statement because they have effects on the parent company's cash flows. Foreign currency balances in a company's own accounts are treated in the same way.

A full account of the rules of FAS 52 can be found in Rubin (1991).

While broadly following the US approach, a number of countries do not take translation gains to profit, instead deferring or excluding such gains.

We have seen above that there is an economic relationship between exchange rates, interest rates, and inflation rates.

As a simple example, during 1989 Brazil experienced inflation of some 1,300 per cent compared with a rate of 6.8 per cent in Spain. Thus the massive devaluation of the Brazilian cruzeiro from 148 pesetas to 9.7 pesetas during 1989 is not surprising.

Let us consider the example of a Spanish company that invested a million pesetas in Brazilian assets at the beginning of 1989. Such an investment would appear very differently in the books of the Spanish company, depending on whether it was translated by the temporal or the closing rate method.

The investment in cruzeiros at the beginning of 1989 would be

$$1,000,000 \times \frac{1}{148} = 6,756 \text{ cruzeiros.}$$

Assuming an investment in non-monetary assets, this would translate back to 1,000,000 pesetas in future years under the temporal method. However, under the closing rate method, at the end of 1989 the cruzeiro balance would translate as

$$6,756 \times 9.7 = 65,533 \text{ pesetas.}$$

Thus a loss of 934,467 pesetas would be recorded.

Assuming that the assets purchased in Brazil kept their value approximately in line with inflation, their real value at the end of 1989 would be

$$\text{cruzeiro } 6,756 \times 1,300\% = 87,828 \text{ cruzeiros.}$$

This would translate as

$$87,828 \times 9.7 = 851,932 \text{ pesetas.}$$

This shows a much less significant loss on the investment of 148,068 pesetas – some 15 per cent, rather than 93 per cent, of the original investment.

The example illustrates why the translation of the historic cost accounts of a company in an environment of hyperinflation gives distorted results under the closing rate method. There are two broad approaches that can be taken in response to this problem:

1. Require use of the temporal method in such situations. The USA adopts this approach.

2. Require inflation adjustments to the subsidiary's accounts before applying the closing rate. This is the UK approach.

INFLATION

In times of inflation the traditional historic cost approach used by accountants can be highly misleading. Both assets and liabilities can be regarded as falling under two broad headings:

1. *Monetary items* These are assets or liabilities where the benefit or obligation is a fixed monetary amount. Examples include bank balances, trade debtors, loans, and trade creditors.

2. *Non-monetary items* These are items where the benefit or obligation is not a fixed monetary amount. Examples of assets include land and buildings, plant, and stock. Examples of liabilities are less common but might include pension obligations under a defined benefit scheme.

Four major problems arise with the use of historic cost accounts in times of inflation:

1. Non-monetary assets are recorded at a historic cost that is lower than current value. Thus the net assets of the business are shown at an unrealistically low amount.

2. When non-monetary assets are consumed, the amount of the related expense charged against profit will be the historic cost figure – again an unrealistically low amount, so that reported profit will be unrealistically high.

3. Because the value of money is falling the benefit to the company of monetary assets declines, and the burden of the obligation liabilities declines. This 'loss' or 'gain' is not recognized in the historic cost account because there is no change in the amount at which the monetary items are shown.

4. When considering successive years' accounts comparison is distorted by the fact that the unit of measurement has a different significance each year.

The simple examples in Table 3.10 illustrate these problems.

Table 3.10

---

1. John bought a new taxi for £10,000 on 1 January 19X4. He expected the taxi to have a five-year life with no residual value. He uses the straight-line basis of depreciation. On 31 December 19X4 the new price of the taxi was £13,000.

2. Mary bought a house for £100,000 on 1 January 19X4, borrowing £90,000 to do so. On 31 December 19X4 the house was valued at £120,000 and the loan still stood at £90,000.

In both the above cases inflation during 19X4 was 25 per cent.

3. Cazuela S.A. sells cooking utensils.

Reported sales were as follows:		
	Year 1	1,000,000
	Year 2	1,100,000
	Year 3	1,320,000
An inflation index showed:	Year 1	100
	Year 2	105
	Year 3	136.5

---

1. John's balance sheet at 31 December 19X4 will show his taxi as

Cost	10,000
Depreciation	2,000
	8,000

However, John owns a taxi with 80 per cent of its life remaining and a current value of £13,000, so perhaps a more realistic figure would be:

$$80\% \times £13,000 = £10,400$$

Similarly John's depreciation charge will be £2,000, but a more realistic figure would be:

$$20\% \times £13,000 = £2,600$$

2. At the end of 19X4 Mary owns one-quarter of the net worth of her house. At the beginning of 19X4 she only owned one-tenth of the net worth of her house. This improvement is not reflected in her accounts.

3. Cazuela S.A. seems to be improving sales – a 10 per cent increase in Year 1, and 20 per cent in Year 2. However, if we restate the value of the sales in terms of Year 3 values a different pattern emerges:

Year 1	1,000,000	$\times$	$\dfrac{136.5}{100}$	$=$	1,365,000
Year 2	1,100,000	$\times$	$\dfrac{136.5}{105}$	$=$	1,430,000
Year 3				$=$	1,320,000

In other words, an economically realistic statement might be that sales rose by 4.8 per cent in Year 1 and fell by 7.7 per cent in Year 2.

There are two broad approaches that can be taken in response to this problem:

1. We can change the unit of measurement. For example, in Germany during the early 1920s accountants responded to massive inflation by translating all amounts into the stable value of the mark before hyperinflation commenced. A number of countries have experimented with Current Purchasing Power (CPP) systems that translate historic cost monetary amounts into CPP units at the balance sheet date by using a general price index and applying the factor:

$$\frac{\text{Index at balance sheet date}}{\text{Index at transaction date}}$$

All monetary items in the balance sheet are then adjusted back to their actual monetary amount, with gains or losses forming part of a gain or loss on monetary items.

2. We can change the basis of measurement, using some concept of 'value' instead of historic cost. Replacement cost as a basis of measurement is used by Philips BV in the Netherlands.

A more complex measure of value is 'deprival value', being the lower of replacement cost and the 'recoverable amount' which is in turn the higher of net realizable value and the 'economic value'. Economic value is the total expected future cash inflow from an asset discounted to present value. Deprival value is the measurement basis for the 'current cost accounting' approach that has been experimented with in a number of countries.

Broadly speaking, three types of countries have developed full inflation accounting sytems:

1. The Netherlands has developed a replacement cost approach, applied by a small number of large companies and discussed in Chapter 12 below.

2. A number of Latin American countries with hyperinflation have adopted crude CPP-type approaches.

3. A number of English-speaking countries, including the US and the UK, developed CCA-type systems in the late 1970s but have now abandoned these as a result of lower inflation. South Africa is a country that has tended to follow the example of these countries, but continues to have high inflation.

Stobie (1989) comments

The inflation accounting debate which raged during the seventies has died down considerably as rates of inflation have dropped in the major Western countries. In South Africa, however, the need for inflation accounting has not abated (it has, if anything, intensified), but our long history as a follower of overseas accounting thought and practice has led to the problem being ignored or shelved pending the discovery of a 'miracle cure' by some overseas gurus (p. 148).

This example offers an interesting illustration of the dangers of developing accounting practice within a 'cluster group' of nations if the economic environment of one nation develops in a different way from others.

TANGIBLE FIXED ASSETS

IAS 16 permits tangible fixed assets to be recorded at depreciated historic cost or at a valuation. The European Community Fourth Directive prescribes historic cost, but does permit member states to allow revaluation on the basis of replacement cost or other current value. Both IAS 16 and the Fourth Directive require depreciation to be provided for on all fixed assets with a finite useful life.

In defining the cost of a fixed asset a problem arises in deciding whether interest costs that accumulate over the period of construction should be treated as part of the cost of the asset and capitalized. IAS 23 puts forward a set of conditions within which capitalization of interest costs may be permitted.

RESEARCH AND DEVELOPMENT

Research and development expenditure is, by its nature, a challenge to traditional accounting principles. On the one hand it is, by nature, prone to uncertainty concerning its outcome. Will the end product be technically feasible? Will it be attractive to the market? Will the financial resources be available to bring the product to the market and take a commanding lead before competitors copy the product? With such a range of uncertainty, it seems that the prudence concept would lead us to a 'write-off policy', charging such expenditure against profit in the year it is incurred. On the other hand, research and development is also, by its nature, intended as an investment for the future. On this basis we might argue that costs should be carried forward as an asset and should be amortized when related profits are earned.

Normally, in a situation of this kind, we would expect the prudence convention to prevail. However, a number of countries have developed rules that permit some use of an amortized policy. This is generally because research and development is seen as a socially desirable activity, promoting employment and economic growth, while a write-off policy discourages such expenditure.

Countries that do permit amortization tend to impose restrictions designed to ensure that due care is taken to guarantee that only expenditure that can reasonably be expected to produce related income in the future is deferred as an asset. Often a distinction is drawn between 'research' which must be written off immediately, and 'development' which may be deferred. Often a time period within which amortization must occur is specified.

IAS 9 distinguishes between 'research', which is original and planned investigation to gain new scientific knowledge or understanding, and 'development', which is the translation of knowledge into a plan or design for the production of some new or substantially improved form of output. Only development expenditure may be deferred and amortized. Deferral is subject to the following conditions:

1. There must be a clearly defined project to which related costs can be clearly attributed.
2. Technical feasibility of the project must be demonstrated.
3. Management must have indicated its intention to complete the project.
4. There must be a clear indication of the future market for, or use of, the output.
5. Adequate resources must be available for exploitation of the project.

The European Community Fourth Directive allows member states to permit deferral of research and development, which should normally be written off over a period of up to five years, though a longer write-off period is permitted if an explanation is given in the notes to the accounts. Normally any deferred research and development costs should be excluded from net assets in computing distributable profit.

STOCK AND WORK IN PROGRESS

Stock is covered by IAS 2 (Valuation and presentation of inventories in the content of the historical cost system) while long-term contracts are covered by IAS 11 (Accounting for construction contracts). Major issues leading to international differences are:

1. There is a problem in deciding what costs should be regarded as part of the cost of stock, particularly in the case of manufactured goods. Clearly, bought in materials and components are part of the cost, and generally direct labour would be included. IAS 2 also requires that the cost of stock should include a systematic allocation of production overheads that relate to putting stock in its current location and condition. Thus stock is valued on a full absorption basis. This approach has been criticized by those who argue that a marginal costing basis is more relevant to decision making.

2. In determining the cost of materials and components held in stock, there is a problem in deciding now to allocate different costs paid. IAS 2 allows first-in first-out (FIFO), last-in first-out (LIFO), average cost (AVCO), specific identification, or base stock. Internationally LIFO, which in times of inflation will tend to depress reported profits, tends to be popular only in those countries where it is used for tax purposes. LIFO is a crude method of giving tax relief for the impact of inflation on stock holding costs.

3. IAS 2 states that stock should be valued at the lower of cost and net realizable value on an item-by-item basis, or by groups of similar items. In some countries, a lower of cost, net realizable value, or replacement cost basis is preferred, and this is permitted by the European Community Fourth Directive.

   Table 3.11 illustrates how these approaches work. Applying the lower of cost and net realizable value rule in IAS 2 gives a stock figure of 9,900. This is an application of the prudence concept – if the lower of *total* cost and *total* net realizable value (10,000) were taken, then the loss of 100 on toffee would be compensated for by the profits on chocolate and biscuits which Sharon expects to earn in the future but has not yet earned. For those countries that also take replacement cost into account, Sharon's stock will be 9,800, a more conservative figure. Critics of this approach would argue that the lower replacement cost of biscuits does not represent a loss to Sharon because she is still able to sell those biscuits at a higher price than cost.

Table 3.11

Sharon owns a sweetshop. On 31 December 19X7 her stock was:

	Cost	NRV	Replacement cost	Lower of cost & NRV	Lowest
Chocolate	5,000	5,400	5,200	5,000	5,000
Toffee	3,000	2,900	3,000	2,900	2,900
Biscuits	2,000	2,100	1,900	2,000	1,900
	10,000	10,400	10,100	9,900	9,800

4. Long-term contracts can be considered in two ways. Under the completed contract method, no profit is recognized in the same income statement until work on the contract is completed. Under the 'percentage of completion' method, part of the profit on a long-term contract may be recognized in the income statement as the contract progresses, in proportion to the amount of work completed. IAS 11 permits either method, subject to clear evidence to justify profit taken under the 'percentage of completion' method. IAS 11 also requires provision for all foreseeable losses on long-term contracts.

LEASES

A lease is an agreement whereby a *lessor*, who owns an asset, conveys the right to use that asset to a *lessee* for an agreed period of time at an agreed rental.

There are two broad categories of lease:

1. Finance leases, covering most or all of the life of an asset. Such a lease is normally designed as a mechanism whereby the lessor finances the acquisition of an asset to be used, in practice, by the lessee.

2. Operating leases, where a lessor acquires an asset to be hired out for successive periods of time to successive users. Such a lease is normally entered into for operational reasons.

An accounting problem arises with finance leases because their legal form as a rental agreement produces an accounting treatment that is very different from their commercial substance as a finance arrangement. Consider the Table 3.12.

Table 3.12 Example

Ost Inc, a Ruritanian company wishes to buy an asset costing 55,404 crowns. A bank is willing to finance this purchase and has offered a choice of three deals, each commencing on 1 January 19X5:

1. The bank will lend Ost Inc the money to buy the asset. The loan will be repaid by instalments of 5,404 crowns per quarter, payable in advance, over a three-year period. Finance charges spread evenly over a three-year period will be:

	Crowns
Year to 31 December 19X5	5,283
Year to 31 December 19X6	3,233
Year to 31 December 19X7	928
	9,444

2. The bank will buy the asset and lease it to Ost Inc for three years for 5,404 crowns per quarter, payable in advance. After three years Ost Inc may purchase the asset for five crowns.
3. The bank will buy the asset and lease it to Ost Inc for three years for 5,404 crowns per quarter, payable in advance. After three years, Ost Inc may continue to lease the asset for as long as it wishes for a payment of one crown per year.

In practice the company expects to use the asset for four years, and after that time the machine will have no value.

Table 3.13 shows how each of the three options in table 3.12 would affect the profit and loss account. The cash flows for each option are virtually identical, the only differences arising being the nominal payments in 19X8 of five crowns under Option 2 and one crown under Option 3.

The profit and loss charges vary for two reasons:

1. Under Options 2 and 3, lease payments are charged to profit and loss over the three years that they are paid rather than the four years that the asset is in use. There is a potential abuse here whereby companies can commit themselves to lease agreements under which the main part of lease payments falls into the years when they prefer to show high expenses. IAS 17 addresses this issue by a requirement that operating lease payments be charged in the income statement on a systematic basis that reflects the benefit to the user, irrespective of the timing of payments in the lease agreement.

2. Under Option 1 the finance cost reduces each year in line with the part of the loan that has been repaid.

The most dramatic difference, however, is in the balance sheet. Option 1, the purchase transaction, shows the asset and related liability indicating an increase in financial leverage. Options 2 and 3, each of which imposes the same pattern of cash flows as Option 1, are not reflected in the balance sheet at all. Consequently they form a kind of 'off balance sheet finance'.

Table 3.13   Profit and Loss Account Related Expenses

Years to:	31.12.X5	31.12.X6	31.12.X7	31.12.X8
	Cr.	Cr.	Cr.	Cr.
Option 1				
Depreciation	13,851	13,851	13,851	13,851
Interest	5,283	3,233	928	
	19,134	17,084	14,779	13,851
Option 2				
Rental	21,616	21,616	21,616	5
Option 3				
Rental	21,616	21,616	21,616	1
Balance sheet amounts				
Option 1				
Fixed assets				
Cost	55,404	55,404	55,404	55,404
Less depreciation	13,851	27,702	41,553	55,404
Net book value	41,553	27,702	13,851	–
Loan				
At 1 January	55,404	39,071	20,688	–
+ Interest	5,283	3,233	928	–
– Instalments paid	(21,616)	(21,616)	(21,616)	
At 31 December	39,071	20,688	–	–

IAS 17 tackles this problem by requiring that finance leases should be 'capitalized'. That means that an asset is recorded as though it had been purchased, and is depreciated in the normal way. The related obligation to pay future instalments is shown as a liability, with related finance costs charged to profit on a systematic basis. The effect is that in our example Options 2 and 3 would be accounted for in the same way as Option 1.

The problem here is to define a 'finance lease'. The principle is that a finance lease is one that transfers substantially all the risks and rewards incident to ownership to the lessee. However, in practice many companies find leasing attractive precisely because it offers the opportunity to conceal leverage. For example, in the UK two studies found that the 'off balance sheet' aspect of leasing was a major reason for companies to lease (Fawthrop and Terry 1975; Sykes 1976). A requirement to capitalize finance leases may, therefore, have two types of effect:

1. Companies may try to restructure lease agreements to avoid classification as a finance lease. For example, one of the conditions that some countries apply in the definition of a finance lease is that there should be a favourable purchase option. In our example – above, a company could therefore avoid finance lease capitalization by choosing Option 3 rather than Option 2. In the UK, Taylor and Turley (1985) found that 50 per cent of a sample of companies planned to avoid new rules on finance lease capitalization by careful structuring of new leases. In the USA, the FASB have found it necessary to produce a 200-page book on the definition of a finance lease in order to curb this sort of avoidance.

2. Companies may change their financial policy as a result of the requirement to capitalize finance leases. In the USA, Abdel-Khalik et al. (1981) investigated the economic consequences of FAS 13 on leasing. They found that managers' reactions included selecting a mix of financial instruments that would increase equity relative to debt, and moving to the purchase of assets in preference to leasing.

IAS 17 also requires disclosure of a range of information about commitments under both finance and operating leases.

IAS 17 requires that lessors should account in a way consistent with the accounting treatment by lessees, i.e. for operating leases the related fixed assets are recorded and depreciated in the normal way, while for finance leases the 'net investment' in the lease is treated as a financial asset.

Different countries may have different tax rules for leased assets, and may take different approaches to whether capitalization of leased assets in the accounts has any impact on tax treatment.

An interesting example of how this can influence accounting regulators arose in the UK and the Republic of Ireland, two countries for which one single body, until recently the Accounting Standards Committee (ASC), formulated accounting regulations. In ED 29 the ASC proposed that finance lease capitalization should be required in the UK but not in the Republic of Ireland, because in the latter country there would be tax implications. This is an interesting example of an accounting regulating body being responsive to 'economic consequences' (see Blake 1989).

European Community directives do not specify any particular accounting treatment for leases.

DEFERRED TAXATION

In countries which do not require the published accounts to be prepared in line with tax law, there may be differences between the accounting profit and the tax profit. These differences may be of two kinds:

1. Permanent differences may arise when a type of expenditure or income shown in one set of accounts simply does not appear in the other. The fact

that such differences arise does not have any accounting implications.

2. 'Timing differences' may arise when a type of expenditure or income appears in accounting profit for one period and in the tax profit in a different period. One example is depreciation. Commonly, tax authorities prescribe depreciation rates to be applied that may differ from those used in the published accounts. Table 3.14 gives a simple example.

Table 3.14 Example

Mijas SA, a Ruritanian company, commenced business on 1 January 19X1. A machine was purchased for $1,000,000. The machine has a four-year life with no residual value, and straight-line depreciation is used. Annual profits before depreciation and tax were $1,200,000. In the next four years, tax rates were:

19X1	50%
19X2	52%
19X3	54%
19X4	53%

Under Ruritanian law, for tax purposes machines are fully depreciated in the year of acquisition.

Liability method

	19X1 $	19X2 $	19X3 $	19X4 $
Profit before depreciation	1,200,000	1,200,000	1,200,000	1,200,000
Depreciation	250,000	250,000	250,000	250,000
Profit before tax	950,000	950,000	950,000	950,000
Tax	(100,000)	(624,000)	(648,000)	(636,000)
Deferred tax	(375,000)	115,000	125,000	135,000
Profit after tax	475,000	441,000	427,000	449,000

Workings

	19X1 $	19X2 $	19X3 $	19X4 $
Accounting value *less* tax value of machine	750,000	500,000	250,000	–
Tax rate	50%	52%	54%	53%
Closing deferred tax balance	375,000	260,000	135,000	–
Opening deferred tax balance	–	375,000	260,000	135,000
P&L charge/recovery	375,000	(115,000)	(125,000)	(135,000)

Deferral method

	19X1	19X2	19X3	19X4
	$	$	$	$
Profit before depreciation	1,200,000	1,200,000	1,200,000	1,200,000
Depreciation	250,000	250,000	250,000	250,000
Profit before tax	950,000	950,000	950,000	950,000
Tax	(100,000)	(624,000)	(648,000)	(636,000)
Deferred tax	(375,000)	125,000	125,000	125,000
Profit after tax	475,000	451,000	427,000	439,000

In 19X1 the actual tax charge will be arrived at after deducting from profit the full cost of the machine, so that in the three subsequent years no tax depreciation is allowed at all. The effect is a very serious distortion of the apparent tax position in the accounts.

There are three broad approaches to accounting for the tax effects of timing differences:

1. The 'flow through' approach, whereby the tax to be accounted for is taken to be the tax assessment for the year, and the question of timing differences is ignored.

2. The 'full deferral' approach, which, following the accruals concept, would charge to the profit and loss account the full tax effects of all timing differences.

3. The 'partial deferral' approach whereby provision is made for the tax effect of timing differences except to the extent that the prospect of these reversing is seen as remote.

There is no European Community guidance on this topic. IAS 12 (Accounting for Taxes on Income) favours a full deferral approach but permits partial deferral.

There are two broad approaches to computing a deferred tax obligation:

1. The liability method applies the current tax rate to the net outstanding differences at the end of each year, taking to the profit and loss account the difference between opening and closing balances.

2. The deferral method involves computing the effect of each timing difference at the time it arises and reversing that effect at the same tax rate in future periods.

Table 3.14 illustrates the difference between the two.

In countries that account for deferred taxation, it is normal, on grounds of prudence, to limit the extent to which deferred tax assets can be carried forward.

PENSION PLANS

Many employers throughout Europe provide a pension as part of the benefits to employees.

Two types of scheme arise:

1. *Defined contribution schemes* These involve an employer in making agreed contributions to a pension scheme. The benefits paid to the employee will then depend on these contributions and related investment earnings. This is a common kind of scheme in small businesses, and the cost to the employer is easy to identify.

2. *Defined benefit schemes* In this case it is the benefits to be paid that are defined, often in terms of the employee's final pay. The level of funding needed to meet benefit requirements is necessarily a matter for estimate. These estimates are made by an actuary and cover such matters as:

   (a) Future pay increases and inflation rates.

   (b) Arrangements to increase pension payments.

   (c) Number of employees joining and leaving the scheme.

   (d) Deaths of employees before and after retiring age.

   (e) Age profile of employees.

   (f) Earnings on investments.

The problem is eased slightly in that some of these estimates may be related and offsetting. One example is that earnings on investments and costs of pension increases may both be related to inflation.

There are substantial variations between different countries as to how precisely pension obligations are defined and the extent to which pension commitments are supported by payments into a separate pension fund. Thus the reader of accounts from different countries has to cope, not only with different accounting rules, but also with different underlying types of commitment.

IAS 19 addresses this issue. For a 'defined contribution' scheme the employer's required contribution should be treated as an expense each year. If a scheme is amended, and an additional payment becomes due to cover benefits granted retrospectively for earlier years of service, then this 'post-service cost' may be treated in one of two ways:

1. Write off immediately,

2. Write off systematically over the expected remaining working lives of participating employees.

For a 'defined benefit' plan, accounting is more complex. An actuary must provide estimates of the 'value' of the obligations implied by the pension scheme, and the pension cost should be expensed systematically over the remaining working lives of employees. Adjustments to the value of the pension fund obligation may arise because of past service costs (as defined above), 'experience adjustments' arising from differences between events as predicted in the previous actuarial valuation and actual experience, and changes in actuarial assumptions for the future. Such gains or losses may be taken to income as they arise or taken on a systematic basis over the expected remaining working lives of participating employees.

POST BALANCE SHEET EVENTS

IAS 10 offers guidance on 'post balance sheet events', namely events, both favourable and unfavourable, that occur between the balance sheet date and the date on which the accounts are authorized for issue. Such events fall into two broad categories:

1. Events providing further evidence of conditions that existed at the year end. For example, stock held at the year end costing 1,000 might subsequently be sold for 900. This is evidence of net realizable value below cost. Such events should be adjusted for in the accounts.

2. Events indicating conditions that arose subsequent to the balance sheet date. An example might be where a fire destroys a building. Such events should not be adjusted for in the accounts, but if material may require disclosure in the notes.

The European Community Fourth Directive does not prescribe any accounting treatment in this area, but does require disclosure in the annual report of important events that occurred since the year end. Although the principles of IAS 10 are not controversial, their application varies.

CONCLUSION

There is a wide range of controversial accounting issues that give scope for major international variations in accounting practice.

REFERENCES

Abdel-Khalik, A.R., Thompson, R.B. and Taylor, R.E. (1981) 'The economic effects on lessees of FASB statement No. 13: Accounting for Leases', FASB.

Baxt, R. (1968) 'True and fair view – a legal analysis', *Accountant's Journal.*, April, pp. 301–10.

Benson, H. (1989) *Accounting for Life*, Kogan Page.

Bircher, P. (1988) 'Company law reform and the Board of Trade', *Accounting and Business Research*, Vol. 18, No. 70, pp. 107–19.

Bird, P. (1984) 'What is a true and fair view?' *Journal of Business Law*, November, pp. 480–5.

Blake, J. (1989) 'Economic consequences in the emergence of SSAP 21: Accounting for Leases and Hire Purchase Contracts' *Managerial Finance*, Vol. 15, No. 1/2 pp. 21–5.

Commission of the European Communities (1987) *The Fourth Company Law Directive: Implementation by Member States.*

Cowan, T.K. (1965) 'Are truth and fairness generally acceptable?', *Accounting Review*, October, pp. 788–94.

Fawthrop, R. and Terry, B. (1975) 'Debt management and the use of leasing finance in UK corporate financing strategies', *Journal of Business Finance and Accounting*, Autumn, pp. 295–314.

Fédération des Experts Comptables Européens (1991).

FEE European Survey of Published Accounts 1991, Routledge.

Felt, H.M. (1968) 'The effort and authority of the AICPA in the development of generally accepted accounting principles', *International Journal of Accounting*, Spring, pp. 11–27.

Giddy, I.H. (1977) 'Exchange risk: whose view?', *Financial Management*, Summer, pp. 23–33.

ICAEW (1958) *Statement N18: Presentation of Balance Sheet and Profit and Loss Account*.

Irish, R.A. (1966) 'Trial by fire', *The Chartered Accountant in Australia*, September, pp. 170–9.

Lorenson, L. (1972) 'Accounting Research Study No. 12 Reporting foreign operations of US companies in US dollars'. AICPA.

McEnroe, J.E. (1991) 'Attitudes towards the term "Generally Accepted Accounting Principles" ', *Accounting and Business Research*, Spring, pp. 157–62.

McMonnies, P. (1967) 'The importance of being English', *The Accountant's Magazine*, February.

Nobes, C.W. (1980) 'A review of the translation debate', *Accounting and Business Research*, Autumn, pp. 421–30.

Nobes, C. (1990) 'EC Group accounting: two zillion ways to do it', *Accountancy*, December, pp. 84–5.

Rubin, S. (1991) 'Consolidation, translation and the equity method' in Carmichael, D.R., Lilien, S.B., and Mellman, M. *Accountants Handbook* Ch. 7, Wiley.

Sauter, D. (1991) 'Remodelling the House of GAAP', *Journal of Accountancy*, July, pp. 30–7.

Stobie, B.S. (1989) 'Inflation accounting in a double digit economy – dormant or dead', *Chartered Accountant*, June, pp. 148–9.

Sykes, A. (1976) *The Lease-Buy Decision*, British Institute of Management.

Taylor, P. and Turley, S. (1985) 'The views of management on accounting for leases', *Accounting and Business Research*, Winter, pp. 59–67.

Williams, D.W. (1985) 'Legal perspectives on auditing' in Kent D., Sherer M., and Turley S. (eds), *Current Issues in Audting*, Harper and Row, pp. 15–32.

CHAPTER 4

Belgium

ABBREVIATIONS

IEC	Institut des Experts Comptables – Professional Accountants' Institute.
IRE	Institut des Réviseurs d'Entreprises – Professional Auditors' Institute.

INTRODUCTION Accounting regulation in Belgium has been radically changed in line with EC directives. One distinctive feature of the Belgian accounting system is the binding link between tax and accounting law. When businesses prepare their annual accounts, fiscal principles tend to take precedence over accounting principles. Another distinctive feature is the role that employee works councils have played in the development of accounting. For example, businesses with more than 100 employees must present a financial report to the works councils.

In Belgium, two languages, French and Flemish, have equal official status. In this chapter French terms are used because they are more commonly understood internationally; each French term used has an official Flemish equivalent.

ACCOUNTING REGULATION

Accounting in Belgium has developed from the French regulations, going back to Colbert's Commercial Code of 1673 and the Napoleonic Commercial Code of 1807. Belgium's first company law was enacted in 1873 followed by a further company law of 1935. One characteristic of this legislation was that accounting disclosure requirements were very limited. Michel et al. (1992, p. 25) explain this tradition with three factors:

1. A small number of very powerful holding companies were reluctant to disclose information to the public.

2. Few shares in companies were held by outside parties, with a consequent low demand for published accounts.

3. The legislators saw accounting disclosure as primarily addressed to the needs of creditors, with a consequent emphasis on a conservative balance sheet.

In the early 1970s representations for more accounting regulation came from a range of sources including trade unions, works councils, financial analysts, accountants and academics. Legislation in 1973 required that workers' councils receive the same information as shareholders. Subsequent legislation included:

1. The accounting law of 1975 provided for criteria for company accounts to be formulated, with penalties for non-compliance.

2. A Royal Decree of 1976 provided detailed disclosure requirements and valuation rules.

3. A Royal Decree of 1978 introduced a chart of accounts, providing a format for presentation.

4. Two Royal Decrees in 1983 brought Belgian accounting law into line with the EC Fourth Directive.

5 In 1990 a Royal Decree on consolidated accounts implemented the EC Seventh Directive.

THE ACCOUNTING PROFESSION

Seabrook (1991) offers a review of the structure of the Belgian profession. There are two professional bodies:

1. The *Institut des Réviseurs d'Entreprises* (IRE), founded in 1953, is the professional body for auditors. Currently there are some 700 members.

2. The *Institut des Experts Comptables* (IEC) is the professional body for accountants offering services such as bookkeeping, preparation of the annual accounts, tax advice and general financial advice. It was founded in 1985, replacing a previous body, the *College National des Experts-Comptables de Belgique*.

The two professions of auditor and accountant are strictly separate and, although the two bodies have similar training schemes, students must choose from the outset which qualification they are pursuing with no option to transfer to the other subsequently. Normally a Belgian firm of accountants will include members of both bodies, but to comply with strict auditor independence requirements the auditing and accounting requirements of the firm must be divided into separate companies with different names.

To qualify as a member of IRE it is necessary to:

1. Pass an examination with 17 papers in line with the EC Eighth Directive on auditor qualifications. Relevant graduates enjoy exemption from some or all papers.

2. Trainees must undergo a period of three years' practical training under the supervision of a qualified auditor. During this period a number of training courses and examinations are undertaken.

3. At the end of the practical training period there is an oral and a written examination.

4. Finally, successful candidates, who must have Belgian residence or nationality, be aged 25 to 65, and not be subject to deprivation of civil or

political rights, must make a solemn oath before the tribunal of the local chamber of commerce.

AUDITING

The auditing law of 1985 responded to the requirements of the EC in relation to audit requirements and auditor qualifications. An audit is compulsory only for large enterprises, and in those cases the auditors must be members of IRE. For any enterprise with more than 100 employees an audited financial report must also be presented to the Works Council. Theunisse (1987) comments on the 'rather unique way' (p. 212) in which Belgian auditors are appointed, arising from the influence of the concept of 'social partners' on Belgian commercial law. Effectively, the members of the Works Council have a power of veto over the appointment of the auditor. If no agreement on the appointment of an auditor can be reached then the final decision is taken by the commercial court.

The auditor's report must cover:

1. How the audit was carried out, including whether or not managers of the company supplied all the explanations and information requested.
2. Whether the accounting records and published accounts comply with all legal requirements.
3. Whether the accounts give an *image fidèle* (true and fair view).
4. Whether the management report includes all information required by law and is in line with the accounts.
5. Whether the proposed dividend is legal.
6. Whether the auditor knows of any illegal transactions or decisions.

CONVENTIONS

There is a basic requirements that accounts should present an *image fidèle*, the French equivalent in the EC Fourth Directive to the UK 'true and fair view'. Michel et al. (1992, p. 43) argue that this principle is interpreted in line with the French approach, as a basis for choosing between alternatives permitted by law, rather than in line with the UK approach as an overriding principle. In particular, the tax-based approach to accounting means that a true and fair view may only be given when the notes to the accounts are considered.

Other accounting conventions prescribed in Belgium include prudence, historic cost and that opening balances must equal previous closing balances.

PRESENTATION

Belgian law provides detailed requirements for the balance sheet, income statement and notes to the accounts. Small and medium-sized companies are allowed to present abbreviated accounts.

A large company is one that exceeds any two of:

Annual sales	145	million francs
Total assets	70	million francs
Number of employees	50	

As in other EC countries, the abbreviated accounts have a similar structure to those for large companies but with much less detail. The accounts must include comparative figures for the previous accounting policy and, if there has been a change in classification or accounting policy, then a note to the accounts must explain this so that the two periods can be compared.

The balance sheet adopts the horizontal format of the Fourth Directive, as shown in Table 4.1.

Table 4.1 Balance Sheet Format

	Current year	Previous year
Fixed assets		
Formation costs		
Intangible fixed assets		
Tangible fixed assets		
Fixed asset investments		
Current assets		
Debtors due over one year		
Stock		
Debtors due within one year		
Short term investments		
Prepayments		
Total		
Capital and reserves		
Share capital		
Share premium		
Revaluation reserve		
Reserves		
Profit and loss		
Capital subsidies		
Provisions for risks and costs		
Provisions for costs and contingencies		
Creditors – over one year		
Creditors – under one year		
Accruals		
Total		

The profit and loss account may be presented on either a horizontal or vertical format. Income and costs must be analysed on a 'type of expense' rather than a functional basis, as shown in Table 4.2.

Table 4.2 Profit and Loss Account Format

	Current year	Previous year
Operating income		
Sales		
Changes in finished stock and WIP		
Capitalized self-construction	_____	_____
Operating expenses		
Purchases		
Changes in raw material stocks		
Other bought-in items		
Remuneration costs		
Depreciations		
Stock and debtor write-offs		
Provisions for contingencies and expenses	_____	_____
Operating profit/loss		
Finance income		
Finance costs	_____	_____
Profit/loss on ordinary activities before tax		
Extraordinary income		
Extraordinary expenses	_____	_____
Profit before tax		
Profit tax	_____	_____
Profit/loss for year		
Transfer to tax-free reserves		
Profit available for appropriation	_____	_____

Belgian accounting law also specifies an extensive range of information to be given in the notes to the accounts.

CONSOLIDATION

A requirement to provide consolidated accounts first appeared in Belgium as recently as 1977. It applied only to listed companies and those with capital in excess of 500 million francs. Currently consolidated accounts are required by a Royal Decree of 1990 which applies to accounting periods commencing after 31 December 1991.

Lefèbvre and Lin (1991) observe an interesting point on the size limits laid down for consolidation. In line with the Seventh Directive these limits are applied in two stages, the lower limit coming into force in the year 2000. Consolidation is required if the group exceeds any two of the following limits:

	Currently		After 2000	
	Belgium	EC directive	Belgium	EC directive
Sales				
Million francs	1450		580	
Million ECU	34.1	20	13.7	8
Total assets:				
Million francs	700		280	
Million ECU	16.5	10	6.6	4
Employees	500	500	250	250

From this table we can see that the Belgian government has set the size limit for both sales and total assets at a higher level than that specified by the EC, thus reducing the number of groups required to provide consolidated accounts. Consolidation is on the following basis:

1. Subsidiaries are normally consolidated on a line-by-line basis.

2. Joint ventures are accounted for by proportional consolidation.

3. Associated companies are accounted for by equity accounting.

Equity accounting is also used for subsidiaries in the following circumstances:

1. Where the 'going concern' position is in doubt.

2. The shareholding is to be sold.

3. The activity of the subsidiary is so different from the rest of the group that consolidation would impair the 'true and fair view'.

4. There is seriously limited control over the subsidiary.

Consolidation is not required for a subgroup within an ultimate holding company preparing accounts in line with EC requirements. Consolidated accounts are prepared on the same basis as individual company accounts, with the important exception that income and expenditure may be analysed by function.

GOODWILL

Goodwill is computed as the difference between the price paid for a subsidiary and the book value of net assets acquired at the accounting date.

As far as possible any difference, positive or negative, is allocated to assets and liabilities with market values above or below book values. Any remaining difference is shown as an asset if positive or liability if negative.

Positive goodwill should be amortized, normally with a maximum life of five years, on a straight-line basis. Any longer write-off period must be justified in the notes to the accounts. Goodwill amortization is tax allowable. Negative goodwill is normally carried indefinitely, although where it can be attributed to expected losses of the subsidiary it may be set off against those losses if they materialize.

FOREIGN CURRENCY TRANSLATION

The Royal Decree on consolidation permits either the closing rate method or the monetary/non-monetary method to be used in translating foreign subsidiaries. Subject to any change in circumstances, once chosen the same method must be applied consistently to each specific subsidiary. No rules for choosing between the two methods are laid down; in practice, similar criteria to those laid down in the USA (see Chapter 3 above) are commonly used. Generally, exchange differences arising from the closing rate method go directly to the balance sheet while differences arising from the monetary/non-monetary method are reflected in the profit and loss account. Thus Belgium has more flexible rules on foreign currency translation than most other countries.

Foreign currency translations in a company's own accounts are translated using the exchange rate at the date they occur, unless covered by an agreed forward rate. Exchange differences on completion of a transaction go to the profit and loss account. Exchange differences on translation of foreign currency monetary items at the balance sheet date are treated as follows:

1. Gains are shown in the balance sheet as deferred income.
2. Losses are first set off against deferred gains, any excess being taken to profit and loss.

INFLATION ACCOUNTING

Historically, Belgium has made some contribution to the development of inflation accounting. McNeill (1961) reports that:

> The Belgians, incidentally, have been something of pioneers in this price-level area. As early as 1936, their government attempted to give relief from taxation of price-level gains on the sale of capital assets.

Currently Belgium has no provision for inflation accounting. Fixed asset revaluations are permitted on the basis discussed below.

FIXED ASSETS

Fixed assets are shown at the lower of historic cost and market value. Revaluation of tangible fixed assets is permitted, with revaluation surpluses credited to a revaluation reserve, provided that it is justified by the profitability of the company. Since 1984, revaluation of intangible assets has not been permitted, although balance sheet amounts relating to such revaluations may still remain from pre-1984 revaluations.

Finance costs relating to construction of a fixed asset may be capitalized up to the point where the asset is ready for use. Depreciation may be on the straight-line or reducing balance basis or may be accelerated in line with tax law. Capital grants are shown as a reserve and are transferred to profit and loss as the related asset is depreciated.

RESEARCH AND DEVELOPMENT

Research and development costs may be capitalized to the extent that they are estimated to be recoverable. The normal maximum write-off period is five years: any longer period must be justified in the notes to the accounts.

STOCK AND WORK IN PROGRESS

Stock is valued at the lower of cost and net realizable value. While the cost is normally computed on an absorption basis, some part or all of the overheads may be excluded. FIFO, LIFO or average cost may be used.

Contracts in progress may be valued on the basis of taking profit in proportion to work done. Alternatively, all profit may be taken on completion of the contract. Full provision for the anticipated losses on contracts must be made.

Given the flexibility of Belgium's accounting rules in this area, it is not surprising that detailed notes on accounting policies for stock and work in progress are required.

LEASING

A finance lease is one which includes a requirement or option to purchase at the end of the rental period. Such lease agreements are capitalized in the books of the lessee, as discussed in Chapter 3 above, with the asset shown under tangible assets. The lessor similarly treats a finance lease as a sale with outstanding lease payments discounted to present value as a financial asset.

DEFERRED TAXATION

As discussed above, Belgian tax and accounting rules are closely linked so that deferred taxation does not normally arise.

PENSION OBLIGATIONS

Since 1986, all companies offering employee pension plans have been required to arrange these with outside independent specialist companies. Thus normally pension obligations will not appear in a company's accounts, other than pre-1986 unfunded outstanding commitments.

CONCLUSION

Belgian accounting regulation follows the French model closely. Two distinctive features emerged compared to other European countries:

1. The strong influence of employees and their representatives.
2. The binding link between tax and accounting rules.

REFERENCES

Lefèbvre, C. (1981) 'Development of Belgian accounting standards within the European Economic Community framework', *International Journal of Accounting*, Autumn, pp. 103–32.

Lefèbvre, C. and Lin, L.–Q. (1991) 'On the scope of consolidation: a comparative study of the EEC Seventh Directive, IAS 27, and the Belgian Royal Decree on Consolidation', *British Accounting Review*, **23**, pp. 133–47.

McNeill, J.H. (1961) 'Accounting for inflation abroad', *Journal of Accountancy*, August.

Michel, P.A. Farber, A. and Ginsburgh, V. (1992) 'Belgium' in Alexander, A. and Archer, S. *The European Accounting Guide*, Academic Press.

Price Waterhouse (1991) *Comparability of Financial Statements. International Survey.*

Seabrook, A. (1991) 'Structures and prospects in Belgium', *Certified Accountant*, January, pp. 36–7.

Theunisse, H. (1987) 'Accounting and reporting in Belgium', *Advances in International Accounting*, pp. 191–248.

CHAPTER 5

Denmark

ABBREVIATIONS

FFR	Føreningen af Registrerede Revisører – the second professional accounting body.
FSR	Føreningen af Statsautoriserede Revisører – the leading professional accounting body.

INTRODUCTION

With a population of just over five million people, Denmark has two important features that influence the accounting environment:

1. As a small country, Denmark has a tradition of incorporating interest groups into the mechanism of government. For accountants this means that the leaders of the accounting profession are also influential as government advisers.

2. Most Danish companies are small and specialized, with a small number of stock exchange listed companies. This has meant that there is not heavy demand for sophisticated accounting regulation.

REGULATIONS

Denmark does not have a long history of accounting legislation. In 1917 the first company law was enacted, with some revision in 1930. This legislation had only brief reference to accounting; published accounts were only obligatory when there were more than 10 equity investors. In 1973 a new company law provided more detailed accounting requirements. Further detail emerged, in response to EC directives, in the Accounting Law of 1981, revised in 1988 and 1990. In 1912 a bookkeeping law covered internal accounting record requirements.

The major professional body for auditors, FSR (see below), publishes International Accounting Standards in both English and Danish with comments and recommendations. Since 1988 FSR has also published National Accounting Standards. There is no attempt to compel members to comply with these. The Copenhagen stock exchange does require listed companies to comply with accounting standards, there being some 260 listed Danish companies.

THE AUDITING PROFESSION

The early history of Danish regulation of the accounting profession offers an instructive illustration both of the force of an individual personality and of the influence of scandal. In 1905 the Minister of Justice, P.A. Alberti, was asked to introduce a scheme for the authorization of auditors. He refused, asserting that such a provision was unnecessary. In 1908, Alberti made a confession to the authorities, admitting major fraud and deception. In 1909 a law for the authorization of auditors, under the supervision of the Ministry of Trade, was enacted (Loft, 1988).

There are now two types of audit qualification:

1. The *Statsautoriserede Revisører* (SR) with a professional body, the *Føreningen af Statsautoriserede Revisører* (FSR). These 'public accountants' qualify by achieving a Master's level degree, covering a range of relevant topics, followed by three years' experience in professional practice and a final exam set by the Ministry of Trade. There is no legal requirement to join the FSR but in practice the overwhelming majority of SRs do so. This qualification allows the practitioner to audit all kinds of company.

2. The *Registrerede Revisører* (RR) with a professional body the *Føreningen af Registrerede Revisører* (FRR). These 'registered accountants' qualify with a Bachelor level degree and have three years' practical experience. Following a transitional period they will, in future, be restricted from the audit of large groups.

FSR is, in practice, an influential body. Senior members of FSR tend to make up the membership of Government committees that revise accounting and audit law.

AUDITING

Auditors are appointed by the shareholders at the Annual General Meeting (AGM) and hold office until the next AGM. They may be reappointed indefinitely. The audit report must explicitly state that the accounts have been audited and that they comply with legal requirements. An unqualified audit report also implies that:

1. There is no occasion for an audit qualification.
2. That the accounts are in accordance with the underlying books and records.
3. That the directors' report covers the matters required by law and is compatible with the accounts.
4. That the accounts give a true and fair view.

CONVENTIONS

In line with the EC Fourth Directive, accounts must give a true and fair view. In order to comply with this requirement any extra information must be given in the notes to the accounts and, if necessary, deviation from other explicit requirements of the law must be made in the accounts; in such a case the notes must provide a full explanation.

Accounting law provides for the conventions of prudence, accruals, going concern, consistency, materiality, and substance over form. It is interesting that in this case the Danish legislation has gone beyond the limits of the EC Fourth Directive to embrace the provisions of IAS 1.

PRESENTATION

Traditionally Denmark has allowed considerable flexibility to companies in their choice of accounting formats. Elling and Hansen (1984) report that during negotiations over the EC Fourth Directive Danish representatives emphasized the need for permitting a variety of formats, and Danish legislation permits the full range of options permitted under the directive (see Chapter 3 above). One distinctive feature of Danish accounting has been that many companies have used a marginal costing approach in the published accounts. Christiansen (1992) explains this:

> most Danish companies are small or medium-sized, with relatively narrow bases of activity, which improves the usefulness of the contribution margin as a subtotal. In 1989, 28 per cent of publicly-listed trade, service, and industrial companies disclosed a contribution margin (p. 111).

A recent National Accounting Standard prescribes a change to absorption costing. However, it is expected that a number of companies will continue to give marginal costing data by way of note.

The variety of formats used in practice in Danish accounts do tend to make comparisons between companies difficult.

CONSOLIDATION

The practice of producing consolidated accounts grew in Denmark during the 1970s. Ernst and Whinney (1984) cite a study that showed, for a sample of 64 listed companies, the number producing consolidated accounts growing from six in 1970 to 61 in 1980. Requirements for consolidated accounts were introduced in accounting law in 1981; the present requirements derive from the 1990 law which responded to the EC Seventh Directive; the 1990 law exempts small groups and minor groups from the obligation to prepare consolidated accounts.

A subsidiary is defined as a company where the investor:

1. Holds more than 50 per cent of the voting ordinary shares.

or

2. Can control more than 50 per cent of the votes at an AGM.

or

3. Exercises control by some form of agreement.

Normally the acquisition method of accounting is used. Merger accounting is permitted, and tends to be used where a full 'legal merger', involving dissolution of the other parties, takes place. Proportional consolidation is often used for joint ventures. Equity accounting is used for non-consolidated subsidiaries and associates.

GOODWILL

Following the implementation of the EC Seventh Directive in 1990, goodwill is computed as the excess of the fair value of the purchase consideration over the fair value of the identifiable net assets acquired. It may be:

1. Written off against reserves at the time of acquisition.

2. Taken through the profit and loss account at the time of acquisition.

3. Recognized as an intangible fixed asset on acquisition and amortized over its useful life. If useful life is estimated at more than five years, the reason for this extended period must be explained in the notes to the accounts.

Comiskey and Mulford (1991, p. 128) noted amongst their sample of 17 Danish companies the following accounting practices:

		Number of Companies
Write off against reserves on acquisition		3
Change of policy from amortization to immediate write-off		1
Amortization of goodwill over:		
5 years	2	
unspecified	1	3
Immediate write-off as extraordinary item		1
		8

Negative goodwill may be:

1. Shown as a provision and matched with any foreseen loss in the subsidiary.

2. Offset against other goodwill.

3. Separately identified as part of the equity as a non-distributable reserve.

FOREIGN CURRENCY TRANSLATION

The Accounting Law does not lay down any rules on foreign currency translation practice. The public accountants recommend IAS 21 with certain amendments, in particular that unrealized gains on long-term items should only be taken to distributable reserves to the extent that they cover previous related losses; any excess should be taken to a special non-distributable reserve. Generally foreign subsidiaries are translated by the closing rate method, with translation differences taken directly to reserves. Foreign currency account balances in a company's own accounts are translated at the closing rate with translation gains or losses taken to the profit and loss account. Foreign currency loans to finance investment in foreign subsidiaries are often regarded as 'hedging' those investments, so that related translation differences are taken direct to reserves. Comiskey and Mulford (1991) quote

> policy disclosures which are pointed and clear (p. 132).

but to Christiansen (1992) the general quality of disclosure appears poor:

> many companies do not disclose full information about their practice in this area, especially about where the differences are placed in the profit and loss account. Supplementary information about hedging or speculating policies and activities is often inadequate. The lack of such information makes it difficult for the financial analyst to evaluate the quality of earnings (p. 116).

INFLATION ACCOUNTING

Denmark has no standard on this topic. Scapens (1973) observes fixed asset revaluation as the only Danish reaction to this issue (p. 36).

TANGIBLE FIXED ASSETS

The basic legal principle is that tangible fixed assets should be shown at depreciated historical cost. Revaluations are permitted, subject to a proviso that where an upward revaluation is made this must be applied to an entire class of assets on a consistent basis. Revaluation surpluses must be transferred to a non-distributable revaluation reserve. When a revalued asset is disposed of the revaluation surplus may be transferred to distributable reserves either by a direct transfer or through the profit and loss account. In practice, revaluation of land and buildings is common, based on official annual valuations carried out for tax purposes.

Companies are free to choose the depreciation methods most appropriate to write off assets over their estimated useful lives, and should not use tax-based depreciation for accounting purposes. Comiskey and Mulford (1991) report a tendency for Danish companies to use the straight-line method and to depreciate buildings over long lives (50–100 years) and plant rapidly (as little as three years), although finding 'a wide disparity of useful lives' (p. 131).

Capitalization of finance costs on self-constructed assets for the period of making the asset ready for use is permitted but is not common.

RESEARCH AND DEVELOPMENT

The accounting act permits deferral of research and development, though this is not common in practice. Where such costs are capitalized they should be written off over a period of up to five years, being matched with related benefits, commencing with commercial production. Any outstanding balance of research and development costs should be reviewed each year and written down to the recoverable amount if necessary. The directors' report should disclose the total research and development cost for the year.

STOCK AND WORK IN PROGRESS

Stock and work in progress are normally shown at the lower of cost and market value. 'Market value' may either be net realizable value or replacement cost. Accounting law allows stock and work in progress to be written up to replacement cost, though this is not commonly done. A range of cost flow assumptions are permitted including FIFO, LIFO and average cost. Danish companies seem to provide little information in their accounts on which accounting policies they have chosen. Comiskey and Mulford (1991) report that out of a sample of 17 large companies only two reported how they defined 'market value' and only five reported their cost flow assumption.

Both marginal costing and absorption costing are permitted in Denmark, with absorption costing being the more common. For long-term construction contracts the percentage of completion method is generally used, with full provision being made for any expected loss. However, where reliable estimates cannot be made, no profit should be recognized until the contract is completed.

LEASING

The only legal requirement is to show rental expenses and lease commitments in the notes to the accounts. Although FSR recommends finance lease capitalization in line with IAS 17, in practice almost all companies treat all leases on an operating lease basis.

DEFERRED TAXATION

Accounting practice in Denmark is divided, with some companies using the full deferral approach and some using the partial deferral approach. Similarly, either the liability method or the deferral method of computation may be used. Curiously, observers differ on what is most common practice. Christiansen (1992) sees full deferral and the liability method as more common. (p. 124), while Comiskey and Mulford (1991) see partial deferral and the deferral method as more common (p. 132).

PENSIONS

Generally pension arrangements do not pose any accounting problem for Danish companies because the Pensions Law requires that pension arrangements be made through insurance companies; only directors may have pension arrangements directly with the company. Consequently there are no accounting rules on pensions. Pensions obligations may appear in Danish balance sheets as a result of foreign subsidiaries.

POST BALANCE SHEET EVENTS

The accounting act draws a distinction between events after the balance sheet date that relate to a condition at that date, which should be reflected in the accounts, and other material events that may require disclosure in the directors' report.

CONCLUSION

Denmark has a highly flexible accounting tradition. EC directives have imposed a more rigid framework on the format of published accounts, but within that framework major variations in accounting practice continue.

REFERENCES

Christiansen, M. (1992) 'Denmark' in Alexander, D. and Archer, S. *European Accounting Guide*, pp. 103–49, Academic Press.

Comiskey, E.E. and Mulford, C.W. (1991) 'Comparing Danish accounting and reporting practices with International Accounting Standards', *Advances in International Accounting*, Vol. 4, pp. 123–42.

Elling, J.O. and Hansen, C.K. (1984) 'The Fourth Directive and Denmark' in Gray, S.J. and Coenenberg, A.G. *EEC Accounting Harmonization: Implementation and Impact of the Fourth Directive*, pp. 29–41, North Holland.

Ernst and Whinney (1984) *The Impact of the Seventh Directive*, Financial Times Business Information.

Loft, A. (1988) 'Regulating the work of accountants and auditors: the case of the State authorisation of auditors in Denmark'. Paper presented to the European Accounting Association, Nice, April.

Scapens, R.W. (1973) *The Treatment of Inflation in the Published Accounts of Companies in Overseas Countries*, Institute of Chartered Accountants in England and Wales.

CHAPTER 6

France

R.T.C. LIBRARY, LETTERKENNY

ABBREVIATIONS

APDC	Association des Directeurs de Comptabilité
CC	Code de Commerce
CNC	Conseil National de la Comptabilité
CNCC	Compagnie National des Commissaires aux Comptes
COB	Commission des Opérations de Bourse
OECCA	Ordre des Experts Comptables et Comptables Agréés

INTRODUCTION **The main feature of French accounting is its legalistic nature, given that the accounting provisions come from commercial and fiscal legislation. Another feature of the French system is that it has a well-developed system of accounting regulation.**

ACCOUNTING LEGISLATION

Accounting legislation in France has a long history. Colbert's Commercial Code of 1673 included detailed regulations concerning bookkeeping. Further accounting provisions were included in the Napoleonic Code, which has had a considerable influence in other countries. At present accounting legislation is in the hands of the *Conseil National de la Comptabilité* (CNC) which was created in 1957. This is a public body which although closely linked to the Ministry of Economy, Finance and Budgets, maintains a certain amount of independence. Its president is a Government official of consequence and its members are Government officers who have been assigned by various ministries and by professionals in accounting and auditing. Among these are representatives of the *Ordre des experts-comptables et des comptables agréés* (OECCA), the professional accounting body, the *Compagnie des Commissaires aux Comptes* (CC) which consists of state registered auditors, the *Commission des Opérations de Bourse* (COB), employers and trade unions.

The main aim of the CNC is to draw up accounting regulations and charts of accounts. Apart from this, the CNC coordinates research related to accounting as well as its dissemination and teaching in collaboration with other public and private bodies. The basic commercial laws which regulate business activity are the Code of Commerce (CC), the 1966 Law of Trading Companies, the 67/236 Decree of 1967 and the 1970 Law of Civil

Companies. Fiscal provisions also have to be considered.

The basic law and regulations related to accounting are described as follows.

The most significant of these is the 1982 General Accounting Plan which has been compulsory for all companies since 1983. This is a development of the 1957 General Accounting Plan, updated and adapted to the EC Fourth Directive, the 1957 plan being itself a revision of the first French General Accounting Plan of 1947.

The Accounting 'Plan' has its roots in the ideas of the German accounting professor Eugen Schmalenbach who proposed a standard national accounting code. In spite of the fact that Schmalenbach was dismissed from his post as professor in Cologne when the Nazis gained power, his system was adopted in Germany in 1937 as an instrument for the national economic plan and it became known as the Goering Plan. In 1942 this plan was adapted in Vichy (France) as the General Accounting Plan (see Standish 1990. Following the liberation of France, the French government saw the concept of the 'Plan' as attractive for two reasons:

1. A large number of companies had been nationalized. Fortin (1991, page 3) emphasizes this fact. 'The Government needed to put some order into the accounting systems of nationalized companies if it wanted to control and manage them properly. What better way to achieve this than to produce a uniform accounting plan?'

2. Advised by Jean Monnet, De Gaulle's government was persuaded of the need for a five-year economic plan to reconstruct French industry. A uniform accounting system would provide information to make this plan possible. Miller (1986) analyses the role of accounting in the French economic plan. This role is so important that it can be argued that French accounting 'is not designed to try and establish minimum principles in accounting data but rather to obtain national statistics which are comparable and reliable' (Filios 1987).

The 1982 Plan which has since been expanded upon by the Decree of 9 December 1986, provides information concerning:

1. The general principles.
2. The terminology.
3. The rules of valuation.
4. The rules of determination of profits and losses.
5. Group accounts.
6. How the accounts function.
7. The annual accounts.
8. Cost accounting.

So as to adopt the EC Fourth Directive, the following provisions have been passed:

1. Law 83/353 of 1983 and its corresponding Decree 83/1020, concerning the harmonizing of the accounting obligations of traders and certain companies.

2. Law 84/148 of 1984 and its corresponding Decree 85/295 which is concerned with the prevention and regulation of company difficulties.

3. Law of 3 January 1985 and its corresponding Decree of 7 February 1985 concerning consolidated accounts in accordance with the EC Seventh Directive.

4. Decree of 17 February 1986 concerning the size of companies. It also takes into account COB regulations which are similar in their functions to the American Securities and Exchange Commission (SEC), with which companies listed on the Stock Exchange have to comply.

In 1975 a new dimension was introduced into French accounting thought with the publication of the 'Sudreau Report' advocating a wide range of new accounting disclosures relevant to employees. These apply to large companies and give France a distinctive position in the field of 'Social Accounting'.

ACCOUNTING PROFESSION

The accounting profession is structured around two large institutions which are government-controlled.

The OECCA, which depends on the Ministry of Finance, joins together accounting experts who are in charge of drawing up annual accounts. They can also carry out auditing as long as it is not compulsory auditing. At the same time, these accounting experts provide consulting services concerning accounts and fiscal matters.

For those wishing to become members of the OECCA, the following are the main requirements:

1. To be 25 or over.

2. To have passed an accounting, economics and law exam (or to be a university graduate).

3. To have passed an auditing exam following this period of training and

4. To have written a thesis.

The CNC, which depends on the Ministry of Justice, is made up of those statutory auditors who are qualified to act in those cases when it is compulsory for a company to be audited.

In recent years there has been a tendency to unite these two institutions and indeed many professionals are members of both of them.

The *Association des Directeurs de Comptabilité* (APDC) made up of accounting directors, as Scheid and Walton point out (1992) is not so much a professional body as a pressure group.

AUDITING

The Ministry of Finance deals with accounting matters, while the Ministry of Justice oversees auditing. By virtue of the 1966 law on trading companies, all limited companies and co-partnerships are obliged to have their accounts audited. This task is entrusted to the *commissaires aux comptes* (accounting commissioners) who are chosen by shareholders to carry out their duties for a period of six years. This period can be renewed indefinitely. Once the auditors have been nominated they cannot be substituted unless there is a judicial verdict which reveals unprofessional conduct on the part of the auditors. If the company's capital exceeds half a million francs or it is listed, it must name two *commissaires aux comptes*. The professional in charge of drawing up the annual accounts (*expert comptable*) must not be the same person who audits them (*commissaire aux comptes*).

Limited partnerships, simply co-partnerships and partnerships need only be audited if they are large.

In France, for accounting purposes, the distinction between small, medium-sized or large companies is made by using the following criteria:

1. Small companies are considered to be those which for two consecutive years do not exceed two of the three following limits:

   (a) Total assets: 1,500,000 French francs

   (b) Net turnover: 3,000,000 French francs

   (c) Average number of employees: 10.

2. Medium-sized companies are those which, without being small, do not exceed two of the three following limits in two consecutive financial years:

   (a) Total assets: 10,000,000 French francs

   (b) Net turnover: 20,000,000 French francs

   (c) Average number of employees: 50.

3. Large companies are those which exceed two of the aforementioned limits in two consecutive financial years. Other companies for which auditing is compulsory include:

   (a) Financial institutions

   (b) Insurance companies

   (c) Agricultural cooperatives

   (d) Investment fund companies

   (e) Sports associations.

CONVENTIONS

The main objective of the accounting system in French companies, in accordance with EC Fourth Directive, is that annual accounts should be prudent, regular, sincere and give a true and fair view of the company's wealth, its financial situation and its profits and losses.

Prudence implies a reasonable appreciation of the facts which can be used so as to prevent current uncertainties from materializing in the future and possibly affecting the company's wealth and its profits and losses.

Regularity refers to the application of legislation and current procedures.

Sincerity implies the honest application of legislation and current procedures which are based on the accountant's knowledge and the importance of the operations.

The *image fidèle* is the translation of the British 'true and fair view' and it is identified as the supreme principle which dominates all the other provisions.

In accordance with the EC Fourth Directive, when the application of the General Accounting Plan fails to achieve the objective of the true and fair view, then the plan may be overridden. These circumstances must be stated clearly in the notes to the accounts, indicating the effect on the financial situation and on profit and loss. However, French accounting is characterized by its extreme conservatism. In practice the true and fair view is not applied literally.

The General Accounting Plan makes the following accounting principles compulsory:

1. Accrued income: the application of revenue and expenses has to be carried out in terms of the real flow that they represent independently of the moment in which they are received or paid.

2. Consistency of uniformity: the accounting policies of valuation and presentation of annual accounts must be maintained as long as there is no change in the circumstances which brought about their choice. If any of the accounting policies should change, it has to be indicated in the notes to the accounts by expressing the qualitative and quantitative effects of such a change.

3. Cost of acquisition: everything has to be valued, at most, at the price of acquisition if the goods have been acquired, or at the production cost if they have been produced in the same company. Fixed assets can be revalued as discussed below.

4. No set-off of assets and liabilities.

5. Identity between the initial balance sheet of one financial year and the final balance sheet of the preceding year: both balance sheets have to coincide. If profits and losses should be identified which correspond to previous years, they cannot be carried out directly against reserves but they have to be carried through the profit and loss account for the year.

6. Independence of the financial years: the profits and losses of each year have to be determined independently of the previous or future ones.

7. Prudence: profits must only be accounted for when they have been gained. On the other hand, losses will be considered as soon as they appear likely. Another consequence of the application of the principle of prudence is that any depreciation has to be accounted independently of whether the company has made a profit or a loss.

8. Going concern: accounting measures are normally as if the life of the company were indefinite. Break-up values must not be used unless the company appears to be approaching liquidation.

9. Materiality: in the attachments to the accounts only information which is relevant to the other annual accounts must be included.

PRESENTATION

The annual accounts are made up of the balance sheet, the profit and loss account and the notes to the accounts. The accounts can be presented in three ways:

1. Abbreviated option: the three accounts (balance sheet, profit and loss account and attachment to the accounts) are presented in summarized form. This option is available to individual businessmen and small companies (according to limits set out in the auditing section).

2. Basic option: apart from the balance sheet, the profit and loss account and the attachment to the accounts, there will be a formulation of company documents. These are composed of the table showing effects on profits and losses, the profit and loss account and other distinguishing elements of the company over the last five years as well as an inventory of the securities portfolio of investments.

3. Developed option: this option which is voluntary includes the accounts in the basic option plus the statement of self-financing capacity for the financial year and the chart of financial changes.

Small companies are able to formulate simplified accounts. The balance sheet is presented as shown in the model contained in Table 6.1.

The profit and loss account which can be drawn up vertically (in the form of a list) or horizontally (in the form of an account), is presented in the format shown in Table 6.2, distributing the costs and income depending on their nature.

Table 6.1

	Current year		Previous year
	Gross	*Net depreciation*	*Net*
Assets			
I Fixed assets			
Intangible			
Tangible			
Investments			
II Current assets			
Inventories			
Advances to suppliers			
Customers			
Investments			
Liquid assets			
III Anticipated expenses			
IV Premiums on repayment of bonds			
V Exchange rate differences			
Total			
Liabilities			
I Shareholders' equity			
Share capital			
Reserves			
Revaluation reserve			
Retained profits			
Capital grants			
Legal provisions			
II Provisions for risks and expenses			
III Loans and other bonds			
Convertible bonds			
Other bonds			
Bank loans			
Advances received			
Accounts payable			
Anticipated income			
Fiscal debts			
IV Exchange rate differences			
Total			

Table 6.2

	Current Year	Previous Year
Expenses (without taxes)		
I Operating expenses		
Purchase		
Variation in stock		
Other external expenses		
Taxes		
Wages and salaries		
Social security		
Amortization		
II Part in losses in joint ventures		
III Financial costs		
IV Non-operating expenses		
V Participation of employees in profits		
VI Company tax		
Profits		
Total		
Income (without tax)		
I Operating income		
Sales		
Variation in stock of finished products		
Construction of own assets		
Operating grants		
Other income		
II Part in profits from joint ventures		
III Financial income		
IV Non-operating income		
Loss		
Total		

The notes to the accounts provide information to make it possible to understand the data supplied by the balance sheet and the profit and loss account. The following is a list of points for which information has to be supplied in the basic model.

1. Accounting rules and methods

    (a) Applied accounting principles.

    (b) Omission of accounting principles so as to attain a true and fair view.

    (c) Criteria of evaluation of assets, such as inventories.

    (d) If the criteria should change, an explanation should be given of the motives which have justified this change and the effect on the annual accounts.

2. Complementary information to that on the balance sheet and the profit and loss account:

    (a) An indication of the accounts with companies in the group and of those accounts to be paid or received.

    (b) Outputs, inputs and balance of tangible and intangible fixed assets with an explanation of the criteria of amortization which has been used.

    (c) Increase, decrease and balance of provisions.

    (d) Information concerning the revaluation carried out on fixed assets.

    (e) Financial expenses capitalized.

    (f) Chart indicating maturity (at under or over one year) of the loans payable and receivable at the end of the financial year.

    (g) Guarantees granted with regard to debts.

    (h) Financial commitments making a distinction between those which affect the directors and related companies.

    (i) Information concerning the leasing operations: value of the goods on signing the contract, payments carried out during the financial year, amortization of the goods if the company owns them and the debt pending payment.

    (j) Information concerning the nature of the goodwill and its amortization.

    (k) Information concerning the difference between the book value and the market value of inventories at the close of the financial year.

    (l) The inclusion of financial costs, research and development and general administration in the cost of acquisition and production of inventories.

    (m) The nature, sum and accounting treatment of the setting up costs, income to be received and costs to pay, the differences in foreign currency translation, income and expenses attributable to other financial years, the profits and losses of operations in common, income and exceptional costs and amortization of premiums of repayment of bonds.

    (n) Distribution of sales turnover by sector of activity and according to geographical market.

    (o) Additional purchasing costs not naturally incorporated in the corresponding accounts of expenses but rather in the accounts of purchases.

    (p) Sharing out of company tax among the exceptional results and other results, indicating the method used.

    (q) Indication of the effect which fiscal provisions have had on profits and losses and their consequences with regard to shareholders' equity.

    (r) Explanation of anticipated and deferred taxes.

3. Other information

    (a) Chart of distribution of profits and losses.

    (b) Chart of shareholders' equity, sales figures, profits and losses, results per share and per employee over the last five years.

    (c) List of affiliated companies, of stakes in each of them of their shareholders' equity and their profits and losses.

    (d) Number and nominal value of shares and other elements which make up the share capital.

    (e) Indication of the rights granted and what they have created or paid up during the financial year.

    (f) Convertible bonds and similar securities issued by the company and the rights which come with them.

    (g) Information concerning companies with which they have consolidated the accounts by the total integration method.

    (h) Indication of investments, rights, debts, income and costs of these related companies.

    (i) Average workforce with a distinction made between temporary and permanent staff.

    (j) Advances, credits, remunerations and commitments such as pensions to members of administration.

    (k) Chart of research and development costs carried out during the financial year.

    (l) Determination of the self-financing capacity of the financial year and the chart of financial changes.

On the other hand, the medium-sized companies have to prepare the balance sheet and the profit and loss account from their basic model but the notes to the accounts can be simplified. However, both the balance sheet as well as the profit and loss account which are published can be abbreviated. The medium-sized companies are those which, without being small, do not exceed two of the three requisites in the section relative to auditing.

The abbreviated notes only have to provide information concerning the following aspects:

1. Trade bills.

2. Expenses to pay and income to be received.

3. Cost paid in advance and income received in advance.

4. Leasing operations.

5. Ownership reserve clause.

Apart from the annual accounts mentioned, the trading companies, and civil companies which draw upon public saving, have to formulate the management report in line with the EC Fourth Directive.

CONSOLIDATION OF ACCOUNTS

In 1986, the decree concerning the drawing up of consolidated accounts was passed. In these accounts, all companies which are controlled must be included. This is implied when the company either directly or indirectly has the majority vote or when it has 40 per cent of the voting rights and nobody has a larger percentage or when apart from having a stake (even if it is not a majority one) the company effectively controls by virtue of some agreement. Affiliated companies which carry out very different activities from the parent company can be excluded from the consolidation although in this case they are consolidated by the application of the equity method. Those affiliated companies whose activities are irrelevant to the group as a whole can also be excluded.

The group must nominate two independent auditors. However, those groups which do not exceed two of the following three limits can be excluded from the obligation to present group accounts:

1. Total assets of group: 100 million francs.

2. Total net income of group: 200 million francs.

3. Average number of employees: 500.

The associated companies in which the holder exercises a considerable influence (which is demonstrated by at least 20 per cent of the voting rights) without having total control, are consolidated by the application of the equity method. Multigroup or joint venture companies are also consolidated with the equity method.

The consolidated accounts are made up of the balance sheet and the profit and loss account. In addition, the groups can voluntarily include the statement of changes in the share capital and the chart of financial changes.

Those subgroups which are included in the consolidated accounts of a larger group are exempt from publishing their consolidated accounts if they publish the accounts of the larger group in French, provided they have been prepared in accordance with the EC Seventh Directive.

GOODWILL

The goodwill contains intangible elements which are not reflected in other items on the balance sheet but which are necessary for the company's development. They can only appear in the assets when a company acquires them. Therefore, following the EC Fourth Directive, the goodwill can only appear when it is exposed by way of a transaction.

In contrast to what is set out in the EC Fourth Directive, Socias (1991) points out that there is no limitation with regard to the period of amortization although this has to be shown in the notes to the accounts. As Scheid and Walton make clear, 66 per cent of the French groups write off the goodwill over a period of between 20 and 40 years, 12 per cent write it off in less than 20 years and 7 per cent do not write it off at all. Some 8 per cent deduct it directly from reserves and the rest of the companies which were researched either do not have goodwill or do not provide information concerning their system of amortization. In the case of the companies which do not publish group accounts, the usual practice is not to depreciate the goodwill.

FOREIGN CURRENCY TRANSLATION

Foreign currency transactions are translated at the exchange rate at the transaction date. At the year end monetary items are retranslated at the closing rate. There is a difference between the accounting treatment of translation gains and losses that illustrates the strength of conservatism in French accounting:

1. Losses are generally charged to profit and loss, although losses on loans to finance fixed asset acquisitions may be written off over the life of the loan.
2. Gains are not normally recorded until realized.

In the consolidated accounts both gains and losses may be taken to the profit and loss account.

For foreign operations, self-sustaining operations are translated by the closing rate or the average rate in the profit and loss account. Translation differences are taken direct to reserves. For foreign operations integrated with the holding company activities the monetary/non-monetary method is used, with translation differences taken through the profit and loss account.

ACCOUNTING FOR INFLATION

In France there are no provisions regarding the accounting of inflation.

However, the Ministry of the Economy and Finance on occasion has permitted the companies to revalue their assets in accordance with certain inflation-based ratios. The last time that fixed assets were allowed to be revalued was in 1978. Before this, revaluations were authorized in 1945 and 1959. When the revaluation ratios are applied, the market value must be considered as the maximum limit.

In the period 1919–27 which was one of high inflation, many French companies prepared their accounts in two ways: in paper francs (which reflected the current values) and in gold francs (which reflected the constant values). To a certain extent, French accountants developed their system of purchasing power in gold francs from the German experience (see Wasserman 1931 for a detailed discussion on the debate in France). A little later, towards the end of the forties, fiscal adjustments were authorized for fixed assets and inventories (Holzer and Schonfeld 1963).

TANGIBLE FIXED ASSETS

Tangible fixed assets have to be shown at their acquisition value or production costs. To the first of these values, transport costs, insurance, facilities and customs duties must be added. As can be seen later, these assets can be revalued so as to reduce the effects of inflation. If the revaluation is not done by virtue of a specific fiscal law the company will have to pay the taxes on the revaluation surplus. These circumstances mean that in practice only the revaluations that are exempt from taxes under the protection of specific laws are carried out. The financial costs involved in financing a fixed asset can be capitalized if they relate to the period of construction. This possibility is allowed both for fixed assets and for current assets, unlike in other countries such as Spain.

Tangible fixed assets have to be depreciated systematically depending on their useful life or the depreciation which occurs when they are in use. The most usual periods of depreciation are 20–30 years for buildings, 10 years for plant and machinery and five years for vehicles.

Since 1960 it has become possible to carry out accelerated depreciation.

In the consolidated accounts these assets tend to be valued according to the amount it would take to replace them.

RESEARCH AND DEVELOPMENT

Research and development costs are generally written off as incurred, but exceptions can be made whenever there are reasonable grounds for anticipating technical success and economic-commercial yield. The projects must be clearly identified and the costs clearly defined. Once capitalized they have to be written off as soon as possible over a maximum of five years except in exceptional cases. If the project does not look profitable it has to be written off immediately. This write-off may not be reversed even though expectations may later improve and the project could prove to be profitable.

Until these costs are totally written off, no dividend payments can be made unless there are sufficient reserves to cover the research and development asset.

STOCK AND WORK IN PROGRESS

These are valued at the lower of cost and market value. In this case, the market value can be either the net realizable value or the replacement cost. The most usual method of cost allocation is weighted average, although FIFO is also authorized. LIFO can only be used in the preparation of consolidated accounts.

If the production cycle exceeds 12 months, related financial costs may be included in work in progress.

LEASING

Financial leasing operations can be capitalized in the consolidated accounts in line with IAS 17. However, there is no concrete definition of what a financial lease is.

In accounts which are not consolidated, only those leasing agreements in which the contract included a purchase clause and the lease holder has exercised it, can be capitalized. The rest of the leasing operations are treated as operating leases.

DEFERRED TAXATION

This is one of the sections in which the treatment of the company accounts is different from that of the consolidated accounts. Deferred tax does not normally appear in the company accounts. However, with regard to the consolidated accounts, the professional accounting bodies recommend the corresponding provision, allowing either partial or total deferral.

PENSION FUNDS

Costs related to pension schemes are fiscally deductible when paid into an independent pension fund. On the other hand, amounts provided by companies for the retirement of their employees are only fiscally deductible when they are paid to the employees. Both these costs and the corresponding debt must appear in the profit and loss account and on the balance sheet respectively.

POST BALANCE SHEET EVENTS

Any relevant facts to indicate the existence of risks and losses, which appear once the accounts have been closed but before the company administrators have drawn them up, have to be set out in the annual records and also in the management report.

If the conditions in which the risks or losses are based, existed on the date that the balance sheet and the profit and loss account are formulated, then adjustments must be made to them.

CONCLUSION

There is a close relationship between French history and accounting developments. As Collins and Pham (1983) observe:

The contradictory influences on French accounting that one sees and feels today spring from the longstanding dichotomy in the country between evolution and revolution . . . Colbert, Napoleon, DeGaulle, and Sudreau.

Colbert, Louis XIV's great minister, legislated to put French business on a competitive footing to support his monarch's military ambitions. A regulated bookkeeping system was part of that scheme. Napoleon developed this concept as part of his grand plan to codify the law. De Gaulle picked up the 'Plan' basis for accounting as part of his reorganization of the French economy. Sudreau introduced the strong 'social' element.

REFERENCES

Collette, C. and Richard, J. (1987) *Le Nouveau Plan Comptable: Comptabilité et Gestion*, Dunod.

Collins, L. and Pham, D. (1983) 'Research into the processes of accounting standard setting in France' in Bromwich, M. and Hopwood, A.G. *Accounting Standard Setting – An International Perspective*, Pitman.

Filios, V.P. (1987) 'The French contribution to the theory of accounting', *Advances in International Accounting*, pp. 136–51.

Fortin, A. (1991) 'The 1947 French Accounting Plan: origins and influences on subsequent practice', *Accounting Historians Journal*, December, pp. 1–23.

Gelard, G. and Pham, D. (1984) *Comprendre le Nouveau Plan Comptable*, Montchrestien.

Holzer, H.P. and Schonfeld, H.M. (1963) 'The French approach to the post-war price level problem', *Accounting Review*, April, pp. 382–8.

Hussey, R. (1978) 'France has a social audit', *Accountancy*, February, pp. 111–12.

Miller, P. (1986) 'Accounting for progress – National accounting and planning in France: a review essay', *Accounting Organizations and Society*, November, pp. 83–104.

Price Waterhouse (1991) *Comparability of Financial Statements. International Survey*, Price Waterhouse.

Scheid, J.C. and Walton, P. (1992) 'France' in Alexander, D. and Archer, S. *The European Accounting Guide*, pp. 151–211, Academic Press.

Socias, A. (1991) *La Normalización Contable en el Reino Unido, Francia, Alemania y España*, AECA.

Standish, P.M. (1990) 'Origins of the *Plan Comptable Général*: a study in cultural intrusion and reaction', *Accounting and Business Research*, Autumn, pp. 337–51.

Wasserman, M.J. (1931) 'Accounting Practice in France during the period of monetary inflation (1919–27)', *The Accounting Review*, March, pp. 1–32.

CHAPTER 7

Germany

ABBREVIATIONS

AG	Aktiengesellschaft – a limited liability company
GAAP	Generally Accepted Accounting Principles
GmbH	Gesellschaft mit beschränkter Haftung. A limited liability company with restricted transfer of shares
IdW	Institut der Wirtschaftsprüfer – Voluntary association of qualified auditors
KGaA	Kommanditgesellschaft auf Aktien – A company where at least one member has full personal liability
StB	Steuerberater – Tax adviser
vBP	Vereidigte Buchprüfer – Approved auditor, being a somewhat less onerous qualification than the WP
WP	Wirtschaftsprüfer – Qualified auditor
WPK	Wirtschaftsprüferkammer – Official body to oversee auditors.

INTRODUCTION **Germany has a strong accounting tradition which, to those accustomed to the Anglo-American tradition, must appear paradoxical. On the one hand, accounting is dominated by legal prescription and tightly linked to the tax system. On the other hand, Germany has a strong and highly trained academic and practitioner accounting community.**

ACCOUNTING REGULATIONS

The three major types of company in Germany are:

1. The *Aktiengesellschaft* (AG), a limited liability company whose shares are freely transferable. The legally prescribed structure for such companies includes a supervisory board made up of equal numbers of shareholder and worker representatives.

2. The *Gesellschaft mit beschränkter Haftung* (GmbH). This is a limited liability company with shares that are not fully transferable and with more legal flexibility than the AG. For example, no supervisory board is required if the workforce is less than 500.

3. The *Kommanditgesellschaft auf Aktien* (KGaA) is a form of company where at least one member must accept personal liability.

Macharzina and Langer (1991) offer a detailed and readable discussion of these and other forms of legal entity (pp. 196–200). Accounting regulations are provided primarily in the *Aktiengesetz* (Company Law) 1965, updated to comply with the European Community Fourth, Seventh and Eighth Directives in the Accounting Directive Law of 1985.

An important element in German accounting law is the *Massgeblichkeitsprinzip*, or principle of bindingness, that aims to achieve tax accounts on the same basis as the commercial accounts. Thus the accounting methods used in the commercial accounts are simultaneously binding for the determination of tax profit unless obviously false or explicitly excluded by tax law. Conversely, any benefit given by tax law can only be enjoyed if reflected in the accounting treatment in the commercial accounts (see Wysocki 1984, pp. 58–60 for a full discussion of this principle).

The Company Law does provide for accounts to be prepared in accordance with 'generally accepted accounting principles' (GAAP). There is no official institution in Germany for the formulation of GAAP. In law this is purely a matter for interpretation by the courts. In practice, most accounting decisions come from the Supreme Tax Court (*Bundesfinanzhof*). (For a discussion of German GAAP see Wysocki 1983.)

The *Institut der Wirtschaftsprüfer* (see below p. 130) does have a professional committee to produce accounting recommendations. While these recommendations are influential on detailed technical matters, the institute has not been successful when advocating major reforms. For example, a detailed set of proposals on inflation accounting failed to persuade either the Government or industry. As Al Hashim and Arpan (1988) observe, 'German accounting practitioners are concerned with complying with the laws that prescribe accounting standards and procedures more than they are concerned with developing those standards and procedures' (p. 31).

Abel (1971) sees two important strands in the development of German accounting practices:

1. The 'ready acceptance of state intervention in economic affairs'.

2. A strong 'tradition of anti-individualism'.

As a result, strong banks rather than individual promoters emerged as the major suppliers of capital. These banks established their own audit companies and forced companies to supply relevant financial information. Thus the banks, as major suppliers of capital, had no occasion to promote improved published disclosure. The central authorities have been perfectly acceptable as regulators of accounting. In the 1930s the National Socialist regime had a strong interest in uniform precise accounting requirements that facilitated national control of economic resources. In particular, the regime did not permit prices to be determined by markets. A detailed and standardized national cost accounting system was therefore required to facilitate national price setting (Singer 1943, p. 16).

This strong tradition of central authority in German accounting regulation helps explain why, despite a highly trained accounting profession and active academic accounting community, the Government continues to dominate accounting regulation.

THE ACCOUNTING PROFESSION

In 1931 the German government introduced a statutory audit requirement for limited companies. Recognized qualified auditors, called *Wirtschaftsprüfer* (WP), organized themselves into a professional *Institut* in 1932. Since 1961 an official regulatory body for the profession the *Wirtschaftsprüferkammer* (WPK), has been established under the Ministry of Economics, and this body maintains a register of all qualified auditors. In addition the *Institut der Wirtschaftsprüfer* (IdW), is a voluntary professional body to which some 84 per cent of the 6,680 individual *Wirtschaftsprüfer* belong. With German unification, some 140 qualified *Wirtschaftsprüfer* in the East are also permitted to register with the WPk provided that they pass examinations in German tax and law. The role of the accountant in the old GDR was clearly very different from that in the West, and is discussed in detail by Graves and Berry (1989). Seabrook (1991) discusses the conversion programme for these accountants. Germany also has some 41,000 *Steuerberater* (StB), or professional tax advisers.

The process of qualifying as a WP is arduous. First, a relevant degree must be taken. Locke (1984) comments on how, as early as 1950, all students in German business schools studied accounting compared to only 500 students at that time in the UK (p. 204). Some 75 per cent of WP candidates have a degree in business and accounting. Next, five years of professional training must be undertaken. Then come exams – seven papers of four to six hours in length. Finally comes a two-hour oral exam in front of an eight person panel, drawn mainly from university professors. The average age of achieving qualification is 35.

Steuerberater sit a more modest set of exams after three years' experience. It is common for aspiring WPs to qualify as StBs first. In response to the demand for an enlarged audit profession, the qualification of *Vereidigte Buchprüfer* (vBP), meaning 'approved auditor' has been revived. This can be achieved by StBs after five years' experience, three of which must be in auditing, on passing one exam paper and a short oral. Some 3,500 vBPs have qualified under these rules.

Nicholson (1991) comments on how traditionally the UK, with 170,000 professional accountants, has been contrasted with Germany and its 7,000 WPs. He argues that a more meaningful comparison is between the UK with 44,000 accountants in professional practice and Germany with some 47,000 WPs and StBs.

AUDITING

An audit is legally required for all medium-sized or large companies. A company is classified in this category if it exceeds any two of the following three criteria for two successive years:

Total assets	3.9 million DM
Sales	8 million DM
Number of employees	50

Dykxhoorn and Sinning (1981) report on some problems that the German audit profession faces in being seen to be independent, including:

1. Some 30 per cent of auditors' income comes from management consulting work. A survey showed that over 70 per cent of business journalists saw this as an impairment of auditor independence.

2. Auditor liability in German law is not extensive, reducing the incentive to demonstrate independence.

3. Uniquely in Europe, German audit firms can have a majority of outside shareholders. An audit client may have a close relationship with the audit firm's controlling shareholders.

CONVENTIONS

In compliance with the Fourth Directive, Germany has introduced a requirement that the accounts should present a 'true and fair view'. If we consider the range of possible meanings attached to this concept in the UK, we can see that they conflict with the German tradition:

1. There is the concept that 'true and fair' allows a degree of flexibility compared with the previous UK 'true and correct' requirement. In Germany, by contrast, regulations should be applied strictly. For example, all required headings in the accounting formats must be used, however small the individual amount to be disclosed.

2. There is the concept that 'true and fair' equates to 'substance over form'. By contrast, German accounting sticks closely to legal form. For example, pension commitments are not normally included in the accounts unless the company itself is legally bound, even though an informal or indirect commitment may be highly likely to affect the company (see p. 138 below).

3. There is the concept that 'true and fair' implies 'neutrality'. German accounting is dominated by one user, the tax authorities, and companies legitimately choose between permitted accounting policies to maximize tax benefits.

4. There is the concept of the 'true and fair view' as reflecting the collective

view of the accounting profession on best accounting practice. By contrast, as we have seen, Germany's accounting profession has no authority and little influence on accounting regulation.

The German authorities have reacted in two ways to the conflict between the 'true and fair view' concept and their own accounting tradition:

1. While the 'true and fair view' requirement is in German law, and companies are required to provide additional information in the notes to the accounts to meet this if necessary, there is no 'true and fair override' provision. In this particular, German law fails to implement the Fourth Directive.

2. The German authorities have deliberately played down the significance of this concept. Thus the official explanatory notes to the German draft law implementing the Fourth Directive referred to the 'true and fair view' requirement in these terms:

> In spite of the pretentious formulation it is supposed that for practice there will be no principle changes. As to now, the content and scope of the general clause will not be changed compared to existing law (cited by Busse von Colbe 1984, p. 123).

Busse von Colbe also offers some views as to why an extreme conservative approach offers an appropriate accounting system in the socioeconomic environment of German companies:

1. The supervisory boards of German companies include shareholder and employee representatives, giving both groups an alternative information source. Bankers also have direct access to companies' internal accounts.

2. Tax benefits can only be enjoyed when reflected in the accounts.

3. Shareholders can claim dividends up to the full profit for a GmbH and half the profits for an AG.

4. Creditor protection is a prime aim of the accounts.

Interestingly, the 1965 Company Law eliminated some of the more extreme opportunities to write down assets and make provisions permitted in earlier legislation. The objective was to force companies to declare more realistic profits, improve opportunities for dividend payment, and thereby stimulate the equity market. Gebhardt (1983) reports a study that compared the predictive ability of accounts under the pre-1965 accounting rules, and found that the pre-1965 accounts were more useful in the prediction of corporate failure.

Other conventions required by German accounting law include going concern, consistency, accruals, prudence, no set-off of assets and liabilities, and that the opening balance sheet must correspond to the previous closing balance sheet.

PRESENTATION

Table 7.1 Income Statement

Type of expenditure format

	Sales	X
+/−	Change in WIP/finished goods	X
+	Own work capitalized	X
		X
+	Other operating income	X
−	Material costs	X
−	Personnel costs	X
−	Depreciation	X
−	Other operating expenses	X
	Operating profit/loss	X
+/−	Financial items	X
	Result from ordinary operations	X
+/−	Extraordinary items	X
−	Taxation	X
	Profit/loss for year	X

Functional format

Sales	X
− Cost of sales	X
Gross profit	X
− Selling costs	X
− Administrative costs	X
+/− Other operating income/costs	X
Operating profit/loss	X
+/− Financial items	X
Result from ordinary operations	X
+/− Extraordinary items	X
− Taxation	X
Profit/loss for the year	X

Table 7.1 shows the two different types of format for the income statement permitted under German accounting law. The 'type of expenditure' format is the traditional and more common one. One peculiarity of German practice is that if a company has chosen to price stocks at direct cost only then, if the functional format is chosen, the difference between direct cost and full absorption cost of stocks may be reflected in other operating costs. There are a number of other differences between common cost allocations using the two formats listed in Seckler (1992) pp. 224–8. Thus German income statements are difficult to compare with each other, let alone on an international basis.

CONSOLIDATION

Since 1 January 1990, German companies have been required to provide consolidated accounts where either:

1. They exercise de facto control over one or more companies where they own more than 20 per cent of the equity.
2. They are able to exercise control by having majority voting rights, a contract of domination, or power to appoint and dismiss board members.

Both domestic and foreign subsidiaries have to be included, although prior to 1 January 1990 only domestic subsidiaries had to be covered. However, there are a number of grounds for exclusion of subsidiaries in order to present a true and fair view, such as materiality or the shares being held with a view to resale.

Where there is control over the subsidiary, full consolidation is required, normally by the acquisition method. Merger accounting is permitted in the case of a subsidiary acquired where at least 90 per cent of the nominal value was acquired by a share exchange, but is not common in practice.

Joint ventures may be accounted for either by proportional consolidation or by equity accounting. Other associated companies are accounted for by equity accounting. The above procedures arise from the introduction of the EC Seventh Directive into German law. This involved major changes from previous requirements; summaries may be found in Ernst and Whinney 1984, pp. 30–5.

GOODWILL

Goodwill on consolidation normally reflects the difference between the market value of net assets acquired and the cost of the investment. Goodwill may be written off against equity reserves on acquisition, or may be amortized. Although the law mentions four years as an appropriate amortization period, periods of up to 40 years are generally regarded as acceptable.

'Negative goodwill' should not normally arise, being commonly applied to reduce asset revaluations. Where it does arise, it should be carried as a liability, only being released if there is a realized profit, e.g. resale of the acquired business, or if future losses can be specifically related to the negative goodwill, e.g. on occurrence of an event anticipated in setting the purchase price.

FOREIGN CURRENCY

In a company's own accounts, and those of domestic subsidiaries, foreign currency receivables and payables are recorded initially at the historic rate. At the balance sheet date:

1. Receivables are reported at the lower amount arrived at by applying the historic rate and the closing rate.

2. Payables are reported at the higher amount arrived at by applying the historic rate and the closing rate.

The only legal requirements for translation of foreign subsidiaries, and related translation gains or losses, are that the accounting policies chosen should be fully disclosed and applied consistently. In practice, all the methods discussed above in this chapter may be found to be used by German companies, with a variety of treatments of translation differences.

INFLATION ACCOUNTING

Scapens (1981, pp. 8–10) offers a brief review of the inflation accounting system used in Germany in the early 1920s. For management decisions replacement costs were commonly used. However, for financial reporting supplementary accounts based on 'balance sheet stabilization in terms of the gold mark' were presented. This assumed that the gold mark had constant purchasing power and a change in its paper mark equivalent was assumed to represent a change in the purchasing power of the paper currency. With the restoration of the gold mark early in 1924 inflation accounting was abandoned.

In 1948, a new monetary unit was introduced in West Germany, the Deutsche Mark, and orderly monetary conditions were restored. The accounting problem of accumulated historic cost figures which were meaningless was resolved by allowing asset revaluation on a replacement cost basis. Companies were allowed a range of discretion in their computation of the new values. In practice the resulting figures tended to be realistic because the tax system imposed competing pressures:

1. The new valuation was to be the basis for tax allowable depreciation, encouraging high values.

2. The new valuation was also to be the basis for a 'war damage equalization levy' of 2 per cent per year for 25 years.

The tax authorities also reviewed the valuation figures used to check that they were reasonable (see Holzer and Schonfeld 1965).

In 1975, the *Institute der Wirtschaftsprüfer* did produce a recommendation for a supplementary statement identifying the impact of inflation on company profits. This was based on a replacement cost approach, developed from

Schmidt's ideas, with an adjustment for the effects of gearing. (See Coenenberg and Macharzina 1976 for a full discussion.) In practice, few companies followed this recommendation and the matter has not been pursued. As in other countries, replacement cost adjustments to fixed assets and stock commanded general support while the gearing adjustment was controversial, with some argument in favour of a CPP-style approach (see Macharzina 1979, p. 230). While little used in the published accounts, there is some evidence that a number of German companies did use the recommended system for cost calculations and dividend policy (cited by Coenenberg et al. 1984, p. 65).

German academics in the 1920s and 1930s devoted a great deal of attention to the inflation accounting issue. Graves (1987) notes the coincidence that in 1921 three major texts on this topic appeared:

1. Walter Mahlberg produced a text arguing the case for a CPP system based on gold mark values, in line with the practice widely adopted at that time.
2. Eugen Schmalenbach also wrote on the merits of CPP, identifying a number of ways of finding a constant purchasing power including gold values, exchange rates with stable currencies, and the use of indices.
3. Fritz Schmidt's *Organic Balance Sheet* argued the case for current value accounting.

Graves (1992) traces the course of the subsequent debate between Schmalenbach and Schmidt, seeing the former as more influential in the prewar period and the latter as more influential postwar. This controversy was important not only in Germany but also in the USA where Henry Sweeney wrote on inflation accounting in terms strongly influenced by both German approaches (see Graves 1991).

It is interesting to observe that, with both practical experience and a strong academic tradition in inflation accounting, postwar German governments have nevertheless strongly resisted any departure from historic cost accounting for fear that inflation may be institutionalized.

TANGIBLE FIXED ASSETS

Expenditure on fixed assets below 800 DM is not normally capitalized, in line with tax law that accepts such costs as revenue expenditure.

Fixed assets are recorded at cost less systematic depreciation. Revaluation is only permitted to the extent that a depreciated asset is put at a figure at or below cost.

There is no legal prescription as to what depreciation methods may be used. 'Straight-line' and 'Reducing balance' are common, while 'Sum of years' digits', and usage based methods are also found. Commonly, asset lives are based on tax tables provided for various industries, and these estimates are normally conservative. Capitalization of interest costs on self-constructed fixed assets is permitted only if there is a close and identifiable relationship between the asset and the related loan capital.

RESEARCH AND DEVELOPMENT

Research and development costs incurred directly by a company must be written off immediately. Where research resulting from R&D costs incurred by a third party has been acquired by a company, the cost must be amortized on a systematic basis.

STOCK AND WORK IN PROGRESS

Stock must be shown at the lower of cost and market value. Market value is taken at the lower of net realizable value and replacement cost. In computing net realizable value, a mark down on the sales price to allow for an adequate profit is also permitted and is commonly applied because it is then recognized for tax purposes. Average cost has been the most commonly used basis for computing cost, followed by FIFO. However, since 1990, LIFO has been allowed for tax purposes and consequently is becoming more popular. For manufactured goods, cost is computed on the basis of absorption costing, but both tax and accounting law permit a range of options as to which costs must be absorbed.

For long-term contracts the 'completed contract' method is almost always used, although in certain circumstances the 'percentage of completion' method is permitted.

The above valuation rules lead to exceptionally conservative valuation of stock, and a number of additional write downs are also permitted in special cases.

LEASING

The commercial code provides for capitalization of finance leases. The definition of a finance lease follows tax law.

Criteria for identification of a finance lease depend on the nature of a leased asset, e.g. whether it is land, buildings or plant. Some criteria used are:

1. Whether bargain purchase or lease extension options have been agreed.
2. Whether the basic lease term covers 40 per cent to 90 per cent of the useful life of the asset.
3. Whether the leased asset is of a special type usable only by the lessee.
4. Whether there is full payment to the lessor during the non-cancellable period.

In practice, it is common for lease contracts to be structured in such a way as to avoid classification as a finance lease.

The commercial code requires lessees to disclose significant operating lease commitments in the notes to the accounts. However, these do not have to be disclosed separately from other commitments, and no analysis of obligations year by year is required.

DEFERRED TAXATION

In most cases, as we have seen, German tax law requires that the same accounting methods be used both for tax law and for accounting. Thus there are relatively few deferred tax 'timing differences' arising in German accounts, and those relate mainly to consolidation adjustments.

In the consolidated accounts, any deferred tax asset or liability must be accounted for in full. In a company's own accounts, any deferred tax liability must be accounted for, but the inclusion in the accounts of any deferred tax asset is optional; where any such asset is recorded it must be deducted from revenue reserves in the computation of distributable profit. The liability method of computation is used.

A peculiarity of German accounting practice is that all taxes are covered together in the profit and loss account, irrespective of whether they are paid in advance or allocated to provisions. This makes it difficult to assess the exact tax position for the year (see Commission of the European Communities 1986, p. 80).

PENSIONS

Accounting for pensions is a rare area where German accounts tend to understate a liability. As Seckler (1992) observes:

> Accrued pensions are one of the most critical issues in analysing German financial statements, since there are significant exceptions from the need to accrue for pensions, and the accruals may be understated because of the calculation methods usually applied (pp. 238–9).

German pension funds are generally of the 'defined benefit' type, and commonly are not externally funded, being supported by pension accruals and company welfare funds. There are three reasons for the common understatement of pension obligations in German accounts:

1. The legal obligation to accrue for pension obligations only applies to pension rights granted to individuals after 31 December 1986. Pension rights granted before that date are often, but not always, covered by an accrual.

2. There is no legal obligation to accrue for pension rights based on indirect

undertakings, such as by a company welfare fund. This applies even though the labour courts have held such undertakings to be legally binding on companies.

3. The actuarial calculation of the pension obligation is normally based on tax regulations. These allow for the following factors to be taken into account:

   (a) Assumed mortality ages

   (b) Disability risks

   (c) A discount rate of 6 per cent

   (d) The impact of employee turnover is only crudely allowed for by excluding employees under 30.

The impact of prospective salary increases is not allowed for in these calculations, as it leads to material understatement.

The accountants' institute strongly recommend full provision for pension liabilities and the law provides for disclosure of such a full provision in the notes to the accounts where the accrual in the balance sheet falls short.

POST BALANCE SHEET EVENTS

German law distinguishes between:

1. Post balance sheet events that indicate conditions existing at the balance sheet date. These should be adjusted for.

2. Post balance sheet events relating to conditions that arose after the balance sheet date. These should be explained in the management report if significant.

CONCLUSION

Within the European Community Germany has a strong influence in the direction of a formal and descriptive approach to accounting regulation.

REFERENCES

Abel, R. (1971) 'The impact of environment on accounting practices: Germany in the thirties', *International Journal of Accounting*, Fall, pp. 29–47.

Al Hashim, D. and Arpan, J. (1988) *International Dimensions of Accounting*, PWS-Kent.

Busse von Colbe, W. (1984) 'A true and fair view: a German perspective in Gray, S.J. and Coenenberg, A. *EEC Accounting Harmonization: Implementation and Impact of the Fourth Directive*, pp. 121–8, North-Holland.

Coenenberg, A. and Macharzina, K. (1976) 'Accounting for price changes: an analysis of current developments in Germany', *Journal of Business Finance and Accounting*, Spring, pp. 53–68.

Coenenberg, A., Möller, P. and Schmidt, F. (1984) 'Empirical research in financial accounting in Germany, Austria, and Switzerland: a review' in Hopwood, A.G. and Schreuder, H. *European Contributions to Accounting Research*, pp. 61–81, Free University Press.

Commission of the European Communities (1986) *The Fourth Company Accounts Directive of 1978 and the Accounting Systems of the Federal Republic of Germany, France, Italy, the United Kingdom, the United States, and Japan*, Commission of the European Communities, Luxembourg.

Dykxhoorn, H.J. and Sinning, K.E. (1981) 'The independence issue concerning German auditors: a synthesis', *International Journal of Accounting*, Spring, pp. 163–81.

Ernst and Whinney (1984) *The Impact of the Seventh Directive*, Financial Times Business Information.

Forrester, D.A.R. (1983) 'German accounting principles applied. A review article', *Accounting and Business Research*, Summer, pp. 215–19.

Gebhardt, G. (1983) 'The usefulness of different accounting disclosure regulations: a German experience', *International Journal of Accounting*, Fall, pp.109–31.

Graves, O.F. (1987) 'Accounting for inflation. Henry Sweeney and the German gold-mark model', *Accounting Historians Journal*, Spring, pp. 33–55.

Graves, O.F. (1991) 'Fritz Schmidt, Henry Sweeney and stabilized accounting', *Accounting and Business Research*, Vol. 21 No. 82, pp. 119–24.

Graves, O.F. (1992) 'Dynamic theory and replacement cost accounting: the Schmalenbach–Schmidt polemic of the 1920s', *Accounting Auditing and Accountability*, Vol. 5 No. 1, pp. 80–91.

Graves, O.F. and Berry, M. (1989) 'Accounting's role in successful economic development: some normative evidence from the German Democratic Republic', *International Journal of Accounting*, Vol. 124, No. 3, pp. 189–220.

Holzer, H.P. and Schonfeld, H.M. (1965) 'The German solution of the postwar price level problem', *Accounting Review*, April.

Locke, R. (1984) *The End of the Practical Man*, Jai Press.

Luck, W. (1982) 'The impact of international standards and other developments on the German accounting profession', *International Journal of Accounting*, Fall, pp. 45–56.

Macharzina, K.R. (1979) 'The impact of inflation on German accounting: theoretical background and professional issues' in Zimmerman, V.K. (ed.) *The Impact of Inflation on Accounting: A Global View*, pp. 225–40, Centre for International Education and Research in Accounting, Illinois.

Macharzina, K. and Langer, K. (1991) 'Financial reporting in Germany' in Nobes, C. and Parker, R. (eds) *Comparative International Accounting*, pp. 194–216, Prentice Hall.

Nicholson, R. (1991) 'The German profession interpreted', *Accountancy*, August, pp. 58–9.

Scapens, R.W. (1981) *Accounting in an Inflationary Environment*, Macmillan.

Seabrook, A. (1991) 'Accountancy in Germany', *Certified Accountant*, May, pp. 53–5.

Seckler, G. (1992) 'Germany' in Alexander, D. and Archer, S. (eds) *European Accounting Guide*, pp. 213–77, Academic Press.

Singer, H.W. (1943) *Standardized Accountancy in Germany*, Cambridge University Press.

Wysocki, K. (1983) 'Research into the processes on accounting standard setting in the Federal Republic of Germany' in Bromwich, M. and Hopwood, A.G. (eds) *Accounting Standards Setting: An International Perspective*, pp. 57–67, Pitman.

Wysocki, K.V. (1984) 'The Fourth Directive and Germany' in Gray, S.J. and Coenenberg, A.G. (eds) *EEC Accounting Harmonization: Implementation and Impact of the Fourth Directive*, pp. 55–61, North-Holland.

CHAPTER 8

Greece

| ABBREVIATIONS | OL | Orkotos Logistis – Qualified Auditor |
| | SOL | Professional body for professional auditors |

INTRODUCTION

As with other EC countries, EC directives have lead to major changes in Greek accounting. In particular, the distinctive monopolistic and state-controlled structure of the auditing profession is likely to be broken down.

ACCOUNTING REGULATION

In Greece, the major sources of accounting regulation are company law, the accounting 'plan' and tax law.

Greek law has included accounting requirements since 1872, with the first company law enacted in 1920 and revised in 1963. In 1986 and 1987, company and accounting law was revised to bring Greece into line with EC directives.

The accounting plan is compulsory for all Greek companies, but it applies at two levels:

1. Above a certain size level, considered below, there is a compulsory audit. In this case, the whole 'plan' applies.

2. For other companies, only those parts of the 'plan' relating to the annual accounts apply.

Finally, tax law has a major influence on Greek accounting. Normally only tax-deductible items are shown as expenses. The 1989 tax law, currently in operation, covers a number of accounting and bookkeeping issues.

THE ACCOUNTING PROFESSION

The accounting profession in Greece has developed along a very different path from that of other European countries. The title *Orkotos Logistis* (OL), translating literally as 'sworn-in accountant', refers to members of SOL, the official accounting organization. Founded in 1955, SOL acts both as a professional body and as an accounting firm, having some 6,000 member/employees. The governing committee of SOL is appointed by the Greek government. Under Greek law, SOL has been the sole authorized body for all compulsory audits. Costouros (1975) explains that each member of SOL acts as a separate firm with total independence in the performance of the audit. Professional fees are both set and collected by the central committee of SOL, without any involvement by the individual auditor.

MacErlean (1992) reports that the Greek government, in compliance with EC directives and under pressure from the international accounting firms, is reviewing SOL's monopoly of the audit roles. Thus it is expected that Greece will develop a system more in line with other EC countries. The impact on SOL in the coming years will be interesting to observe.

AUDITING

An independent audit is required for all enterprises which exceed two of the following three limits:

Total assets	400 million drachma
Turnover	800 million drachma
Number of employees	50

CONVENTIONS

While conventions such as historic cost and prudence apply, the strong tax link means that accounting conventions do not apply in the normal way to Greek accounts. However, as Price Waterhouse (1991, p. 11) report, when there is deviation from a normal accounting method for tax purposes, then the effects on income must be disclosed in a note to the accounts.

PRESENTATION

Greek requirements for the publication of accounts are somewhat unusual. The notes to the accounts do not have to be published, being filed with the Ministry of Commerce. Companies subject to a compulsory audit must publish their accounts with the audit report in two newspapers and the official Gazette. The permitted formats follow EC requirements, with analysis of expenses in the profit and loss account by function. Notes to the accounts included details of departures from normal accounting evaluation for tax purposes.

CONSOLIDATION

A requirement to provide consolidated accounts was introduced in 1991 in line with the EC Seventh Directive. Consolidated accounts are required where the Group exceeds two of the following three limits:

Total assets	500 million drachma
Turnover	1,000 million drachma
Number of employees	250

Otherwise, consolidation is not normally practised in Greece.

Consolidation is on a line-by-line basis for subsidiaries and equity accounting is applied to associates.

GOODWILL

Positive goodwill is treated as an intangible asset and is amortized over a maximum life of five years, the write-off being tax-deductible. Negative goodwill is shown as a consolidation reserve, but may be transferred to profit and loss if set off against an anticipated loss as it occurs.

FOREIGN CURRENCY TRANSLATION

In a company's own accounts, the monetary/non-monetary method is used. Exchange differences, except as discussed below, are taken to profit and loss. Differences on amounts owed and owing are accounted for:

1. All exchange losses are taken to the current profit and loss account.
2. Gains on short-term items are deferred to the following year's income statement.
3. Gains on long-term items are deferred, matched with any subsequent losses and taken to profit and loss as the related amounts are discharged.

Differences on long-term loans financing fixed assets are taken to profit and loss over the life of the related asset.

INFLATION ACCOUNTING

Greece has not developed any form of comprehensive inflation accounting system. On several occasions the law has prescribed revaluation of land and buildings, and on one occasion permitted revaluation of plant, in all cases using specific indices.

FIXED ASSETS

Historic cost is the normal basis of measurement, with write-downs to reflect any permanent diminution of value. Depreciation, although supposed to reflect an estimated economic life, is based on methods prescribed by tax law. Interest on borrowings relating to construction of an asset may be treated in one of two ways:

1. Immediate write-off.
2. Capitalization and amortization over five years.

RESEARCH AND DEVELOPMENT

Research and development may be written off immediately or capitalized and amortized over five years.

STOCK AND WORK IN PROGRESS

Stock is shown at the lower of historic cost and replacement cost. Cost includes indirect costs, other than interest, as well as direct costs. FIFO, LIFO, base stock and average cost are all permitted; in this respect Greek rules are among the most permissive in Europe; LIFO is common.

LEASING

All leases are shown in the accounts in accordance with strict legal form, i.e. as operating leases. However, details on a finance lease basis must be recorded by both lessor and lessee in memorandum accounts where there is a determined rental and a purchase option.

DEFERRED TAXATION

There is little occasion for this to arise under Greek regulations, and no system of accounting for deferred tax.

PENSIONS

Few company pension schemes exist in Greece, although the law does provide for a payment to employees who retire. As Casely (1992, p. 291) observes:

Many companies, based on an opinion issued by the Legal Counsel of the State, record an accrual only for the severance pay due to those employees retiring in the following year. Therefore, users of financial statements should be aware of the policy adopted, since the unrecorded liability can be significant.

CONCLUSION

EC membership has meant a greater culture change for Greek accountants than in any other country. More changes, such as that in the auditing requirements, are still to come.

REFERENCES   Casely, R.H. (1992) 'Greece' in Alexander, A. and Archer, S. (eds) *The European Accounting Guide*, pp. 279–315, Academic Press.

Costouros, G.J. (1975) 'Accounting education and practice in Greece', *International Journal of Accounting*, Fall, pp. 95–106.

McEarlean, N. (1992) 'Greek firms poised for audit explosion', *Accountancy*, August, p. 101.

Price Waterhouse (1991) *Comparability of Financial Statements International Survey*.

CHAPTER 9

Ireland

ABBREVIATIONS

ICAI	Institute of Chartered Accountants in Ireland.
ICPAI	Institute of Certified Public Accountants in Ireland.

INTRODUCTION

Accounting regulation and practice in the Republic of Ireland is closely linked to that in the United Kingdom for three reasons:

1. Until 1921 all Irish company law was enacted at Westminster. Subsequently Irish company law tended to be modelled on that in the UK. In particular the Companies Act 1963 was strongly influenced by the UK Companies Act of 1948 and the report in the UK of the Jenkins Committee that was to have a major influence on the UK Companies Act of 1967.

2. Both the UK and the Republic of Ireland are members of the European Community, and so are obliged to implement the accounting directives.

3. Until 1990 the UK and the Republic of Ireland had a common system for the formulation of accounting standards, and in practice Irish accountants continue to follow UK standards.

Accordingly this chapter only covers the regulatory environment and specific variations from UK practice. For other specific requirements reference should be made to the chapter on the UK (Chapter 16).

REGULATION

A series of Companies Acts from 1963 to 1990 include regulations for accounting, while regulations issued in 1992 by the Minister for Industry and Commerce implement the Seventh Directive on group accounts.

Brennan et al. (1992, pp. 74–81) report the history of the involvement of the Irish accounting profession with the UK accounting standard-setting process. Along with the Institute of Chartered Accountants in Scotland, the Institute of Chartered Accountants in Ireland joined with the English Institute in the Accounting Standards initiative of 1970 (see p. 203 below).

When the UK moved to a new accounting standard-setting process in 1990 involving legislative backing, and an element of Government funding and involvement, the Irish government declined an invitation to participate in this process. Instead, the Irish Institute of Chartered Accountants issues new standards, formulated in the UK, in its own name. Compliance with these standards is not an explicit legal requirement but is considered to be implied by the 'true and fair view' requirement and is required from members of the Irish Institute with disciplinary sanctions.

THE ACCOUNTING PROFESSION

The Institute of Chartered Accountants in Ireland (ICAI), founded in 1888, has developed as the major professional accounting body in the Republic of Ireland. The Institute also covers Northern Ireland and so operates under two national jurisdictions. Robinson (1983) offers a history of the Institute. Most, but not all, entrants to training with the Institute are graduates, not necessarily with relevant degrees. To qualify as members, trainees must complete a period of structured practical experience and pass examinations set by the Institute. The ICAI has shown a particular interest both in monitoring the quality of educational courses and in encouraging full-time postgraduate courses that give major exemptions from the Institute's own examinations (see Walsh 1988 for a full discussion). Some 50 per cent of members of the ICAI work in public accounting practice.

AUDITING

All incorporated companies are required to appoint an independent auditor from one of the following bodies:

1. The Institute of Certified Public Accountants in Ireland.
2. The Institute of Chartered Accountants in Ireland.
3. The Chartered Association of Certified Accountants.
4. The Institute of Chartered Accountants in England and Wales.
5. The Institute of Chartered Accountants in Scotland.

In general, the audit procedures and requirements are similar to those in the UK. The one significant difference is that in the Irish Republic the audit report must refer explicitly to whether, in the auditor's opinion:

1. The accounts give a true and fair view of the state of affairs at the year end and of the profit and loss for the year, both for the company and the group.
2. The accounts give the information required by the Companies Acts.
3. The auditor has obtained all information and explanations required for the audit.
4. Proper books of account have been kept.
5. Proper returns have been received from branches not visited during the audit.
6. The company's balance sheet and profit and loss account agree with the books of account.

7. The information in the directors' report is consistent with the accounts.

CONVENTIONS

Both the 'true and fair view' and specific accounting conventions apply in a similar way to the UK.

PRESENTATION

As in the UK, the whole range of formats permitted by the EC Fourth Directive are allowed. Brennan et al. (1991) report that in practice the vertical formats are rarely used in Ireland.

CONSOLIDATION

Following implementation of the EC Seventh Directive, consolidation in the Irish Republic will be similar to the UK. The major exception is that Irish company law effectively does not permit merger accounting.

GOODWILL

Requirements are similar to those in the UK.

FOREIGN CURRENCY TRANSLATION

Requirements are similar to those in the UK.

INFLATION ACCOUNTING

As part of the UK standard-setting community, Irish accountants participated in the debate over inflation accounting discussed in Chapter 16 below. One major Irish company, P. J. Carroll, produced current cost accounts from 1975 to 1988.

FIXED ASSETS

Requirements are similar to those in the UK.

RESEARCH AND DEVELOPMENT

Accounting requirements are similar to those in the UK. One difference is that company law explicitly requires disclosure of the R&D expense for the year, although non-disclosure is permitted where disclosure may be prejudicial to the company's interests.

STOCK AND WORK IN PROGRESS

Accounting requirements are similar to those in the UK.

LEASING

Accounting requirements are similar to those in the UK. However, in the early 1980s this topic posed a serious problem in achieving an agreed common accounting standard for Ireland and the UK.

The reason was that in Ireland, unlike the UK, the company showing a leased asset in the balance sheet was regarded as the purchaser for tax purposes. A number of Irish companies found this inconvenient, and the Irish Institute used its power of veto to block the issue of SSAP 21 on leasing until Irish tax law changed (see Brennan et al. 1992, pp. 75–6, Blake 1992, p. 321).

DEFERRED TAXATION

Accounting requirements are similar to those in the UK.

PENSIONS

Accounting requirements are similar to those in the UK. Because of a shortage of actuaries with experience of pension scheme valuation the full requirements of SSAP 24 will only apply to unlisted companies from 1993.

POST BALANCE SHEET EVENTS

Accounting requirements are similar to the UK.

CONCLUSION

While Irish accounting rules are very similar to those in the UK, there are minor differences. Now that the link between the accounting standard-setting systems of the two countries has been weakened these diffences may expand in the future.

REFERENCES

Blake, J. (1992) 'A classification system for economic consequences issues in accounting regulation', *Accounting and Business Research*, Autumn, pp. 305–21.

Brennan, N., O'Brien, F.J. and Pierce, A. (1991) *Financial Accounting and Reporting in Ireland*, Oak Tree Press.

Brennan, N., O'Brien, F.J., and Pierce, A. (1992) *European Financial Reporting – Ireland*, Routledge.

Robinson, H.W. (1983) *A History of Accountants in Ireland*, Institute of Chartered Accountants in Ireland.

Walsh, A. (1988) 'The making of the Chartered Accountant' in Rowe, D. (ed.) *The Irish Chartered Accountant. Centenary Essays* 1888–1988, pp. 155–72.

CHAPTER 10

Italy

ABBREVIATIONS

CNDCR   Consiglio Nazionale dei Dottori Commercialisti e dei Ragionieri.

INTRODUCTION   **Italy has been remarkably dilatory in the implementation of the European Community directives. In 1991 it became the last member state to implement the Fourth Directive, albeit in the same year the Seventh Directive was also implemented, ahead of Ireland and Portugal. The Eighth Directive is yet to be applied. In consequence, new practices in line with the new legislation have yet to emerge. This is particularly important because, in Italy, there is a well-established tradition that accounting rules are applied more flexibly than the strict legal position implies (Busse von Colbe 1983, p. 125). Thus, it is not possible to give a clear and comprehensive view of the new Italian accounting scene at this time. Accordingly, this chapter will necessarily be brief.**

ACCOUNTING REGULATION

During the period of Napoleon's domination, the French Civil Code was applied throughout Italy. When, following the fall of Napoleon, the various Italian states were restored, the French code tended to be adopted into local legislation. Accounting regulation has continued to be provided within the framework of the Civil Code. However, the most important source of authority has been from tax law. Expenses can only be claimed for tax purposes if they are shown in the statutory accounts, so that tax law tends, in practice, to determine accounting treatment. There is a professional body, the *Consiglio Nazionale dei Dottori Commercialisti e dei Ragionieri* (CNDCR) that issues some accounting standards which tend to be 'broad and generic' (Coopers and Lybrand 1991, pp. 1–31). These have been recognized by the Stock Exchange Commission and apply to listed companies. From 1993, the new law implementing the EC Fourth Directive will apply, as will the new law implementing the EC Seventh Directive from 1994.

THE ACCOUNTING PROFESSION

The Ministry of Justice exercises a general oversight over the Italian accounting profession, including explicit regulation of professional conduct and the basis for charging fees. There are two types of accounting qualification:

1. *Ragionieri e Periti Commerciali*, translating roughly as 'accountants and commercial appraisers'. To achieve this qualification, requirements include a business school diploma, three years' relevant work experience, and success in state-controlled examinations. These accountants each join a local *Collegio*, being a body to oversee its members. Italy has about 100 *Collegi* with a national supervisory body.

2. *Dottori Commercialisti*, roughly translating as Doctors in Commerce. To achieve this qualification it is necessary to complete a lengthy process of relevant education, culminating in a four-year university course for a doctorate. Then a further university examination for membership of an *Ordine dei Dottori Commercialisti* is required. There is no professional experience requirement. Each *Ordine* is a local organization, there being over 100, with a National Council overseeing these *Ordini*.

In practice, both these types of accounting qualification are recognized in the business world as equally valid. Neither, however, fully meets the provisions of the EC Eighth Directive on auditor qualifications. Accordingly, some restructuring and reform of the Italian accounting profession is likely in the near future.

AUDITING

A form of audit process is legally required for all companies above a certain size, but no professional qualification is required and the auditors' duties, as laid out in the Civil Code are very limited. An independent professional audit is only required for:

1. Stock exchange limited companies
2. Financial institutions
3. Public bodies.

ACCOUNTING CONVENTIONS

In implementing the EC Fourth Directive, a requirement for accounts to present a *quadro fedele*, the 'true and fair view' requirement, was proposed and discussed in the academic journals. As Canziani (1988) observes, this is an ill-defined concept in the UK, where it originates, and appears to be inherently contradictory to the Italian legal tradition of clarity in regulation. He suggests that the new concept is likely to be interpreted in the light of an existing Italian requirement that accounts be presented with *chiarezza e precisione* (exactness and precision). In fact, the more restricted requirement for accounts to be *veritiero e corretto* (truthful and correct) has now been introduced (Took 1992). On this basis the new convention is unlikely, in practice, to change the tendency of Italian accounting.

PRESENTATION

The legally required annual accounts comprise the balance sheet, the profit and loss account, and the notes to the accounts. Only large companies have to publish the formats in full, both small and medium-sized companies being allowed to present abridged accounts. A large company is one that exceeds two of the following three limits:

Total assets	2 billion lire
Total sales	4 billion lire
Number of employees	50

As in most EC countries, the abridged and the full accounts have the same basic structure with more detail in the latter. Comparative figures are required for both the balance sheet and the profit and loss account. Any change in the accounting policy or analysis should be explained in the notes to the accounts with sufficient detail to enable comparison of the current with the preceding accounting period to be made.

In Italy, the balance sheet formats are similar to those in Germany. The balance sheet is in the horizontal format, as permitted in the Fourth Directive (see Chapter 3 above). The profit and loss account is on a vertical basis, classified on a 'type of expense' rather than a functional basis. The notes are part of the accounts.

CONSOLIDATION

Legislation on consolidated accounts, enacted in compliance with the EC Fourth Directive, will be in force from 1994. Until that date, group accounts will only be required for listed companies and certain special sectors.

The obligation to provide consolidated accounts will only apply to groups which, after normal consolidation adjustments, exceed two of the following limits:

Total assets	10 billion lire
Total sales	20 billion lire
Number of employees	250

In addition to the parent company, three types of investee are included:

1. Subsidiary companies, which must be included where the holding company has controlled a majority of the voting rights in the two most recent general meetings. Line-by-line consolidation is used in this case.

2. 'Multigroup' or 'joint ventures' where proportional consolidation is used.

3. Associated companies, where there is significant influence but not control.

Significant influence is deemed to arise where the shareholding exceeds 20 per cent of voting rights, or 10 per cent in the case of a listed company. Equity accounting is used in this case.

Certain exemptions from inclusion in the consolidated accounts exist, subject to disclosure and explanation in the notes to the accounts:

1. Where an investment is not material it may be excluded from consolidation.

2. Equity accounting may be used in place of line-by-line or proportional consolidation in any of the following circumstances:

    (a) The investee is in receivership or liquidation.

    (b) Investments where there is an intention to sell in the near future.

    (c) Companies engaged in activities so different from the rest of the group that their consolidation would impair the true and fair view.

    (d) Investments for which the necessary information can only be obtained with disproportionate delay or expense.

In line with the Seventh Directive, subgroups are not required to prepare consolidated accounts if the ultimate holding company does so in another EC member state. The format of the consolidated accounts is generally similar to the individual company accounts, with two major differences:

1. The balance sheet must show minority interests.

2. The profit and loss account may show costs analysed by function.

GOODWILL

Goodwill is reported in an individual company's accounts where a price has been paid for it in an acquisition and that price is shown in the purchase contract. Such goodwill is normally amortized over a five to ten-year period, and is a tax-deductible expense.

In the consolidated accounts, goodwill is computed as the difference between the fair value of the purchase consideration and the fair value of the identifiable assets acquired. Positive goodwill may either be written off immediately against retained profits or capitalized. In the latter case, amortization should normally be over a maximum of five years. Negative goodwill should be shown as a reserve or as a provision for future losses.

FOREIGN CURRENCY TRANSLATION

Transactions in a foreign currency are initially accounted for at the exchange rate ruling at the transaction date, unless a hedging transaction makes use of a forward rate more appropriate. At each balance sheet date monetary assets and monetary liabilities are translated at the average rate for the final month of the year. Translation gains are shown in the liabilities section of the balance sheet as deferred income. Translation losses are offset against this deferred income and, to the extent that this does not cover the loss, are taken to the profit and loss account. When foreign currency monetary items are repaid, realized gains or losses go to the profit and loss account. For foreign currency investments, it appears that the principles of IAS 21 are to be applied.

INFLATION ACCOUNTING

In Italy, no form of inflation accounting has emerged. However, in response to the inflation problem, revaluations by specified indices have been permitted. The last such revaluation was in 1983.

FIXED ASSETS

The normal basis for fixed asset valuation is historic cost. Finance costs relating to fixed asset construction may also be capitalized up to the date that the asset is complete. Depreciation is determined by tax law and in practice is often accelerated. The accounting treatment of government grants is, in some cases, determined by legislation; in other cases the principles of IAS 20 tend to apply.

RESEARCH AND DEVELOPMENT

Either a write-off or a deferral policy may be applied. In the latter case, the deferred amount, which must not exceed the expected net income to be generated, must be amortized over a maximum of five years.

STOCK

Stock is valued at the lower of cost and market value. Market value may be taken as either net realizable value or as replacement cost. Cost is computed on an absorption basis which should be explained in the notes to the accounts. FIFO, LIFO and weighted average are all permitted.

For long-term contract work in progress, either the completed contract method or the percentage of completion method may be used.

LEASING

Italian practice has normally been to treat all leases as operating leases.

DEFERRED TAXATION

Because of the close links between tax and accounting rules, deferred tax timing differences do not normally arise.

PENSIONS

State pensions are earnings related, based on contributions paid by companies. These costs are charged to the profit and loss account as incurred.

CONCLUSION

While Italy has formally moved to an accounting system in line with European Community practice, there is a national tradition of low levels of compliance. As Ernst and Whinney (1984) observe:

> A mentality has developed in Italy whereby the law has been interpreted in both a literal and limited way, and the need to provide sufficient information about the company has been neglected (p. 39).

REFERENCES

Alexander, D. and Latini, R. (1992) 'Italy' in Alexander, D. and Archer, S., *The European Accounting Guide*, Academic Press.

Andrei, P. (1990) 'Some considerations relevant to the practice of external auditing and legal control of financial statements in Italy', EIASM, Workshop on Accounting in Europe, May.

Busse von Colbe, W. (1983) 'A discussion of international issues in accounting standard setting in Bromwich, M. and Hopwood, A.G., *Accounting Standards Setting – An International Perspective*, pp. 121–6, Pitman.

Canziani, A. (1988) 'Italy and the Seventh Directive' in Gray, S.J. and Coenenberg, A.G. (eds) *International Group Accounting*, pp. 105–16, Croom Helm.

Coopers and Lybrand (1991) *International Accounting Summaries*.

Ernst and Whinney (1984) *The Impact of the Seventh Directive*, Financial Times Business Information.

Hagigi, M. and Sponza, A. (1990) 'Financial statement analysis of Italian companies: accounting practices, environmental factors, and international corporate performance comparisons', *The International Journal of Accounting*, Vol. 25, No. 4, pp. 234–51.

Nobes, C. (1992) 'Accounting harmonization: Italy completes the picture', *Management Accounting*, July-August, pp. 32–3.

Nobes, C. and Zambon, S. (1991) 'Piano, piano: Italy implements the directives', *Accountancy*, July, pp. 84–5.

Price Waterhouse (1991) *Comparability of Financial Statements. International Survey*.

Rivola-Clay, A.M. and Doupnik, T. (1987) 'The progress of international accounting: allegro ma non troppo', *International Journal of Accounting*, Spring, pp. 87–102.

Took, L. (1992) 'The new Italian accounting laws', *Management Accounting*, February, pp. 48–9.

CHAPTER 11

Luxembourg

ABBREVIATIONS

| IRE | Institut des Réviseurs d'Entreprises – The professional body for qualified auditors. |

INTRODUCTION **With a population of under 400,000 Luxembourg is the smallest country in the European Community. The country has a tradition of little legal regulation of accounting and, although EC directives have been applied, generally options allowing a wide range of discretion have been chosen.**

ACCOUNTING REGULATION

Prior to the implementation of the EC directives Luxembourg's only legal accounting requirements were to be found in the Company Law of 1915 as amended in 1933. Apart from a requirement that the annual accounts should consist of a balance sheet and profit and loss accounts, no specific accounting requirements were included. Gebhard (1992) quotes a comment on such accounts as consisting of 'some lines of vague and imprecise headings with numbers against them' (p. 367). In 1984 the law was amended to comply with the Fourth Directive and in 1988 to comply with the Seventh Directive.

ACCOUNTING PROFESSION

In 1984, the professional qualification of *Réviseur d'entreprises* was established. This is under the supervision of the Ministry of Justice, and requires a university degree, three years' practical training, and examination passes. Qualified auditors from other EEC countries may also be admitted subject to tests in Luxembourg law, tax, and standards. Once approved by the Ministry each *Réviseur* becomes a member of the *Institut des Réviseurs d'Entreprises*, a professional body responsible for supervising the conduct of auditors.

AUDITING

Audit and accounting requirements depend on company size. Companies are classified in the 'small' or 'medium' category if they do not exceed two out of three criteria:

	Small	*Medium*
Total Assets	77 million francs	310 million francs
Turnover	160 million francs	640 million francs
Number of Employees	50	250

Since 1984 all large and medium-sized enterprises have been required to have a member of IRE as auditor. Small companies continue to be required to appoint a *Commissaire aux Comptes* (statutory auditor) under the legislation of 1915, with no requirement for a professional qualification.

Archer et al. (1989) observe: 'Not surprisingly, a number of multi-listed Luxembourg countries have strong links with other financial centres, including London. Accordingly, it is difficult to speak of a Luxembourg norm in audit reporting, since practice tends to reflect more the influence of other countries' (p. 44).

CONVENTIONS

In line with the EC Fourth Directive, the true and fair view requirement has been adopted as the basic objective of company accounts. Other conventions in the Fourth Directive, as outlined in Chapter 3 above, are:

1. Prudence
2. Going concern
3. Accruals
4. Consistency
5. No set-off.

PRESENTATION

The full range of formats under the EC Fourth Directive are permitted in Luxembourg. Exemptions within the size limits presented in the section on auditing above apply differently to accounts presented to shareholders and accounts filed for public record. Medium-sized companies must present a full balance sheet to shareholders, but may omit some detail in the publicly filed accounts, while presenting an abridged profit and loss account in both cases. Small companies may present an abridged profit and loss account to shareholders and need not file the profit and loss account publicly, while they present an abridged balance sheet in both cases.

CONSOLIDATION

As Ernst and Whinney (1984) observe, the introduction of a requirement to produce consolidated accounts in response to the EC Seventh Directive has been a major change in Luxembourg law. However, of 7,400 registered limited companies 5,800 are financial holding companies which enjoy exemption from this rule. Moreover, a number of Luxembourg holding companies are in turn subsidiaries of other holding companies in other countries presenting group accounts in line with the EC Seventh Directive. Consolidation is commonly on a line-by-line basis by the acquisition method, although in certain circumstances merger accounting is permitted.

GOODWILL

Goodwill is computed as the difference between the fair value of the purchase consideration and the fair value of the net assets acquired. It should be written off within five years; if a longer period of amortization is applied then this must be explained in the notes to the accounts.

FOREIGN CURRENCY TRANSLATION

An interesting feature of Luxembourg accounting is that company accounts may be expressed in any freely convertible currency. There are no legal provisions on foreign currency translation methods, and in practice both the closing rate method and the temporal method are used.

INFLATION ACCOUNTING

Luxembourg has no tradition in this field.

FIXED ASSETS

While initial measurement of fixed assets is at historical cost, revaluation is permitted. Depreciation must be on a systematic and realistic basis, with the straight-line method in common use.

RESEARCH AND DEVELOPMENT

Deferral of research and development costs is permitted, and amortization should normally be within five years. Dividends may only be distributed to the extent that distributable reserves exceed unamortized research and development costs.

STOCK

The lower of cost and net realizable value rule applies. Cost may be ascertained by a variety of methods, e.g. FIFO, LIFO, average cost, but tax rules are more restrictive leading to potential timing differences.

LEASING

Capitalization of long-term finance leases is common.

DEFERRED TAXATION

A number of differences between accounting practices and tax rules can give rise to timing differences. Full provision for deferred taxation on these is made.

PENSION COSTS

Full provision for pension costs is usually made.

POST BALANCE SHEET EVENTS

Non-adjusting post balance sheet events are not normally reported.

CONCLUSION

Luxembourg continues to have one of the least regulated accounting systems in the European Community.

REFERENCES

Archer, S., Dufour J.B. and McCleay, S. (1989) *Audit Reports on the Financial Statements of European Multinational Companies: A Comparative Study*, Institute of Chartered Accountants in England and Wales.

Ernst and Whinney (1984) *The Impact of the Seventh Directive*, Financial Times Business Information.

Gebhard, G.H. (1992) 'Luxembourg' in Alexander, D. and Archer, S. (eds) *The European Accounting Guide*, Academic Press.

CHAPTER 12

The Netherlands

ABBREVIATIONS

AA Accountants	Administratie consulenten. An accountancy qualification.
NIVRA	Nederlands Instituut van Register Accountants – The leading Dutch professional accountancy body.
NOVAA	Nederlandse Orde van Accountants – Administratie consulenten – A Dutch professional accountancy body.
RA	Register accountants – The leading accountancy qualification.

INTRODUCTION   **As home to a number of the world's major multinational enterprises, it is not surprising that the Netherlands has a strongly international approach to accounting. International accounting standards are well respected, while traditionally accounting regulation is flexible. A distinctive Dutch approach to accounting, particularly in the use of replacement costs, has its roots in the thinking of Theodore Limperg.**

ACCOUNTING REGULATION

The first Dutch accounting legislation was enacted in 1928. This contained some requirements relating to the disclosure of assets in the balance sheet. In 1970 an accounting law was enacted, applicable to all limited companies, cooperatives, and mutual guarantee associations. This law provided some general rules for the preparation of accounts, but left most accounting issues to the professional judgment of accountants with a requirement that accounts should present a 'true and fair view' and should be in accordance with 'principles acceptable in economic and social life'. Van Hoepen (1984) comments on the importance of the term 'acceptable'.

> *Acceptable* practice was preferred because it was felt that *accepted* practice, especially if laid down by the law, would hamper further development of financial accounting and business economics. It was clear from the then Exploratory Memorandum that the Minister of Justice expected the employers and the trade unions together with the accountants' organization (NIVRA) to inventory and examine the financial accounting policies adopted in commercial practice (p. 69).

In response to this expectation an accounting standards committee, with representatives of employers, employees, and professional accountants, was set up in 1971. In 1982 this was renamed the Council for Annual Reporting (*Raad voor de Jaarverslaggeving*). The accounting standards produced by this body tend to be flexible in character. Although not legally binding they are regarded as authoritative, and would constitute evidence of 'acceptable' accounting practice. Bloom and Naciri (1988) report that, although this system appears to give employees a significant role, some union seats on the council were vacant in the mid-1980s. They conclude that 'this indicates that until recently there was some reluctance on the part of the unions to participate in the council's work' (p. 78). This is curious given that Schreuder (1981) found that some 70 per cent of a sample of Dutch employees did read their company's social reports. The Accounting Act of 1970 set up a new court, called the 'Enterprise Chamber'. This court considers cases where a complaint is made that companies fail to comply with the accounting law, and it may order the issue of revised accounts. The plaintiff must have a financial interest in the company; the court has held that employees and their representative have such an interest. Klaasen (1980) discusses a number of cases considered by the court and points out that in some cases the decisions reached differ from the pronouncements of the accounting standards committee.

In 1984, Dutch accounting law was amended to comply with the EC Fourth Directive, and in 1988 was amended to comply with the EC Seventh Directive. However, the tone of Dutch accounting law continues to be flexible. For most continental European countries, the Anglo-American accounting system seems flexible and permissive. It is interesting to note that, by contrast, a comparison of Dutch and US accounting law found the Dutch approach to be more flexible in a number of ways (Beekhuizen and Frishkoff 1975).

THE ACCOUNTING PROFESSION

In 1895, a professional body for Dutch accountants, the *Nederlands Instituut van Register Accountants* (NIVRA), was founded. In 1962, a law on accounting qualifications provided for the regulation of accounting exams and reserved the audit role for RAs, who are required to be members of NIVRA and therefore are subject to that body's ethical code and disciplinary system. RAs normally qualify by taking a five-year business economics degree followed by some three years of part-time study; there is no practical training requirement.

In 1974, a further law established the qualification of *accountant-administratieconsultant* (AA). AAs are not qualified to carry out audits, and tend to serve small and medium-sized clients. They have a professional body, NOVAA, membership of which is voluntary.

The Netherlands is currently in the process of implementing the EC Eighth Directive on auditor qualifications. This is likely to create a new professional audit qualification embracing existing RAs, and also AAs who pass a transitional exam. A practical training requirement will also be introduced.

AUDITING

All companies, except for those classified as 'small', must be audited. To be 'small' a company must meet at least two of the following requirements.

Total assets less than 4 million guilders
Net turnover less than 8 million guilders
Average number of employees less than 50

In addition to the public audit report attached to the accounts, a fuller report on the audit examination must be made to the company's supervisory board.

CONVENTIONS

The true and fair view requirement was prescribed in the Accounting Law of 1970. Thus compliance with the EC Fourth Directive on the true and fair view did not pose problems of interpretation for Dutch accountants. Accounts must give a true and fair view, with extra information given in the notes to achieve this and, if necessary, override specific legal requirements supported by an explanatory note.

The general principles of going concern, consistency, accruals, prudence, substance over form, and materiality are also prescribed.

PRESENTATION

The law permits companies to choose between the formats allowed in the Fourth Directive. In practice, most companies present a horizontal balance sheet and a vertical profit and loss account.

CONSOLIDATION

A holding company is normally required to present consolidated accounts except where

1. The limits for definition as a 'small company' (see 'audit' above) would not be exceeded if consolidation took place

and

2. None of the group companies is listed

and

3. The company is not a credit institution

and

4. No notice of objection is lodged by 10 per cent of shareholders or the holders of 10 per cent of share capital.

A subsidiary company is one that meets one of the following three conditions:

1. The holding company exercises more than half the voting rights.
2. The holding company is entitled to appoint or discharge more than half of the board of directors.
3. The holding company is fully liable as a partner.

Normally the purchase method of consolidation is used. The 'pooling of interests' method is only applicable in the very unusual circumstance that a separate acquirer cannot be identified. For joint ventures, proportional consolidation is used. The equity method is used for associated companies.

GOODWILL

When a company is acquired, the identifiable assets and liabilities are valued on the same basis as is in the acquiring company's accounts. The difference between the group share of the net assets and the purchase consideration is goodwill. Goodwill is credited to revaluation reserve if negative, while an asset may be:

1. Charged directly against profit
2. Written off against reserves
3. Amortized over a period up to five years.

Any period of amortization over five years must be justified in the notes to the accounts.

FOREIGN CURRENCY

A company's own foreign currency holdings or liabilities should be translated at the closing rate, except where forward transactions to cover the position have been entered into. All exchange losses must, and all exchange gains may, be taken to the profit and loss account as they arise. As an alternative, exchange gains on long-term items may be allocated over the period to payment.

Foreign based operations are of two types:

1. For 'self-sustaining' operations, where the foreign entity is regarded as being independently managed, the closing rate method applies. Balance sheet translation gains and losses are taken direct to reserves while gains or losses arising from the profit and loss account translation, which may be by either the average rate or the closing rate, are taken either through profit or direct to reserves.

2. For 'integrated' foreign operations, which are regarded effectively as an extension of the parent company's activities, the temporal method is used, with all translation gains and losses taken through the profit and loss account.

INFLATION ACCOUNTING

The Netherlands is the only country in the world with a modest inflation rate where a system of replacement cost accounting has developed and is in use by a number of major companies. Van Seventer (1975, p. 70) points out that in Germany in the 1920s and 1930s the debate over alternatives to historical cost was a response to the problems of inflation, 'to remedy an immediate and pressing problem of the entire business community'. Much the same might be said of the 'inflation accounting' debate in most other countries of the world. By contrast, replacement value theory in the Netherlands:

1. Has developed on the basis of theory of business economics, not as a response to the inflation problem.
2. Has evolved over a number of years, with Limperg's first writings advocating replacement value appearing in 1917.

The thoughts and influence of Theodore Limperg (1879–1961) play a dominant part in the evolution of Dutch replacement value theory. From 1922 to 1950 he headed the business economics school at Amsterdam University. He was the guiding spirit of a group of scholars, many of them colleagues or former students, known as the Amsterdam school. (See Van Seventer 1984, pp. 348–56 on the influence of Limperg.)

Van Seventer (1969) sees the 'continuity' postulate as the basis for Limperg's theory. This is similar to, but wider than, the 'going concern' concept of the Anglo-American literature. It is derived from economic theory rather than accounting analysis. It involves envisaging the operating process of the business as a stream of activity where the means of production enter the business, are processed, and at the time of sale the means of production must be replaced if the stream is to continue to flow. This 'duty to replace' makes replacement cost the relevant measure of the value of all inputs to the firm. In circumstances where it is no longer appropriate to continue a line of activity, the net present value of future income streams from the asset will become important. The lower of the two values is the one relevant to the business because it represents the extent to which the business is dependent on the asset for its continuance.

Burgert (1972) summarized some criticisms of Limperg's approach to replacement value accounting. In particular, he identified certain unresolved problems of application:

1. The theory fails to address the problem of accounting for the impact of inflation on monetary items.

2. The theory fails to address the problem of technological change when the replacement is not identical to the asset consumed.

3. While the theory addresses specific price charge levels, it fails to address the relationship between these and general price levels.

These comments are concerned with the questions of how to apply a replacement cost approach rather than the fundamental principle of its utility. A survey of Dutch companies listed on the Amsterdam stock exchange as at 31 December 1985 (van Offeren 1990) found three out of 147 companies producing pure current cost accounts and only 15 producing a current cost operating income figure. However, the majority of companies gave some element of current cost data in their accounts. An earlier survey (Klaasen 1979) looked at why company accountants opted for their chosen approach. A number of companies did not apply revaluations to stocks because stock levels were generally low, making adjustments immaterial. Three out of 31 companies did not adjust stock valuations because price fluctuations were regarded as so erratic as to create unrealistic fluctuations in profit. An interesting point for analysis is that several companies reported concern that automatic revaluation of assets would increase depreciation charges above an acceptable level, so had limited the percentage of revaluation.

One company which had led the way in promoting replacement cost accounting is Philips. There are a number of published descriptions of the company's experience including Goudeket (1960), Holmes (1972) and Spinosa Cattela (1979). Some important elements in Philips' approach are:

1. Internally generated indices are used to compute replacement costs of fixed assets and stock. The computation of these is part of the purchasing function.

2. The same system of accounting is used in the management accounts and the published accounts.

3. The publication of replacement cost accounts is seen as an important element in persuading unions of the real level of company profit, and in urging tax authorities to be aware of the impact of taxation on company profits.

FIXED ASSETS

Dutch accounting law identifies five categories of tangible fixed asset. The first three relate to assets used in the production process:

1. Land and buildings
2. Plant and machinery
3. Other operating fixed assets
4. Assets under construction
5. Assets not used in the production process.

This separate identification of assets used in the production process is characteristic of the business economics approach.

Assets may be valued either on a historical cost or on a current value basis. The basis adopted must be applied consistently, so that revaluation of only part of the assets within an overall historical cost approach is not permitted. Production cost of an asset may include interest on capital borrowed for the period of production.

Depreciation must be computed on a consistent and economically realistic basis, and accounting depreciation is not linked in any way to depreciation for tax purposes.

RESEARCH AND DEVELOPMENT

These costs may be capitalized where there is a 'well-founded expectation' that future benefits will result. To meet this condition:

1. The product and related costs must be clearly identifiable.

2. Technical feasibility must be proven.

3. Management must be committed to implementing the project.

4. There must be evidence of the market for, or usefulness of, the product.

5. Adequate funds for implementation must be available.

Amortization should be over a maximum period of five years. The total research and development cost for each year must be disclosed.

STOCK AND WORK IN PROGRESS

Stock and work in progress may be shown on either a historical cost or a current value basis. Current value is defined as the lower of replacement cost and net realizable value. Historic cost is the lower of actual cost and net realizable value. Cost may be computed on an average, FIFO, LIFO or base stock basis; if either of the latter two bases is used, then current value must also be shown. Production costs are computed on a full absorption basis, and may even include attributable interest costs. For long-term contract work in progress both the percentage of completion and the completed contract methods are used in practice.

LEASING

Finance leases are defined, in principle, as those where the legal ownership of the asset remains with the lender but the economic risks are borne, almost entirely, by the lessee. Not surprisingly, given the Dutch 'substance over form' tradition, the definition of such a lease is a broad one covering the following situations:

1. A situation where the lessee enjoys a purchase option at a bargain price.
2. The primary lease period covers substantially the full economic life of the asset.
3. After the primary lease period there is an option to extend the lease for the full economic life of the asset on favourable terms.

The lessee should capitalize finance leases. Where operating lease rentals involve substantial commitments for the future these should be disclosed in the notes to the accounts.

DEFERRED TAXATION

In the Netherlands there is a well-established tradition of a distinction between accounting income and taxable income. Thus it is not surprising that there is also a well-established practice of providing for deferred taxation. Such provision is normally made on a full deferral basis, although there is no specific rule against a partial deferral approach. Provision is generally made by the liability method, as recommended by an accounting standard.

PENSION LIABILITIES

Dutch law requires employee pension rights to be covered by an independent pension fund or insurance company. Companies are required to provide in the accounts for the full pension obligation arising each year, so that the pension expense may not match exactly with pension contributions paid into the fund, with a consequent asset or liability arising. If a change in the pension scheme creates a pension entitlement relating to earlier years' service then this may be charged directly against the equity.

CONCLUSION

Broadly speaking, the Netherlands has an accounting environment in line with the Anglo-American model of flexibility in the pursuit of economically realistic reports. Two distinctive features of the Dutch accounting environment are:

1. A major role for employees both in the formulation of accounting rules and as respected users.
2. A well-developed inflation accounting system.

REFERENCES

Beekhuizen, T. and Frishkoff, P. (1975) 'A comparison of the new Dutch Accounting Act with generally accepted accounting principles', *International Journal of Accounting*, Spring, pp. 13–22.

Bloom, R. and Naciri, M.A. (1988) 'An analysis of the accounting standard setting framework in two European countries: France and the Netherlands', *Advances in International Accounting*, pp. 69–85.

Burgert, R. (1972) 'Reservations about Replacement Value Accounting in the Netherlands', *Abacus*, December, pp. 111–26.

Enthoven, A.J.H. (1976) 'Replacement value accounting: wave of the future'. *Harvard Business Review*, Jan–Feb, pp. 6–8.

Goudeket, A. (1960) 'An application of replacement value theory'. *Journal of Accountancy*, July.

Holmes, G. (1972) 'Replacement value accounting', *Accountancy*, March, pp. 4–8.

Klaasen, J. (1979) 'The practice of current value accounting in the Netherlands' in Wanless, P.T. and Forrester, D.A.R. (eds) *Readings in Inflation Accounting*, Wiley.

Klaasen, J. (1980) 'An accounting Court: the impact of the Enterprise Chamber on financial reporting in the Netherlands', *Accounting Review*, April, pp. 327–41.

Kleerekoper, I. (1963) 'The economic approach to accounting', *Journal of Accountancy*, March, pp. 36–40.

Mey, A. (1966) 'Theodore Limperg and his theory of values and costs', *Abacus*, September, pp. 3–23.

Schreuder, H. (1981) 'Employees and the Corporate Social Report: the Dutch case', *Accounting Reivew*, April, pp. 294–308.

Schreuder, H. and Klaasen, J. (1984) 'Confidential revenue and profit forecasts by management and financial analysts', *Accounting Review*, January, pp. 64–77.

Scott, G.M. (1970) 'A business economics foundation for accounting: the Dutch experience', *International Journal of Accounting*, Spring, pp. 117–31.

Spinosa Cattela, R.C. (1979) 'An introduction into Current Cost Accounting and its application with Philips' in *Notable Contributions to the Periodical International Accounting Literature – 1975–8*, pp. 102–17, American Accounting Association.

Van Hoepen, M.A. (1984) 'The Fourth Directive and the Netherlands' in Gray, S.J. and Coenenberg, A.G. (eds) *EEC Accounting Harmonization: Implementation and Impact of the Fourth Directive*, pp. 69–80, North-Holland.

Van Offeren, D. (1990) 'Accounting for changing prices in Dutch annual reports' in Most, K.S. (ed.) *Advances in Interntional Accounting – Vol. 3*, Jai Press.

Van Seventer, A. (1969) 'The continuity postulate in the Dutch theory of business income', *International Journal of Accounting*, Spring, pp. 1–19.

Van Seventer, A. (1975) 'Replacement value theory in modern Dutch accounting', *International Journal of Accounting*, Fall, pp. 67–94.

Van Seventer, A. (1984) 'Accounting in the Netherlands' in Holzer, H.P. *International Accounting*, pp. 345–68, Harper and Row.

Vos, J. (1970) 'Replacement value accounting', *Abacus*, December, pp. 132–4.

CHAPTER 13

Portugal

ABBREVIATIONS

APC	Associaçao Portuguesa de Contabilistas
APCTEC	Associaçao Portuguesa de Tecnicos de Contas
CNC	Comissao de Normalizaçao Contabilistica
POC	Plano Oficial de Contabilidade
ROC	Revisores Oficiais de Contas
SPC	Sociedade Portuguesa de Contabilidade

INTRODUCTION **The reform of the Portuguese accounting system began in 1970 and was in-spired like other southern European countries such as Spain or Greece, by the French model and particularly by the French General Accounting Plan of 1957. Apart from the French influence, it was also inspired by certain aspects of the United Kingdom's system.**

Portugal's entry into the EEC in 1986 has been the main force in bringing the Portuguese accounting system up to the level of most other community countries.

LEGAL FRAMEWORK

One of the distinguishing features of the Portuguese accounting system is that only the accounting principles which are in the commercial and fiscal laws are used. Therefore, unlike other countries there is no such thing as a tradition in which the profession and practice of accounting make certain accounting principles valid other than those which are a product of current legislation.

This legislation is basically composed of the Code of Commerce, *Plan Oficial de Contabilidade* (POC) or General Accounting Plan and the fiscal laws.

The first Portuguese accounting plan, the POC, was passed in 1977 following the creation of a commission to normalize accounting methods a year earlier. The *Comissao de Normalizaçao Contabilistica* (CNC) was a body which was dependent on the Ministry of Finance. As a consequence of the political and economic convulsions which the country underwent in these years, the POC was not specifically regulated until 1980 and the CNC was not effectively constituted until 1983.

The CNC is a body which depends on the Ministry of Finance. In fact, the President of the CNC is nominated directly by the Ministry of Finance. His functions are:

1. To advise the Ministry of Finance on the establishment of accounting principles and procedures.

2. To constantly update the POC and make the corresponding sectorial adaptations.

3. To deal with consultations made by companies as to how the POC works and other provisions which affect accounting.

4. To represent the country in the international accounting bodies.

As has been pointed out previously, the POC is clearly inspired by the French model.

The POC was revised in 1989 in order to adapt it to the EC Fourth Directive.

THE ACCOUNTING PROFESSION

In Portugal there is a clear distinction between accounting and auditing professionals. Accounting professionals, known as *Tecnicos de Contas* must have a law or economics degree and be registered at the Ministry of Finance. The auditors, known as *Revisores Oficiais de Contas* (ROC) are registered at the Ministry of Justice.

Annual accounts which have to be presented for fiscal reasons must be signed by a *Tecnico de Contas* who is nominated by each company for that purpose.

There are various professional accounting organizations although none of them is officially recognized. The most influential of these is the *Associaçao Portuguesa de Tecnicos de Contas* (APOTEC) which is the Portuguese Association of Accounting Technicians which brings together the finest professionals in accounting. Other such associations are the Portuguese Accounting Society which is the oldest, having been founded in 1930, and the Portuguese Association of Accountants.

The Accounts and Business Magazine first appeared in 1933 and is one of the key points of reference for Portuguese accounting.

AUDITING

As has been explained previously, auditors or ROCs are registered with the Ministry of Justice and belong to the Board of Official Accounts Auditors. This body is officially recognized and its members must have a law or economics degree and have passed an exam after three years training.

The incorporated companies must have statutory auditors. The exact requirements vary, depending on the size of the incorporated company. So those companies with capital which is equal to or more than 20 million escudos must have three statutory auditors, one of whom is a ROC, while companies with capital under 20 million escudos need only have one statutory auditor who has to be an ROC.

Individual companies and limited companies need only be audited if two of the following three points apply:

Net assets:	180 million escudos
Net turnover:	370 million escudos
Average number of employees:	50

Statutory auditors cannot be employees of the same company or any company within the group and they cannot work for rival companies.

CONVENTIONS

Accounting principles are defined clearly in the General Accounting Plan of 1989 and also in the Code of Commerce. With regard to fixed assets and provisions, fiscal legislation has to be considered.

The main objective of the accounting of Portuguese companies in accordance with SFAC 2, is that their annual accounts should be useful and they must therefore be reliable, comparable and comprehensible. Apart from this, in line with EC Fourth Directive, the previous characteristics along with the main accounting principles have to ensure that accounts present the true and fair view of the company's wealth and its profits and losses.

The Portuguese General Accounting Plan or POC following the EC Fourth Directive, rules that various accounting principles should be followed:

1. Prudence: Profits should only be accounted for when they have been realized. On the other hand, losses will be considered as soon as they are known. Another consequence of the application of the principle of prudence is that depreciation has to be considered independently of whether the company makes a profit or loss. However, with regard to the differences in foreign currency translation, there are some cases in which the principle of prudence is not applied, as will be shown later.

2. Going concern.

3. Historic Cost: Items are shown at the price of acquisition unless the market price is lower. However, in some cases the replacement cost may be applied.

4. Accruals: The application of income and expenses has to be done in terms of the real flow that they represent independently of the moment at which they are received or paid.

5. Consistency: The accounting criteria have to be maintained as long as the assumptions which brought about this choice do not change. If any of the accounting criteria should change, the changes should be indicated in the annual report, expressing the qualitative and quantitative effect of such changes.

6. Substance over form: Accounting of transactions must be based on their real content and not on the legal framework. The accounting of leasing contracts is a good example of this principle, as will be seen later.

7. Materiality: The annual accounts must provide all the relevant information that might affect the opinion of those using the accounting data.

One of the peculiarities of the Portuguese system is that it makes a reference to the profits and losses of previous years which were not accounted for at the time. When these results are known they can be accounted in the profit and loss account of the current financial year, or the reserves in the balance sheet can be modified directly.

The importance of the fiscal regulations in the Portuguese accounting system has been shown previously. An example of this situation is pointed out by Fernandes (1992, p. 472), who states that in the case of a discrepancy between a POC accounting principle and the fiscal regulations, the latter will be given preference in spite of the fact that in the notes to the accounts it is stated that the accounting and fiscal differences should be made known.

PRESENTATION

The annual accounts, in accordance with POC which is based on the EC Fourth Directive, are composed of the balance sheet, the profit and loss account and the notes to the accounts. The annual accounts have two possible formats: the normal one and the abbreviated one. As a rule, all companies are obliged to use the normal format unless they fulfil the conditions which allow them to use the abbreviated one. Those companies which do not exceed two of the three following limits over two consecutive years can formulate the abbreviated models:

Total assets	180 million escudos
Total sales	370 million escudos
Average number of employees	250

The balance sheet is structured in the same way; it takes the horizontal form in both normal and abbreviated models, although in the latter there is less detail. It must also be pointed out that the balance sheet has four columns. The first three apply to the financial year which has just ended: one for gross income, another for depreciation and the last for net income. The other column is for the net income of the previous year (see Table 13.1).

The compulsory profit and loss account which, like the balance sheet, has to be presented along with the annual figures which close the previous year, also has the same structure which is horizontal in the two models (normal and abbreviated). In it, the revenues and expenses are classified according to the nature of the expenses. Therefore, the profit and loss account is structured in the shape of an account and naturally, it is one of the four options accepted by

Table 13.1

Balance sheet
Assets

Fixed assets
Intangible assets (includes starting up costs)
Tangible assets
Permanent investments
Fixed assets in course of construction
Current assets
Inventories
Debtors
Temporary investments
Cash at bank and in hand
Accrued income and prepaid expenses

Total assets

Stockholders' equity and debts
Stockholders' equity
Share capital
Revaluation reserves
Reserves
Profits after tax
Provisions for liabilities and charges
Long-term debts
Current liabilities
Deferred income and deferred expenses

Total liabilities

the EC Fourth Directive. As in the balance sheet, the normal and abbreviated models of the profit and loss account have the same structure. The difference is in the fact that the normal model provides much greater detail.

The results are divided into operating profit, financial results, ordinary and extraordinary profits and losses. The latter includes transactions which do not come from the company's ordinary commercial activity, in the same way as in the Spanish system (see Table 13.2).

Apart from the compulsory profit and loss account, companies can voluntarily draw up a statement on the analytical model, which is also described in the EC Fourth Directive. In this model, revenues and expenses are not grouped together but are categorized depending on function. This functional profit and loss account is optional and therefore cannot replace the compulsory model.

Table 13.2

Cost and losses	Products and earnings
Operating expenses (A)	Operating income (B)
Material cost	Sales
External services	Supply of services
Personnel costs	Work for fixed assets
Depreciation	Operating grants
Provisions	
Taxes	
Financial expenses (C)	Financial income (D)
Extraordinary expenses (E)	Extraordinary income (F)
Tax on profits	
Total costs and losses	Total products and earnings
Summary:	
Operating profit or loss	B – A
Financial profit or loss	D – C
Current profit or loss	Operating profit or loss plus financial profit or loss
Results before taxes:	Current profit or loss + F – E
Liquid profit or loss of financial year: Profit or loss before tax – G	

The notes to the accounts provide further information apart from that supplied by the balance sheet and the profit and loss account. So as not to repeat information which is similar to that of other European countries, the following points which are of special interest are listed as follows:

1. Modifications carried out in the annual profits and losses to gain fiscal incentives (accelerated depreciation, for instance).
2. Doubtful trade debts.
3. Grants and tax incentives received.

CONSOLIDATION OF ACCOUNTS

At the time of writing, it is not compulsory to draw up consolidated accounts in Portugal. However, the modifications which are going to be produced will be in accordance with the EC Seventh Directive. Below, the main aspects of the rough draft which the CNC is working on to enlarge the General Accounting Plan or POC are discussed.

Those groups in which the controlling company has more than 50 per cent of shares with voting rights, or of which most of the board members are in control, will be obliged to consolidate their accounts whenever the group exceeds two of the three following limits:

Total assets:	1,500 million escudos
Total sales:	3,000 million escudos
Average no. of employees	250

However, the previous exemption is not applicable to those groups in which one or more of its companies are listed on an EEC stock exchange.

Neither is it compulsory to consolidate in the following circumstances:

1. When the subsidiary company is not material.
2. When it is necessary to incur very high costs to obtain this information and these are not justified.
3. When the subsidiary company is in a country in which Government policy limits the control on the part of the parent company.
4. When it has been acquired to be sold immediately or
5. When it carries out very different activities from those of the controlling company.

The consolidated accounts comprise the balance sheet, the profit and loss account and the notes to the accounts. The format of these accounts is identical to those which have already been displayed (see presentation), with the difference that the minority shareholders' interests of the participating companies must be shown.

Besides this, the formulation of a statement of source and application of funds is recommended.

The accounts of the group (controlling and dependent) are consolidated on a line-by-line basis.

If a group also has associated companies, these stakes are valued by the application of the equity method.

The difference between an associated company and a subsidiary one is that in the former the investor has some influence while in the latter, the group has control.

If the group has stakes in multigroup companies (companies directed simultaneously by two or more companies) the method of proportional consolidation is applied. According to this method, the percentage of assets and liabilities of the multigroup company which corresponds to its stake is added to the group. The difference of first consolidation between the value paid for the stake and its net book value on the balance sheet of the company being controlled will be considered goodwill (if it is positive) and a consolidation reserve (if negative). The goodwill of consolidation has to be written off over a maximum period of five years.

However, this period can be prolonged if the expected useful life is thought to be greater.

GOODWILL

Goodwill can only appear in the assets when a company acquires another one and pays more than the book value (assets minus debts) of the acquired company. Therefore, following the EC Fourth Directive, goodwill can only appear when it is shown through a transaction.

The goodwill has to be amortized over a maximum period of five years unless it is reasonably considered that its useful life will be longer. In this case, the maximum period is 20 years but this must be stated in the notes to the accounts.

Like other European countries such as the United Kingdom, France, Spain, Denmark and Eire, the amortization of the goodwill is not tax-deductible.

FOREIGN CURRENCY TRANSLATION

Transactions in foreign currency are translated by using the current exchange rate at the time they are made. At the end of the financial year, monetary items are translated by using the current exchange rate on the closing day of the year.

In the case of gains or losses on foreign monetary assets, these are taken direct to the profit and loss account. However, for translation differences on foreign currency liabilities only losses and realized gains are taken through the profit and loss account. Unrealized gains are shown as a balance sheet liability, unless there is good reason to regard a gain as irreversible, in which case it may be taken to profit. Exchange differences on loans financing fixed asset construction may be treated as part of the asset cost.

ACCOUNTING FOR INFLATION

Fiscal legislation allows for the revaluation of fixed assets. To do this, revaluation ratios based on the consumer price index can be used.

These revaluations are optional and have to be made under the provision of updating laws from the Ministry of Finance which are passed annually. From the fiscal point of view, companies can only deduct 60 per cent of the additional amortization from the revalued fixed assets. However, in the annual accounts the total amortization has to be shown in spite of the fact that one part is not tax-deductible.

FIXED ASSETS

The acquisition price or production cost is the basis of valuation, with transport, insurance, starting-up costs and customs duties added to this. Also, the financial expenses of the loans which finance assets during their production can be included in the cost of the tangible fixed assets. This is only allowed for fixed assets and does not apply to current assets.

The tangible fixed assets have to be depreciated systematically over their useful life on a time or usage basis.

RESEARCH AND DEVELOPMENT

These expenses can be capitalized when there are reasonable indications that the company can benefit in the future from this research. When this is so, information must be given in the notes to the accounts and they have to be written off as soon as possible with five years being the maximum period of time allowed. If write-off takes longer, this must be made clear in the notes to the accounts.

INVENTORIES

The lower of cost or market rule applies. The market price is that of the replacement of raw materials and the net worth of producing the goods.

Not only are the direct costs included in the inventories but also the allotted part of the fixed production costs. On the other hand, the distribution, general administration and financial costs are not included.

The valuation methods accepted for inventories are the FIFO, LIFO, the weighted average, standard and other similar methods.

Retail companies can value their inventories according to the sale price minus the gross margin.

For raw materials the base stock method can be used for a determined quantity and value when the following circumstances apply: if they are not material to the company as a whole, if the balance, value or composition does not vary greatly and if they have a high rotation.

In current contracts it is possible to calculate the profits gained before the operation has been completed by using the percentage of completion method. This method is not compulsory, however, and if preferred the profits can be calculated at the end of the operation.

LEASING

As Magalhães states (1990, p. 267) accounting for leasing in Portugal is a clear example of the application of the principle of the priority of substance over form in accordance with NIC 17.

From the point of view of leasing, when it is a financial lease, whereby there is an option to buy in the contract, the value of what is being leased is included in the assets and the liabilities. As the rentals are paid, they are allocated between repayment of the liability and the financial costs which are shown in the profit and loss account as expenses. The assets which have been capitalized will be depreciated depending on their period of useful life, or the term stated in the lease contract if it is not certain that the option to buy is going to be employed.

In the case of operating leases the rental payments are accounted as expenses as they become due.

DEFERRED TAXATION

As has been shown previously, fiscal legislation in Portugal has a considerable influence on accounting. This is especially so with regard to the obsolescence of stocks, revaluation and amortization of fixed stocks, provisions for depreciation of assets, confidential expenses, cultural donations, capital gains and capital loss and tax contingencies. Some of these are hereby set out in further detail:

1. Provisions for stock obsolescence: These are set out in much greater detail in the tax regulations than in the General Accounting Plan (POC).

2. Revaluation of fixed assets: Only 60 per cent of the additional amortization is tax-deductible. However, in the annual accounts all the amortization is to be accounted for, whether tax-deductible or not.

3. Amortization of fixed assets: The methods allowed are the straight-line and decreasing methods. The method of the sum of digits is not allowed. Accelerated depreciation is allowed when a fixed asset is used daily in two or more shifts. Fixed assets which are worth less than 20,000 escudos can be passed directly as expenses from the moment they are acquired.

4. Provisions for the depreciation of investments: These provisions are not tax-deductible. This implies a contradiction between the aim of a true and fair view and the tax regulations.

5. Amortization of the goodwill: This is not tax-deductible as has been shown previously.

6. Provisions for insolvencies: Some 25 per cent of the debts which expired between six months and one year previously are tax-deductible. After two years, some 100 per cent can be deducted. In the case of the former there are two exceptions in which there is no possible tax deduction:

   (a) when the client is a Government-dependent company

   (b) when there is a minimum stake of 10 per cent in the client's capital or vice versa.

   When the client goes bankrupt the total of the balance is considered a tax loss.

7. Confidential expenses: Those expenses which are not revealed require an additional 10 per cent even if the company has losses.

8. Cultural donations: These are limited to 0.2 per cent of the net income of the financial year unless the receiver is the State or a state institution in which case there are no limits.

PENSION FUNDS

To calculate how much is paid into pension schemes, actuarial techniques are used. In these transfers, up to 15 per cent of the salary cost is tax-deductible. The transfers are accounted as an expense in the profit and loss account and as a debt in the liabilities on the balance sheet.

CONCLUSION

The Portuguese accounting system is greatly influenced by the French tradition both in its structural norms as well as its connections with the fiscal system. However, in matters such as voluntary acceptance of the principle of the substance over form concept, some English influence is also apparent.

REFERENCES

Fernandes, R. (1990) 'Le crédit-bail au Portugal: caractérisation et importance économique', *Cahiers de Droit Fiscal International*, Vol. LXXV.

Fernandes, L. (1992) 'Portugal' in Alexander, D. and Archer, S. *The European Accounting Guide*, pp. 457–511, Academic Press.

Magalhães, R.M. (1990) 'Considerações sobre a contabilização do leasing', *Jornal do Técnico de Contas e da Empresa*, Vol. 302 November.

Price Waterhouse (1991) *Comparability of Financial Statements. International Survey.*

CHAPTER 14

Spain

ABBREVIATIONS

AECA	Asociación Española de Contabilidad y Administración
ICAC	Instituto de Contabilidad y Auditoria de Cuentas
ICJC	Instituto de Censores Jurados de Cuentas
PGC	Plan General de Contabilidad
ROAC	Registro Oficial de Auditorias de Cuentas

INTRODUCTION **Accounting regulation in Spain has developed rapidly as a result of Spain's joining the European Community in 1986. Since then, the whole range of accounting legislation has been reformed in line with the EC directives. Until this time, accounting practices in Spain have varied substantially from most other countries (see Price Waterhouse 1991). The review of Spanish accounting below excludes the special rules applying to banks and insurance companies.**

ACCOUNTING REGULATION

In Spain, accounting regulation is the responsibility of the Ministry for the Economy and Finance. The Ministry has created a special body to fulfil this role, the *Instituto de Contabilidad y Auditoria de Cuentas* (ICAC).

Business activity is regulated by the commercial code and company law (see Ribalta et al. 1990). These were reformed in 1989 in line with the EC directives. This legislation includes the basis for accounting principles, presentation of the accounts, auditing, and publication of the accounts. Detail is provided in the *Plan General de Contabilidad* (PGC) of 1990, largely based on the French Plan of 1982.

The plan includes:

1. Compulsory sections on accounting principles, valuation bases, and accounting formats.

2. Voluntary sections on accounting definitions and ledger accounts.

Spain first followed the French Plan approach in 1973, without the same compulsion.

ICAC periodically publishes a *Boletín*, which may amend or add to accounting regulation. ICAC also promotes the publication of books and papers on accounting issues.

Legislation in 1989 also included provision for public filing of Spanish accounts.

A Royal Decree of 1991 implemented the EC Seventh Directive on Group Accounts.

THE ACCOUNTING PROFESSION

ICAC is responsible for overseeing auditing as well as accounting matters. For this purpose an official register of authorized auditors, the *Registro Oficial de Auditores de Cuentas* (ROAC) is maintained. In practice most authorized auditors join one of two private professional bodies:

1. The *Registro de Economistas Auditores* (REA)

2. The *Instituto de Censores Jurados de Cuentas* (ICJC).

These bodies both formulate auditing standards, but these are not binding on auditors until officially adopted by ICAC.

Gabas et al. (1990) have traced the growing influence of a private sector accounting body, the *Asociación Española de Contabilidad y Administración* (AECA). AECA, a voluntary body, draws its membership from accountants, auditors, and academics. AECA develops recommendations on accounting issues. Although without legal backing, in practice these are highly influential. Often ICAC uses AECA recommendations as the basis for developing regulations. The universities and business schools are also influential on Spanish accounting development.

AUDITING

The auditing law of 1988 and subsequent regulations of 1990 implement the EC Eighth Directive and cover the issues of which businesses must be audited, auditor qualifications, and the audit process.

The basic objective of an audit is to form an opinion on whether the accounts provide a 'true and fair view' (*imagen fiel*) of the equity and the financial position of the business and on whether the accounts show the profits and flows of funds in the period under review in compliance with legislation. The auditor must also check that the directors' report is in accordance with the accounts. In addition, the audit report must cover a range of detailed issues of compliance.

The audit requirement applies to large and medium-sized companies, being those which fall above two of the following three size limits:

Total assets	230 million pesetas
Total sales	480 million pesetas
Number of employees	50

These criteria include some 70,000 out of about 1,000,000 Spanish companies. The audit requirement also covers banks, companies in the finance and insurance sector, and all those where at least five per cent of shareholders call for an audit.

In addition to the audit report on the annual accounts, the auditors must also report in a variety of special situations, such as auditing the accounts in the case of a merger or demerger, and valuing shares in the case where the company regulations control transfers of shares.

Auditors, who must be totally independent, are appointed by the shareholders for a period of between three and nine years. They may be reappointed within a total nine-year period but, after that, may not be reappointed for at least three years. Auditors cannot be dismissed within their specified period of office unless there is 'good cause'.

To qualify for inclusion in ROAC, the Register of Auditors, it is necessary to:

1. Have a university degree.
2. Gain three years' practical experience including appropriate training programmes.
3. Pass a final professional exam recognized by the state.

The audit report is deposited with the registry of companies with the annual accounts.

CONVENTIONS

In line with the EC Fourth Directive, the primary objective of the annual accounts is to present an *imagen fiel*, literally 'faithful image', the Spanish equivalent of the English term 'true and fair view'. Spanish accountants have studied the English language literature to ascertain the significance of this term and, as discussed in Chapter 3 above, have found that there is no clear, unambiguous, definition. Moreover, the implication that accounting principles should evolve from professional accountants rather than explicit legislation is in conflict with the Spanish accounting tradition and the spirit of Roman law. Tua Pereda (1985, p. 48) refers to 'Controversies whose origin is nothing other than the differences between continental and Anglo-Saxon legal approaches'.

However, the PGC follows the Fourth Directive in requiring that in order to ensure an *imagen fiel* any necessary extra information must be given in the notes to the accounts and, in extreme cases, the accounts must depart from specific accounting rules with a full explanation. Amat et al. (1991, p. 114) offer a diagram (Fig. 14.1) to summarize this rule.

Despite its ambiguity, the *imagen fiel* requirement is seen as more important than the previous prescription that accounts should show *claridad* (clarity) and *exactitud* (precision).

Fig. 14.1 Summary of the *imagen fiel* rule

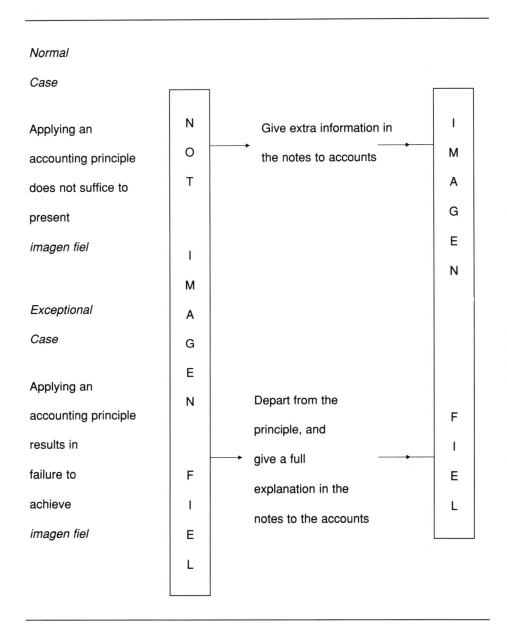

The PGC includes nine other specific conventions:

1. Prudence, that profits should only be accounted for when realized while losses should be accounted for as soon as their incidence is anticipated. This principle takes priority over others.
2. Going concern.

3. *Registro*, that a transaction must be recorded in the accounting records as soon as it gives rise to rights and obligations.

4. Historic cost, being that historic cost should be the basis of measurement unless the market value is lower.

5. Accruals, that income and expenditure should be shown in the period to which it relates rather than when received or paid.

6. Matching, that as far as possible expenditure should be matched with related income.

7. No set-off of assets against liabilities or income against expenditure.

8. Consistency, so that accounting policies may only be changed if the circumstances that gave rise to their choice change. The notes to the accounts must explain and quantify the effects of any change in accounting policy.

9. Materiality.

PRESENTATION

The PGC of 1990 provides for annual accounts to consist of a balance sheet, profit and loss account and notes alongside which a director's report is also required. Cea (1990, p. 422) observes that the formats provided in the PGC are somewhat inflexible. Two models are laid out, one full, the other abridged. Companies may use the abridged format if they fall below two of the following three size limits:

	For the balance sheet and notes to the accounts	For the profit and loss account
Total assets	230 million pesetas	920 million pesetas
Total Sales	480 million pesetas	1920 million pesetas
Number of employees	50	250

It is interesting to observe that a business that is required to present a full balance sheet and notes may be allowed to present an abridged profit and loss account. As Lizcano (1990) points out, the structure of the full and abridged formats is similar, the difference between the two being in the amount of detail required.

The abridged balance sheet shows:

Assets	*Liabilities*
(A) Calls on Share Capital not yet made	(A) Equity
(B) Fixed Assets	(B) Deferred Income
(C) Prepaid Expenses	(C) Provisions for contingencies and costs
(D) Current Assets	(D) Long-term creditors
	(E) Short-term creditors

The profit and loss account is presented on a 'type of expenditure basis'. It is analysed under three broad headings:

1. Income and expenditure from ordinary operating activities
2. Finance income and expenditure
3. Income and expenditure seen as 'extraordinary'. This term covers all items outside the ordinary business activities and is therefore akin to what in the UK would be termed 'exceptional' as well as 'extraordinary' items. Thus a summarized profit and loss format would identify:

   (a) An operating profit and loss
   (b) An ordinary profit and loss, after finance items
   (c) Profit and loss after 'extraordinary' items
   (d) Profit and loss after tax.

In addition, companies may, if they wish, produce a profit and loss account on an operational basis.

Further details must be included in the notes to the accounts. In the following list of topics the asterisks (*) show those also required in the abridged model:

1. The business activity*
2. Bases of presentation*
3. Appropriations of profit*
4. Valuation bases*
5. Establishment costs*
6. Intangible fixed assets*
7. Tangible fixed assets*
8. Financial investments*
9. Stock
10. Movements in equity*
11. Grants
12. Pension provisions
13. Other provisions
14. Non-trading debts*
15. Tax position
16. Guarantees
17. Income and expenditure*
18. Transactions with directors*
19. Post balance sheet events
20. A statement of balance sheet changes.

The accounts must be supported by a directors' report. Basically this discusses developments in, and prospects for, the business. In particular it considers research and development activity.

Each year the accounts and directors' report must be filed at the companies' registry, where they are open to public inspection. The PGC does not impose any special requirements on listed companies, but the stock exchange requires three-monthly interim accounts.

CONSOLIDATION

The requirements to present group accounts is a recent one in Spain, in response to the EC Seventh Directive. A Royal Decree on consolidated accounts in 1991 drew heavily on IAS 27 and IAS 28.

Group accounts are required where two of the following three limits are exceeded:

Total assets	2,300 million pesetas
Total sales	4,800 million pesetas
Number of employees	500

A holding company is held to have an investment in a subsidiary where more than 50 per cent of voting shares are held, or where it controls the majority of the board of directors. Exemptions from the obligation to consolidate a subsidiary arise where:

1. The subsidiary is not material.
2. The subsidiary is under some form of legal administration, having suspended payment of obligations.
3. Excessive expense is involved in obtaining necessary information.
4. The subsidiary has been acquired with a view to early resale.
5. The activities of the subsidiary are very different from those of the group.

Consolidation is on a line-by-line basis. For associated companies, where 20 to 50 per cent of the equity is held, the equity method is used, for 'multigroup' holdings, where two or more companies exercise joint control, proportional consolidation is used.

GOODWILL

Where the purchase price of a business exceeds the net book value of the assets acquired, the excess may be applied in writing up the assets of the business acquired to their market value. Any remaining excess should be amortized over five years or, if justified in a note to the accounts, up to a maximum of ten years. As Socias (1991, p. 204) observes, these requirements are less flexible than in most other European countries.

If there is a goodwill balance in the accounts, then dividend payments are not permitted if they reduce distributable profits below the goodwill balance.

FOREIGN CURRENCY TRANSLATION

For foreign operations the normal approach is the closing rate method, with translation differences taken direct to a special reserve in the balance sheet. Where the activities of a subsidiary are fully dependent on those of the Spanish holding company, the monetary/non-monetary method is used, with translation differences shown in the profit and loss account. Foreign currency items in a company's own accounts are entered at the exchange rate prevailing when the transaction occurs. At each balance sheet date monetary items are retranslated at the closing rate. Losses on translation are taken to the profit and loss account, as are realized gains. Unrealized gains are carried forward as a liability in the balance sheet.

INFLATION ACCOUNTING

Spain has no experience of applying a comprehensive inflation accounting system. From time to time, as a response to the inflation problem, *actualización* has been allowed. This involves permitted revaluations, tax-free, by Government determined indices. Subsequent related depreciation is then tax-allowable. The most recent general *actualización* was in 1983. In 1992, an interesting new development was announced, that *actualización* would be permitted each year under a special tax incentive scheme in the Basque region. Thus, as a result of Spain's close links between tax and accounting rules, just one region of Spain will have a regular system of asset revaluation.

Until 1989 it was common for businesses to revalue their assets up to original historical cost. Such revaluation surpluses had to be taken through the profit and loss account, and provided a mechanism for extending tax losses. Such revaluation surpluses may still affect Spanish accounts.

FIXED ASSETS

Fixed assets are recorded at cost, including all costs relating to acquisition and installation. Moreover, finance costs relating to the period of construction can also be included in the cost of fixed assets, but not current assets. Depreciation must be on a systematic basis over the useful life on a time or usage basis, and is no longer tied to rates permitted for tax purposes.

RESEARCH AND DEVELOPMENT

Capitalization of research and development costs is permitted when there is good reason to expect commercial success. There must also be clearly identified projects and related costs. Amortization should be over as short a period as possible, with a maximum of five years. As with goodwill, dividends should not reduce distributable profits below the level of this intangible asset.

STOCK AND WORK IN PROGRESS

The lower of cost and market value rule applies. Market value is the lower of net realizable value and replacement cost, an example of the strength of the prudence concept in Spanish accounting. Cost includes direct costs and some production overheads.

The PGC is flexible in permitting FIFO, LIFO, weighted average, or other similar methods. However for tax purposes only FIFO or weighted average are acceptable, giving rise to potential deferred tax timing differences.

LEASING

There is an interesting contrast between lessor and lessee accounting. Lessors do not distinguish between finance and operating leases, following legal form in all cases with the leased asset recorded in fixed assets and being subject to depreciation. Lessees, by contrast, distinguish between:

1. Finance leases, defined as those where there is an option to purchase at a bargain price, are capitalized as discussed in Chapter 3 above.
2. Operating leases are accounted for in line with their legal form, with rentals charged to the profit and loss account.

DEFERRED TAXATION

The reforms of Spanish accounting in line with EC directives has broken the traditional link between accounting and tax rules. For example, Cañibano (1990) comments that the PGC is no longer a 'fiscal instrument'. Timing differences can arise from such items as depreciation, stock valuation, and leasing (see Carenys and Sambola 1991, pp. 227–41). Deferred taxation should therefore be provided in full by the liability method, although deferred tax assets should only be shown where future recovery is confidently expected.

PENSIONS

The requirement to recognize future pension liabilities in the accounts only came into Spanish accounting with the PGC of 1989. As a transitional arrangement, companies have been given the following time periods to accumulate provision for the full actuarial liability for pensions:

Employees still working	15 years
Retired employees	7 years

POST BALANCE SHEET EVENTS

Material non-adjusting events must be shown in the notes to the accounts and the directors' report.

CONCLUSION

Spain's membership of the European Community has brought about major changes in accounting. The main innovations have been:

1. The formulation of a new plan with a major expansion in disclosure requirements and a move away from a tax-based accounting system.

2. The general introduction of a requirement for consolidated accounts for groups above a certain size.

3. The introduction of a compulsory audit for large and medium-sized businesses.

While the formal regulation of accounting and auditing remains firmly in the hands of the Government, the Spanish accounting body has played a major part, particularly through AECA, in developing and improving audit and accounting practices.

REFERENCES

Amat, O., Carenys, J., Monfort, E., Prior, D. and Sambola, R. (1991) *Comprender el Plan General de Contabilidad*, Ediciones Gestión 2000 SA.

Cañibano, L. (1990) 'El proyecto del Plan General de Contabilidad', AECA, *Revista Española de Financiación y Contabilidad*.

Carenys, J. and Sambola, R. (1991) *Guía de Aplicación Práctica del Nuevo Plan General de Contabilidad*, Ediciones Gestión 2000 SA.

Cea, J.L. (1990) *Revisión Panorámica de los Modelos de Cuentas Anuales*, AECA.

Equipo Fundemi (1991) *Manual de Contabilidad*, Ediciones Gestión 2000.

Gabas, F., Condor, V., Latinez, J.A. and Pina, V. (1990) 'Private accounting standard setting in Spain', XIII Annual Congress of the European Accounting Association.

Lizcano, J. (1990) 'Cuentas anuales: balance y cuenta de pérdidas y ganancias', AECA, *Revista Española de Contabilidad y Financiación*.

Price Waterhouse (1991) *Comparability of Financial Statements. International Survey*.

Ribalta, J. et al. (1990) *La Nueva Legislación Mercantil*, Fomento Formación, Ediciones Gestión 2000.

Socias, A. (1991) *La Normalización Contable en el Reino Unido, Francia, Alemania y España*, AECA.

Tua Pereda, J. (1985) 'Los principios contables de la regulación profesional al ámbito internacional', *Revista Española de Financiación y Contabilidad*, January–April, pp. 25–56.

CHAPTER 15

Sweden

ABBREVIATIONS

AB	Aktiebolag	– Limited Liability Company
ABL	Aktiebolagslagen	– The Companies Act
BFL	Bok föringslagen	– The Accountancy Act
BFN	Bok föringsnämnden	– Accounting Standards Board
FAR	Föreningen Auktoriserade Revisörer	– Professional Accountants' Body

INTRODUCTION

Sweden is home to a substantial number of multinational enterprises, out of proportion to the size of its population and its economy. These rely on international capital markets (see Hornell and Vahlne, 1986, for a discussion on how this situation has developed). This leads to a demand for high quality financial reports in line with best international practice. At the same time Swedish accounting law is dominated by the aim of keeping accounting rules in line with tax law. In the face of this conflict the Swedish accounting profession contrives to produce financial reports that command international respect. Stilling et al. (1984) compared some 175 companies from 19 countries. They found that overall Swedish companies had the second best record compliance with International Accounting Standards, with Volvo A.B. as the best overall company. It should be emphasized that this high level of disclosure is based on a survey of large, multinational, listed companies – the category of Swedish company that Cooke (1989) has identified as having particularly high quality disclosure.

ACCOUNTING REGULATIONS

The most common form of business organization in Sweden is the *Aktiebolag* (AB), the limited liability company. The Companies Act 1975 (*Aktiebolagslagen*, ABL) and the Accounting Act 1976 (*Bokföringslagen*, BFL) currently provide the legal framework for accounting. In 1990 the Swedish government set up a committee to review the Companies Act and propose amendments in line with European integration.

The Accounting Act 1976 established an Accounting Standards Board (*Bokföringsnämnden*, BFN). This is a body under the Ministry of Justice made up of representatives including the accounting profession, the national tax board, the industrial organizations, the trade unions, and academics, and is supported by a small, full-time secretariat. The board advises the Government and parliament on proposed accounting legislation. It also issues public, non-mandatory, recommendations on accounting matters.

FAR, the professional body for auditors (see below), issues recommendations on accounting and auditing matters. Although not mandatory, these recommendations are highly influential.

During the late 1980s the Accounting Standards Board, FAR, and the Swedish Federation of Industries joined together to form an organization to produce high quality accounting standards for public companies. This new body, the Swedish Financial Accounting Standards Board (*Redovisningsrådet*), issued its first statement, on consolidated accounts, in 1991.

THE ACCOUNTING PROFESSION

Since 1973, the Government has handled the task of authorizing public accountants through the Board of Trade (*Kommerskollegium*).

The qualification of 'authorized public accountant' (*auktoriserade revisörer*) is granted on the basis of an approved relevant degree and five years' professional audit experience. The lower qualification of 'registered accountant' is granted on the basis of relevant technical educational qualifications and five years' experience. There is a professional body for authorized public accountants, the *Föreningen Auktoriserade Revisörer* (FAR), with some 1,400 members. Although membership of FAR is not a legal obligation for authorized public accountants, most do in fact join, even though fees are high. FAR has a firm ethical code, and is notably more speedy than the Board of Trade in taking action in the rare instances of erring members. FAR publishes audit and accounting recommendations, and also offers a range of useful publications in English explaining the Swedish accounting environment.

Academic accounting theorists have a strong influence on the development of Swedish accounting practice. In the first half of the twentieth century the first professors of accounting at both the Stockholm School of Economics and the Göteborg School of Economics were German, and both their successors had studied in Germany under Schmalenbach and Schmidt respectively. This strong German influence helps to explain Sweden's traditional attachment to a binding link between tax and accounting rules. From the 1960s onwards, particularly under the leadership of Professor Sven-Erik Johansson at the Stockholm School of Economics, the influence of the leading American theorists has become stronger. Jönsson (1984) sees this move from German to American academic influence as explaining the powerful role of FAR as a private sector body interpreting 'good accounting practice' (pp. 13–14).

One other aspect of Swedish life is important in understanding how Sweden's accounting profession works. As Lawrence and Spybey (1986) observe: 'The Swedish ethic of competence and the Swedes' attachment to acting correctly may appear to be a vague formula, but it is important. It leads to people doing the right things for the right reasons' (p. 122).

This analysis is compatible with our own experience of interviewing members of Sweden's Accounting Standards Board. In particular:

1. Differences of opinion do not normally emerge between representatives of different interest groups.

2. Non-accountant members of the board see their role as a technical one. For example, a trade union nominee referred to drawing on his own accounting training, and the technical expertise of his accountant members.

It is because of this honest pursuit of a common aim that Swedish accountants can achieve highly professional reports based on guidance from a variety of authorities, some compulsory and some voluntary.

AUDITING

All Swedish limited liability companies must appoint qualified auditors. For large companies, and certain other sensitive categories, the auditor must hold the higher level of qualification of the *auktoriserade revisörer*.

An interesting feature of the Swedish audit report was identified by Archer et al. (1989, p. 73). In a sample of 18 Swedish audit reports they found that they were signed as follows:

Only audit firm name shown	1
Only name of responsible audit partnership shown	11
Both firm name and individual name shown	6
	18

To the international analyst the name of the accounting firm is likely to be more interesting. However, in the context of a society like that of Sweden with a close knit business community, knowing the name of the partner personally responsible for the audit is likely to give an insight into the way in which work has been done.

CONVENTIONS

Sweden does not have a 'true and fair view' requirement but does use the term 'god redovisningssed', which translates loosely as 'generally accepted accounting principles'.

PRESENTATION

Swedish accountants face a dilemma. On the one hand, the benefits of tax laws that allow artificially conservative expense levels can only be enjoyed if those expense levels are recorded on the face of the accounts. Sweden's professional accounting body refers to 'the unique stranglehold Swedish taxation law has on financial reporting practices' (*Föreningen Auktoriserade Revisörer* 1988, p. 2). On the other hand, international capital markets demand economically realistic accounts based on best international practice. The highly simplified Example 15.1 illustrates this dilemma.

Example 15.1

Kungshatt A B has the following simplified income position for the year to 31 December 19X1.

	SKr millions
Sales	500
Cost of sales	420
Depreciation	26

In addition, extra tax allowances of SKr 20 million cost of sales and SKr 24 million depreciation are available. The tax rate is 50%

	Income Statements	
	Internationally acceptable accounting	*Tax based accounting*
	SKr m	SKr m
Sales	500	500
Cost of sales	(420)	(440)
Depreciation	(26)	(50)
Profit before tax	54	10
Tax at 50%	27	5
Net income	27	5

We can see from the example that on a 'tax-based accounting' system profit before tax is less than 20 per cent of that on an 'internationally acceptable accounting' basis. On the other hand, preparation of the accounts on an 'internationally acceptable accounting' basis would increase the legal obligation to pay tax by a corresponding amount. Swedish accountants have solved this problem by developing the format shown in Example 15.2. This format effectively splits the income statement into two parts:

1. Down to the line 'profit before appropriations' the income statement follows internationally accepted accounting principles.

2. In the 'appropriations' section of the income statement are shown the differences between profit computed on a normal accounting basis and profit computed on a tax basis. The double entry is completed by equivalent adjustments to the 'untaxed reserves', shown on the balance sheet between equity and liabilities.

Thus the need to show profit on a basis in line with internationally acceptable accounting practice is met by the 'profit before appropriations' figure. However, after the 'appropriations', the final 'profit before tax' is on a 'tax-based accounting' basis that results in the desired tax obligation.

This form of presentation, devised in the 1960s, recognized in the Accounting Act 1975, and followed as an example by other Scandinavian countries, has enabled Swedish companies to maintain a high quality of disclosure while complying with national tax-based accounting legislation. Choi and Mueller (1984) commend this Swedish approach as a 'promising model for bridging the gap between domestic and international user needs' (p. 307).

However, as Sweden enters the 1990s a new approach to this problem has emerged. By way of illustration, the 1989 Volvo accounts were presented in the style shown above. In 1990, however, the *consolidated* income statement was prepared on a basis that excluded these 'appropriations' altogether. In the consolidated balance sheet the 'untaxed reserves' have been recorded as part of the ordinary equity after a transfer to deferred taxation at the tax rate predicted for the coming year (30 per cent for 1991). This approach is legal and has no tax effects as long as it is only applied to the *consolidated* accounts. In the company's own accounts the traditional approach outlined above continues to be followed.

Example 15.2 The Swedish format simplified

	SKr m
Sales	500
Cost of sales	(420)
Depreciation	(26)
Profit before appropriations	54
Appropriations:	
Increase in inventory reserve	(20)
Book depreciation	(24)
Profit before tax	10
Tax	5
Net income	5

CONSOLIDATED ACCOUNTS

The Companies Act provides a brief requirement that a company with subsidiaries should present consolidated accounts in accordance with the accepted accounting policies for the parent and subsidiary companies' accounts. A subsidiary is an entity in which the parent company holds, directly or indirectly, more than 50 per cent of the voting shares. When the parent company has both a decisive influence over an entity and a considerable share in its results then that entity will also be a subsidiary.

FAR has issued detailed guidance on consolidation techniques. Acquisition accounting is normally used, but merger accounting is permitted where a group has been formed after a non-cash issue.

Swedish multinationals operating in the European Community have faced a major problem as a result of the Seventh Directive. This is because 'subgroups' operating within the European Community are obliged to prepare their own consolidated accounts unless the ultimate holding company outside the Community prepares consolidated accounts on a basis 'equivalent' to the requirements of the Seventh Directive. At first it was thought that Swedish law effectively barred equity accounting for associated companies, as required in the Seventh Directive (see above).

For example, Ernst and Whinney (1984) bluntly state that for Sweden a 'major difference from the Directive' is that 'equity-accounting of associates (is) not permitted' (p. 49). However, in 1986 FAR issued an exposure draft providing for equity accounting treatment for associated companies, but *only* in the consolidated accounts. Some critics have argued that this in turn is a breach of the legal provision that consolidated accounts should follow the accounting policies for the parent and subsidiary companies' accounts. However, an increasing number of Swedish companies are following the approach of the FAR exposure draft. This is an interesting example of the European Community's power to influence the accounting practices of major trading partners.

GOODWILL

The Accounting Law provides that where goodwill arises in a company's own accounts (e.g. on acquisition of an incorporated business) then it may be recorded as a fixed asset, of which at least 10 per cent should be amortized each year. An FAR recommendation states that consolidation goodwill should be treated on a similar basis, and be recorded as a fixed asset and amortized with a maximum life of ten years. This seems to be the most common practice, although in recent years there has been a tendency for some companies to use longer estimated lives up to 40 years. Some companies write off goodwill on acquisition against the equity.

FAR recommend that negative goodwill, often translated from the Swedish as 'badwill', should be accounted for in a way that depends on how it arose. Cooke (1988, p. 85) cites three examples of ways in which Swedish companies treat negative goodwill:

1. Deduction from acquired fixed assets.

2. Inclusion in restricted equity.

3. Recording as a long-term debt to be released to equity over a number of years.

FOREIGN CURRENCY TRANSLATION

An accounting standards board recommendation provides that foreign currency monetary items should be translated at the closing rate. Exchange differences should be shown in the profit or loss account except that unrealized exchange gains on long-term monetary items should be shown in an untaxed currency reserve in the balance sheet, and unrealized losses in the same or a closely related currency should be set off against any related unrealized gains on the untaxed currency reserve.

The recommendation also covers a range of 'hedging arrangements'.

FAR have issued a proposed recommendation on the translation of foreign subsidiary accounts that closely follows IAS 21 (see above).

An 'independent subsidiary company' is one where operations are substantially independent of the current company, even if they are in the same business. The accounts should be translated using the closing rate method and any translation difference should be taken direct to the equity.

An 'integrated subsidiary company' is one where operations are closely linked to the parent company. The accounts should be translated using the temporal method and the resulting exchange of differences (normally only relating to monetary items) should be included in the consolidated income statement.

Subsidiaries operating in areas of hyperinflation should be translated by the temporal method. However, the alternative of translating inflation adjusted accounts by the closing rate method is permitted.

INFLATION ACCOUNTING

In 1980 FAR produced an exposure draft on inflation accounting. This was based on the measurement of non-monetary assets at current cost in the balance sheet, with corresponding adjustments to depreciation and cost of sales in the computation of current operating profit. Realized and unrealized gains/losses were then to be added to arrive at current cost profit. Several versions of the income statement were then suggested, including the possibility of adjustments to reflect the amount necessary to maintain shareholders' equity in terms of general purchasing power. Thus the possibility of a 'current cost' basis of measurement combined with a 'real terms' capital maintenance concept was put forward. This was a distinct advance on the worldwide inflation accounting debate which had tended to polarize between CPP and CCA-type solutions. In this sense Tweedie and

Whittington (1984) argue that 'Sweden could claim to be a world leader in inflation accounting practice' (p. 224).

Ostman (1984, p. 37) describes the range of academic research in the 1970s underlying this achievement. However, as in other developed countries where inflation has been kept under control, Swedish companies have generally chosen not to develop inflation accounting.

TANGIBLE FIXED ASSETS

Normally a fixed asset should not be recorded at an amount in excess of cost. The Accounting Act does permit revaluation to offset a write-down of other fixed assets where there are special reasons for the offset. The Companies Act extends those provisions to allow revaluations to be used for bonus share issues or for appropriation to a non-distributable revaluation reserve. In practice most revaluations in Sweden apply to real estate and investments (see for example *Föreningen Auktoriserade Revisörer* 1988, p. 83).

The Accounting Act requires that fixed assets be depreciated on a systematic basis. In practice, the straight-line method is normally used. In the property industry it is common not to depreciate investment properties, or to apply a symbolic rate of one per cent. An FAR recommendation permits capitalization of actual interest costs paid as part of the cost of construction and installation, but does not permit capitalization of imputed interest costs.

RESEARCH AND DEVELOPMENT

Section 17 of the Accounting Act allows the cost of expenditure on items such as technical assistance, research and development, test runs, and market research to be recorded as a fixed asset. Items capitalized under this heading tend to be shown in the balance sheet as 'Research and Development' or 'Organizational Expense'. At least 20 per cent of such costs must be amortized each year unless a longer write-off period is justified by 'special circumstances'. BFN have issued detailed guidance on the circumstances in which R&D capitalization may be justified.

In practice capitalization of R&D expenditure is rare because immediate write-off is fully tax-allowable. Swedish companies also tend to provide minimal accounting disclosure on research and development for competitive reasons (see Cooke 1988, p. 97).

STOCK AND WORK IN PROGRESS

The accounting law requires stock and work in progress to be shown at the lower of cost and market value. Market value is normally taken to be net realizable value, but is sometimes taken to be replacement cost less any appropriate deduction for obsolescence. FIFO is the most common basis for computing cost and is favoured by tax law. For manufactured goods, cost is computed on the basis of absorption costing.

An FAR recommendation permits the 'percentage of completion' basis for long-term contracts provided that the revenue and costs to completion are determinable. In practice, most companies apply the 'completed contract' method.

LEASING

The only official guidance on leasing in Sweden is in an FAR recommendation. This advocates capitalization of finance leases only where there is an *obligation* for the lessee to purchase the related asset. There is also provision for disclosure of the estimated cost of leased assets and the rental charge where a 'significant proportion' of the company's fixed assets are held under leases.

DEFERRED TAXATION

Neither the Accounting Act nor the Companies Act recognizes deferred taxation. This is not surprising, given that the bottom line of the income statement represents taxable income. However, deferred taxation may appear in the consolidated accounts because of consolidation adjustments and because of foreign subsidies.

PENSIONS

Most of Swedish companies' pension costs relate to fully funded schemes run jointly by the employers' associations and the trade unions. Such costs are clearly identifiable as the amount payable into the fund each year. Where employers take direct responsibility for pension arrangements there is little explicit guidance in the Accounting Act on accounting arrangements, but FAR have issued a recommendation that provision should be made for the entire pension obligation on an actuarial basis.

POST BALANCE SHEET EVENTS

The Companies Act requires that the annual report includes information on material events after the year end or events that significantly affect the company's financial position or income.

CONCLUSION

In accounting, Sweden, as in many aspects of its social policy, has developed a distinctive style of its own. Drawing on a strong academic accounting tradition that includes both German and American influences, Sweden's accountants have contrived to reconcile a tax-based highly legalized approach to accounting law with the demands of the international capital markets.

REFERENCES

Archer, S., Dufour, J.B. and McLeay, S. (1989) *Audit Reports in the Financial Statements of European Multinational Companies. A Comparative Study*, Institute of Chartered Accountants in England and Wales.

Choi, F.D.S. and Mueller, G.G. (1984) *International Accounting*, Prentice Hall.

Cooke, T.E. (1988) *European Financial Reporting*, Institute of Chartered Accountants in England and Wales.

Cooke, T.E. (1989) 'Disclosure in the Corporate Annual Reports of Swedish Companies,' *Accounting and Business Research*, Spring, pp. 113–24.

Ernst and Whinney (1984) *The Impact of the Seventh Directive*, Financial Times Business Information.

Föreningen Auktoriserade Revisörer (1988) *Survey of Accounting Practices in Larger Swedish Companies 1987*.

Hearlin, S. and Peterssohn, E. (1991) 'Sweden' in Alexander, D. and Archer, S. (eds) *European Accounting Guide*, pp. 767–824, Academic Press.

Hornell, E. and Vahlne, J.E. (1986) *Multinationals: The Swedish Case*, Croom Helm.

Jönsson, S. (1984) 'Accounting elite and accounting policy making – the Swedish case', *Scandinavian Journal of Management Studies*, August, pp. 3–32.

Lawrence, P. and Spybey, T. (1986) *Management and Society in Sweden*, Routledge & Kegan Paul.

Ostman, L. (1984) 'Some impressions of accounting research in Scandinavia during the 1970s', in Hopwood, A.G. and Schreuder, H. (eds) *European Contributions to Accounting Research*, Free University Press, Amsterdam.

Stilling, P., Norton, R. and Hopkins, L. (1984) *Financial Times World Accounting Survey*, Financial Times Business Information.

Tweedie, D. and Whittington, G. (1984) *The Debate on Inflation Accounting*, Cambridge University Press.

CHAPTER 16

The United Kingdom

ABBREVIATIONS

ASB	Accounting Standards Board
ASC	Accounting Standards Committee
AIA	Association of International Accountants
CACA	Chartered Association of Certified Accountants
CCAB	Consultative Committee of Accounting Bodies
CIMA	Chartered Institute of Management Accountants
CIPFA	Chartered Institute of Public Finance and Accountancy
ED	Exposure Draft
FRC	Financial Reporting Council
FRS	Financial Reporting Standard
ICAEW	Institute of Chartered Accountants in England and Wales
ICAS	Institute of Chartered Accountants in Scotland
I ComA	Institute of Company Accountants
RQB	Registered Qualifying Body
RSB	Registered Supervisory Body
SSAP	Statement of Standard Accounting Practice
UITF	Urgent Issues Task Force

INTRODUCTION

The United Kingdom (UK) has a number of distinguishing features in its accounting environment that make the country distinctive within the European Community:

1. **A strong and independent accounting profession.**
2. **A tradition of broad legal requirements with detailed accounting methods formulated by private sector regulators.**
3. **Strong links with US accountants, sharing a common language and with close connections between US and UK offices of the international accounting firms.**

THE ACCOUNTING PROFESSION

Six UK accounting bodies each have the status of incorporation by a Royal Charter and have formed a joint representative body, the Consultative Committee of Accounting Bodies (CCAB). These are:

1. The Institute of Chartered Accountants of Scotland (ICAS) which traces its roots back to the Edinburgh Institute founded in 1853.

2. The Institute of Chartered Accountants in England and Wales (ICAEW) founded in 1880.

3. The Institute of Chartered Accountants in Ireland, founded in 1888.

The above three bodies are independent, but in practice are similar in character. Almost all of their students train in public practice, but after qualifying about half remain in public practice while about half move to other forms of employment.

4. The Chartered Association of Certified Accountants (CACA), founded in 1904 as the London Society of Accountants, allows students to train in public practice or in commercial organizations.

Under company law members of each of the above bodies may be appointed to audit the accounts of a limited company.

5. The Chartered Institute of Management Accountants (CIMA) requires its students to train in commercial organizations, where most of its members are employed.

6. The Chartered Institute of Public Finance and Accountancy (CIPFA) operates in the public sector.

Historically there has been a tendency for the older established bodies to fight hard to suppress those established more recently, particularly in the area of public accounting practice. For example, the journal of the ICAEW in 1908 described the newly formed London Association of Accountants as 'questionable characters who make the dregs of the profession' (Edwards 1989, p. 282).

More recently the umbrella organization of the CCAB has been effective in producing a coordinated approach from these bodies. For example, from 1976 to 1990 Statements of Standard Accounting Practice (SSAPs) were formulated by the Accounting Standards Committee (ASC), a joint committee of the CCAB. However, SSAPs were still formally issued by each individual professional body to its own members. For example, issue of a UK accounting standard on leasing was delayed because the Institute of Chartered Accountants in Ireland refused to sanction publication until the Irish government clarified certain tax issues (see *Accountancy*, February 1984, p. 15).

Two other well-established bodies are the Association of International Accountants (AIA) and the Institute of Company Accountants (I ComA).

ACCOUNTING REGULATIONS

In 1844, the first UK Companies Act required an audited balance sheet. However, in 1856 this ceased to be a legal requirement, apparently because the Government took the view that accounting requirements should be the subject of private agreement rather than legislation. In 1900, an audited balance sheet was again required. Subsequent Companies Acts, particularly those of 1948 and 1967, substantially expanded accounting disclosure and audit requirements but left most issues of accounting measurement to the discretion of companies and their accountants. In compliance with EC directives, UK legislation has prescribed formats and certain rules of accounting measurement; these provisions are now contained in the Companies Acts of 1985 and, for group accounts, 1989. However, the tone of UK legislation continues to be flexible, tending to adopt the full range of options allowed by the EC, and relying on the accounting profession to develop detailed guidance.

In 1969, the ICAEW launched an initiative for the formulation of Statements of Standard Accounting Practice (SSAPs). The other CCAB bodies joined in to support the Accounting Standards Committee (ASC), which became a subcommittee of CCAB in 1976.

The ASC formulated a series of SSAPs on a range of topics, many of which are briefly summarized below. These were issued by the individual professional bodies on their own authority, the major incentive for compliance being that auditors were expected to comment adversely on significant non-compliance.

The Companies Act 1989 introduced a new legal requirement for large companies to comply with accounting standards or explain departures in the notes to the accounts. Failure to comply with the Act can result in a court order to publish revised accounts and the possibility that the costs or revision be charged to the responsible company directors personally. In 1990, the ASC was replaced with a new regulatory regime.

Fig. 16.1 The UK regulatory structure

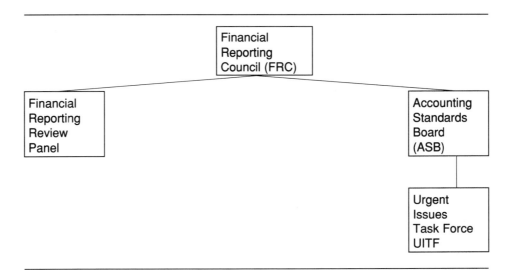

Figure 16.1 outlines the new regulatory structure. The Financial Reporting Council (FRC) has a chairman appointed jointly by the Minister for Trade and Industry and the Governor of the Bank of England. The FRC oversees the whole process of standard setting. Finance comes from the Government, the professional bodies, and private sector contributions. The review panel, headed by a lawyer, investigates apparent breaches of accounting standards by large companies. The Accounting Standards Board (ASB) formulates, issues, and withdraws accounting standards. The ASB has a full-time chairman and technical director. The Urgent Issues Task Force (UITF) seeks to find consensus solutions to new problems that emerge.

AUDITING

All UK companies, without exception, are required to have their annual accounts audited by professionally qualified auditors. Since 1948, members of four professional bodies, the ICAEW, the ICAS, the ICAI, and the CACA, have been recognized by the Government as qualified auditors. Following the Companies Act 1989 a new audit regulation regime has emerged with the following elements:

1. 'A Recognized Supervisory Body' (RSB) regulates and maintains a register of auditors.
2. A 'Recognized Qualifying Body' (RQB) establishes entry and training requirements, examination procedures, and other qualifying criteria.

All four of the established professional bodies now have RSB and RQB status.

3. A 'Qualified Person' is a member of an RQB holding a practising certificate, a person qualified under previous UK legislation benefiting from transitional provision, or a person with an equivalent overseas qualification.
4. A 'Registered Auditor' is a firm or individual granted registration by an RSB.

RSBs monitor audit firms' quality procedures. Woolf (1992) reports on the range of issues expected to be addressed in inspection procedures.

ACCOUNTING CONVENTIONS

The 'True and Fair View' (TFV) requirement was introduced into UK law in 1947. As discussed in Chapter 3 above, the UK professional accounting bodies find this an attractive convention and lobbied vigorously, and successfully, to have it included in the EC Fourth Directive. UK company law now follows the directive both in requiring any additional information needed to provide a TFV to be included in the notes to the accounts, and in requiring departure from detailed company law requirements on accounting where this is necessary to present a TFV. During 1992 two of the UK's leading accountants were interviewed on television concerning accounting practice and were asked to define the term 'true and fair view'. Their difficulty in answering the question resulted in increased public awareness of the inherent ambiguity of the expression.

UK company law provides that there should be no 'set-off' between liability and assets in the balance sheet and, alongside SSAP 2, also provides for the conventions of 'accruals', 'going concern', 'prudence', and 'consistency'. 'Substance over form' has not been explicitly adopted as a convention in company law or an accounting standard but has some recognition by virtue of inclusion in IAS 1, and is explicitly applied in accounting for leases.

PRESENTATION

Traditionally UK legislation has not prescribed any particular format for the presentation of accounts. In line with the EC Fourth Directive, formats were prescribed in the Companies Act 1981, covering the whole range of formats permitted in the Directive. In October 1992, the ASB issued FRS 3, 'Reporting Financial Performance', which required certain disclosures and classifications of items in the profit and loss account. FRS 3 includes suggested formats which comply with the standard. One of these is shown in Table 16.1.

Key elements of FRS 3 are:

1. The operating results of continuing operations, acquisitions, and discontinued operations should be separately identifiable.

2. 'Exceptionable items', being material items deriving from events or transactions that fall within the ordinary activities of the enterprise and by virtue of their size or incidence need to be disclosed to give a true and fair view. These are shown before the figure of profit or loss on ordinary activities, on the face of the profit and loss account 'if that degree of prominence is necessary', or otherwise by way of note.

3. After the figure of profit on operations, and before the figure of profit on ordinary activities before interest, three items are shown:

   (a) Profits or losses on termination of an operation.

   (b) Costs of a fundamental reorganization or restructuring.

   (c) Profits or losses on a fixed asset disposal.

4. Extraordinary items are 'material items possessing a high degree of abnormality which arise from events or transactions that fall outside the ordinary activities of the reporting entity and which are not expected to recur'. These are shown immediately before appropriations and should be 'extremely rare'.

Table 16.1 Profit and Loss Format as in FRS 3

	1993	1993	1992 as restated
	£m	£m	£m
Turnover			
Continuing operations	550		500
Acquisitions	50		
	600		
Discontinued operations	175		190
		775	690
Cost of sales		(620)	(555)
Gross profit		155	135
Net operating expenses		(104)	(83)
Operating profit			
Continuing operations	50		40
Acquisitions	6		
	56		
Discontinued operations	(15)		12
Less 1992 provision	10		
		51	52
Profit on sale of properties in continuing operations		9	6
Provision for loss on operations to be discontinued			(30)
Loss on disposal of discontinued operations	(17)		
Less 1992 provision	20		
		3	
Profit on ordinary activities before interest		63	28
Interest payable		(18)	(15)
Profit on ordinary activities before taxation		45	13
Tax on profit on ordinary activities		(14)	(4)
Profit on ordinary activities after taxation		31	9
Minority interest		(2)	(2)
[Profit before extraordinary items]		29	7
[Extraordinary items] (included only to show positioning)		–	–
Profit for the financial year		29	7
Dividends		(8)	(1)
Retained profit for the financial year		21	6
Earnings per share		39p	10p
Adjustments		xp	xp
[to be itemized and an adequate description to be given]			
Adjusted earnings per share		yp	yp

[Reason for calculating the adjusted earnings per share to be given]

5. Earnings per share (EPS) is computed by reference to profit after tax, minority interest, extraordinary items and preference dividends.

FRS 3 makes two particularly important changes to the previous rules in force:

1. Under SSAP 6 (now withdrawn) extraordinary items were defined more widely.
2. Under SSAP 3 (now amended) earnings per share were computed by reference to profit before extraordinary items.

The combined effect was that companies could manipulate their reported EPS figure, considered to be very influential with analysts, by classifying profit and loss items as extraordinary. Smith (1992) offers a review of apparent abuses of this position (p. 63–75).

GROUP ACCOUNTS

The UK has a well-established tradition of presenting consolidated accounts, required in legislation since 1947. Thus, as Ernst and Whinney (1984) observed, of all the EC member states the UK was the one least affected by the requirements of the EC Fourth Directive. Detailed requirements emerged in the Companies Acts 1985 and 1989, FRS 2, 'Accounting for Subsidiary Undertakings' and SSAP 1 'Accounting for Associated Companies'. Gee (1992) offers a useful summary of FRS 2.

A company is held to be a subsidiary (S) of a holding company (H) if one of the five following conditions applies:

1. H holds a majority of the voting rights in S.
2. H is a member of S and has the right to appoint or dismiss directors with a majority of the voting rights.
3. H is entitled to exercise a dominant influence in S.
4. H is a member of S and, by agreement, controls a majority of the voting rights.
5. H has a 'participating interest' (more than 20 per cent) in S and has a dominating interest or management is on a unified basis.

There is a requirement to prepare consolidated accounts subject to three exemptions:

1. Small and medium-sized groups are excluded from the requirements.
2. The 'EC parent exemption' exempts certain subgroups which are part of a larger group preparing consolidated accounts in line with EC requirements.
3. Where all the subsidiaries fall into categories that lead to their exclusion from consolidation.

Circumstances where an individual subsidiary is excluded from consolidation are:

1. Severe long-term restrictions inhibit control over the subsidiary. In this case the subsidiary is treated as a fixed asset investment.

2. The interest in the subsidiary is held exclusively with a view to resale. In this case the subsidiary is shown as a current asset at the lower of cost and net realizable value.

3. The subsidiary's activities are so different from those of other undertakings that inclusion in the consolidation accounts would impair the true and fair view. In such case the equity method should be used. FRS 2 discourages exclusion on these grounds, arguing that generally clear segmental reporting solves this problem.

4. Company law allows exclusion of a subsidiary where 'disproportionate expense' or 'undue delay' would result from obtaining the necessary information to include a subsidiary in the consolidated accounts. FRS 2 adds a proviso that this exemption should not apply where a subsidiary is material to the group accounts.

An accounting standard, SSAP 1, provides for equity accounting to apply in the case of an associated company. An 'associated company' is normally one where the investor has a long-term substantial investment and is able to exercise 'significant influence' over the investee. Generally 'significant influence' is assumed to arise at 20 per cent of voting shares but associated company treatment can be applied below this level where significant influence can be 'clearly demonstrated' and the investee concurs; conversely an equity holding above 20 per cent need not be treated as an associate where a lack of 'significant influence' can be demonstrated.

Merger accounting, permitted in the UK since the Companies Act 1985, is governed by SSAP 23 'Accounting for Acquisitions and Mergers'. This aims to permit merger accounting where 'only limited resources leave the group', and accordingly lays down a range of conditions such as that:

1. The offeree company must have at least 90 per cent of shares taken up in the offer.

2. At least 90 per cent of the consideration given must be in the form of equity capital.

Because companies find merger accounting attractive, some UK companies have found ingenious ways to stay within these rules. For example, a 'vendor placing' arrangement involves issuing new equity to acquire another company while providing arrangements for a third party to be willing to buy those shares immediately. Blake (1991, pp. 204–8) discusses these arrangements in detail.

GOODWILL

SSAP 22, 'Accounting for Goodwill', requires that goodwill should be computed as the difference between the fair value of the purchase consideration and the fair value of the identifiable items acquired. Positive goodwill can be accounted for in one of two ways:

1. An immediate write-off to reserves.
2. Amortization through the profit and loss account over the useful estimated economic life.

Negative goodwill should be taken directly to reserves.

FOREIGN CURRENCY TRANSLATION

SSAP 20, 'Foreign Currency Translation', was formulated in cooperation with US and Canadian standard setters and is broadly in line with FAS 52 discussed in Chapter 3 above.

When translating accounts of foreign enterprises for inclusion in the consolidated accounts the approach depends on the relationship with the subsidiary:

1. Where the trade of the foreign enterprise is more dependent on the economic environment of the investing company's currency than that of its own reporting currency the temporal method should be used. Translation gains or losses are taken through the profit and loss account. A similar approach is taken to foreign currency balances in a company's own accounts.
2. In other cases, translation is by the closing rate method, with a choice in translating the profit and loss account between the average rate and the closing rate. Translation gains or losses go direct to the reserves.

Where loans in a company's own accounts finance investment in a foreign subsidiary then, subject to certain conditions, translation gains or losses on the loans may be matched with related translation gains or losses on the investment.

INFLATION ACCOUNTING

UK inflation accounting proposals have included:

1973 ED 8 proposed a system of CPP accounting, whereby the effects of general price level movements on shareholders' funds would be shown in statements supplementary to the historic cost accounts.

1974 SSAP 7, issued as a provisional statement and therefore not binding on members of the professional accounting bodies as SSAPs usually are, followed ED 8.

1975 The Sandilands Report being the report of a committee set up by the Government to investigate the problem of accounting for inflation, rejected CPP and recommended a CCA approach.

1976 The ASC proposed, in ED 18, a full system of CCA accounts to replace historic cost accounts.

1977 Members of the ICAEW voted to reject ED 18, despite intense lobbying from leaders of the accounting profession.

1978 An interim report, the 'Hyde Guideline', recommended a supplementary statement to the accounts showing CCA profit adjustments.

1979 In ED 18 the ASC produced a proposal for a full CCA set of accounts to be presented either as the main accounts or as a supplementary statement to the historic cost accounts.

1980 The CCAB accounting bodies together issued SSAP 16, based on ED 24.

1984 ED 35 proposed some minor amendments to SSAP 16.

1985 SSAP 16 ceased to be mandatory.

1986 The ASC withdrew SSAP 16 and published a handbook on inflation accounting considering a broader range of options.

This brief history shows the range of approaches considered during the UK 'inflation accounting' debate.

Westwick (1980) offers an interesting and authoritative review of the UK inflation accounting debate. Amongst the points of interest that he notes are:

1. Historically there has been little interest in the UK in inflation accounting while inflation rates have been below 10 per cent. This helps to explain why, since the early 1980s, UK accountants have lost interest in the topic.

2. The UK government appears to have deliberately sabotaged efforts to promote a CPP-type system. One suggested reason for this is that it might lead to a general trend towards indexation and, consequently, higher tolerance of inflation.

FIXED ASSETS

The accounting rules on fixed assets illustrate the permissive character of UK accounting regulation. Such assets may be shown at either historic cost or at a valuation; different assets, even within the same category, may be shown on a different basis. Capitalization of borrowing costs during construction of a fixed asset is permitted.

Where revaluation occurs there are no rules on the frequency or basis of valuation. An exposure draft issued in 1990 did propose that valuation should be on a net realizable value basis, but in practice replacement cost is more commonly used.

Depreciation is the subject of an accounting standard, SSAP 12. This provides that depreciation should be allocated on a systematic basis over an asset life estimated on a realistic basis. For tax purposes the Inland Revenue disallows a company's own calculation of depreciation and substitutes a standard computation of 'capital allowance'. In defining fixed assets subject to depreciation SSAP 12 specifically includes buildings.

An accounting standard, SSAP 19, applies a special set of accounting rules for investment properties. This standard arose because property companies lobbied vigorously against the requirement in SSAP 12 to depreciate buildings. While a variety of arguments were put forward to support this position, the basic problem appears to have been that the provision of depreciation would have reduced reported profits to the point where payment of dividends would have been difficult (see Blake 1991, pp. 165–6). Accordingly SSAP 19 provides that no depreciation is required on investment properties, except for leases with less than 20 years to run. Instead, such properties must be revalued each year. Revaluation surpluses and deficits are taken direct to a revaluation reserve except that, to the extent that a deficit exceeds the balance on the revaluation reserve, such an excess deficit must be changed in the profit and loss account. To have such a distinctive set of rules for just one type of fixed asset does seem inconsistent. Nevertheless, Weetman and Gray (1992) report that this pragmatic approach is popular with both the property companies and investment analysts.

RESEARCH AND DEVELOPMENT

SSAP 13, 'Accounting for Research and Development', distinguishes between research expenditure, aimed at gaining new scientific or technical knowledge, and development expenditure, aimed at using scientific or technical knowledge for a specific commercial project. All research expenditure must be written off as it is incurred. For development expenditure, companies are allowed to choose between a write-off policy and a deferral policy, but where the latter policy is chosen then deferral is only permitted to the extent that the related project can meet a number of stringent tests to assess viability. In practice, most UK companies opt for a write-off policy. Blake (1990, pp. 35–6) suggests a list of factors that companies might consider when choosing which policy to adopt.

In formulating a standard on this topic the ASC initially opted for only allowing a write-off policy. A factor that influenced the ASC in permitting a deferral policy is reported by Eccles and Lifford (1979, p. 9). In the 1970s, Government contracts for development work on defence projects allowed an agreed profit percentage to be charged on capital employed in projects by developers. The Government would only allow development expenditure to be counted as part of such capital employed if it was shown in the published balance sheet. Therefore defence contractors lobbied, successfully, for a deferral policy to be permitted.

STOCK AND WORK IN PROGRESS

An accounting standard, SSAP 9, provides that stock should be valued at the lower of cost and net realizable value; replacement cost is specifically excluded except in the context of a current cost accounting system. Cost should be computed on a basis that includes apportioned overhead costs. Company law permits a full range of cost-flow methods to be applied, but SSAP 9 excludes LIFO and base-stock; there is little interest in LIFO in the UK because the Inland Revenue does not accept it for tax purposes. Where borrowings can be related to specific long-term contracts, interest on those borrowings *may* be treated as part of the cost of the related work in progress.

Long-term contract work in progress should be treated on the 'percentage of completion method' so that attributable profit should be taken to the profit and loss account as work progresses, while 'foreseeable losses' should be written off as soon as they are foreseen.

LEASING

SSAP 21, 'Accounting for Leases and Hire Purchase Agreements', covers this topic. A distinction is made between two types of lease:

1. A 'finance lease' is one 'that transfers substantially all the risks and rewards of ownership of an asset to the lessee'. Normally that will arise where 'at the inception of a lease the present value of the minimum lease payments, including any initial payment, amounts to substantially all (normally 90 per cent or more) of the fair value of the leased asset'.

2. An operating lease is any lease other than a finance lease.

A finance lease must be accounted for by the lessee as an asset and as an obligation to pay future rentals. The asset is subject to depreciation. Finance charges on the lease obligation are allocated over the period of the lease agreement, normally on an actuarial basis. The lessor treats the amount due from the lessee as a financial asset. By contrast, in the case of an operating lease, the lessor records the leased asset as a fixed asset, providing depreciation, while operating lease rentals are allocated to profit and loss on a straight-line basis both by the lessor and the lessee.

The UK definition of a finance lease is, in principle, a wide-ranging one. However, many UK companies are attracted by the idea of keeping lease commitments 'off-balance sheet'. Accordingly, lease agreements are often constructed so as to justify 'operating lease' status even though their basic character is as a financing measure. SSAP 21 also requires that future commitments for both finance and operating leases are shown in the notes to the accounts. Thus analysts who observe large 'operating lease' commitments for some years ahead will normally regard these as financing arrangements and adjust their estimates of the true gearing position accordingly.

DEFERRED TAXATION

The potential for difference between accounting and taxable income in the UK is particularly substantial. From 1958 the ICAEW recommended full deferred tax provision by the liability method, and this recommendation was widely followed. In 1975 the ASC produced SSAP 11 prescribing full deferral, permitting either the deferral or the liability method. At that time the UK tax authorities allowed two particular deductions, for 100 per cent first year allowances (abolished in 1984) on capital investment, and for stock relief (abolished in 1981) on inflationary increases in stock values. Companies objected to the impact of full deferred taxation on their accounts, some having difficulty with debt covenants in particular. As reported by the then Head of the Government Accounting Service, the UK government was persuaded to put pressure on the ASC to take a more flexible approach (Sharp 1979). In response, the ASC withdrew SSAP 11 and issued SSAP 15 which now prescribes only partial deferral to the extent that a liability is expected to crystallize, computed by the liability method. Hope and Briggs (1982) review this debate.

PENSIONS

SSAP 24 addresses the complex issue of accounting for pension obligations. The accounting objective is that all pension obligations, whether legally binding or discretionary, should be accounted for. The accounting objective is to allocate the expected costs of providing pensions on a systematic and rational basis over the period of the employees' services. For large UK companies, pension schemes are generally on a 'defined benefit' basis, with contributions paid into a separate pension fund. As a result of a buoyant stock market and a tendency for companies to slim down workforces, pension funds have tended to be more than adequate to cover a full actuarial valuation of pension obligations.

POST BALANCE SHEET EVENTS

SSAP 17, 'Accounting for Post Balance Sheet Events' makes a similar distinction between adjusting events and non-adjusting events in line with IAS 10. In practice there is a greater tendency towards treating events as adjusting in the UK than in many other countries.

CONCLUSION

The appearance of UK accounts has changed substantially as a result of EC directives but, thanks the ambiguous formulation of the 'true and fair view' convention, the underlying accounting practices continue to be the most flexible and the least conservative in Europe.

REFERENCES

Blake, J. (1990) 'SSAP 13: Accounting for Research and Development', *Accountants Record*, June, pp. 32–6.

Blake, J. (1991) *Accounting Standards*, 3rd edn, Pitman.

Eccles, G.W. and Lifford, W.C. (1979) *Accountants Digest Guide to Accounting Standards. Accounting for Research and Development*, ICAEW.

Edwards, J.R. (1989) *A History of Financial Accounting*, Routledge.

Ernst and Whinney (1984) *The Impact of the Seventh Directive*, Financial Times Business Information.

Gee, P. (1992) 'Consolidated accounts. The new standard', *Company Accounts*, October, pp. 19–21.

Hope, A. and Briggs, J. (1982) 'Accounting policy making – some lessons from the deferred tax debate', *Accounting and Business Research*, Spring, pp. 83–96.

Hope, A. and Gray, R.H. (1982) 'Power and policy making: the development of an R&D standard', *Journal of Business Finance and Accounting*, Winter, pp. 531–58.

Sharp, K. (1979) 'The Whitehall perspective: Government and accounting standards', *Accountant*, July 19, pp. 67–9.

Smith, T. (1992) *Accounting for Growth*, Century Business.

Weetman, P. and Gray, S.J. (1992) *SSAP 19: Accounting for Investment Properties*, Institute of Chartered Accountants of Scotland.

Westwick, C. (1980) 'The lessons to be learnt from the development of inflation accounting in the UK', *Accounting and Business Research*, Autumn, pp. 353–72.

Woolf, E. (1992) *Preserving Your Right to Audit*, CCH.

CHAPTER 17

Eastern Europe

INTRODUCTION **In this chapter we briefly consider the accounting approaches that have developed in the centrally controlled economies of Eastern Europe. Specifically, we review:**

1. The distinctive features of accounting in a socialist economy.

2. The characteristics of the accounting profession.

3. Special issues in accounting for joint ventures.

DISTINCTIVE FEATURES OF SOCIALIST ACCOUNTING

Bailey (1988, pp. 1–18) reviews the factors that make accounting different in a Socialist as compared to a market economy. In a Socialist 'command' economy, economic resources are state-owned. The management of each State enterprise is allocated economic resources and instructed to use these to achieve production. The enterprise, in pursuing maximum production, is 'resource constrained', by the limits on the inputs of resources allocated by the central planners. The primary concern of the management is with technical feasibility. By contrast, in a market economy most firms are 'demand constrained', limiting production to what they can sell. The prime concern of the management is with commercial viability. Specific effects on accounting within a Socialist economy are:

1. Prices are set centrally, and do not respond to supply and demand. As Gorelik (1973) observes:

   Accounting profits and profitability can be used as measures of economic efficiency only if prices are a measure of economic efficiency. Since Soviet prices do not reflect economic efficiency, Soviet accounting profits also fail to measure the economic efficiency of enterprise operations (p. 142).

2. Accounting reports, rather than being published, are submitted to specific supervising organizations. Berry (1984) reports that at 1 January 1980 in the Soviet Union, accounts had to be submitted to:

   (a) Superior organizations.

   (b) 'Gosbank', responsible for cash management, and 'Stroybank', responsible for investment.

   (c) The Central Statistical Administration.

(d) The Ministry of Finance.

Deadlines for enterprises were tight:

Monthly and quarterly balance sheets	12 days after reporting period
Annual reports and balance sheet	By January 20

To meet these tight deadlines, Kupzhasar (1974) reports that the accounting in the Soviet Union was the first management function to use computers.

3. The enterprise may undertake a range of activities in the field of social provision for its workforce that require separate accounting. Satubaldin (1976) reports that in the USSR at that time profit was analysed into three headings:

(a) Profit or loss from the basic productive activity.

(b) Profit or loss from subsidiary productive activity.

(c) Other items, examples including profits or losses from housing and communal household operations, and expenses of 'buildings, quarters, structures, gardens, parks, and pioneer camps transferred to trade unions for use without compensation' (p. 98).

4. Bailey (1988) observes:

The Socialist enterprise is not autonomous and, in principle, its corporate plan is a component of the national economic plan. Consequently 'the national economy, or its industrial segment, becomes the accounting entity and the individual enterprise is represented as an accounting subentity' (p. 10).

For one accounting entity there can only be one set of accounting policies. Thus there is not the opportunity for accounting policy choice at the enterprise level that we find in market economies – Gorelik (1973) cites Tatur (1959):

The statutes, which are binding on all Union Republics, ensure a uniform system of bookkeeping at all enterprises in the Soviet Union, and as a result accounting data can be compiled for the individual branches of the national economy and for the national economy as a whole.

By contrast, in Yugoslavia, the central control of the economy was relaxed to permit some degree of control by workers at the local level. The consequence was that while standardized accounting returns to the Government were prescribed by a Governmental body, the Social Accountancy Service, reports to the workers could be on a more flexible basis. Turk (1976) explained:

The Social Accountancy Service demands quarterly statements of financial result and annual statements; the latter must be filed, on uniform schedules, by the end of February of the next year. These external accounting statements must be made up not only for the work organization as a whole, but also for each basic organization of associated labor within its scope. For the rest, accounting is to be mainly directed to the requirements of the organization of associated labor, of its workers in their capacity of self-managers, and of those who are in charge of operations. The accountant is obliged to make the content of internal and external reports uniform. The schedules of the former may be adapted to the requirements of the organization of associated labor; hence they differ from the latter (p. 117).

5. Brzezin and Jaruga (1988) offer the following definition of the role of the accountant:

> In a Socialist economy, accounting services the following functions exclusively: preparation of documents and recording of clearing transactions, preparation of documents and recording of revenues and expenditures of the Government and all institutions financed directly by the State Budget, recording national assets assigned to business entities and recording the persons (cashier, store-keeper, etc.) responsible for a certain part of these assets (p. 50).

> While these are important functions – Lenin explicitly acknowledged the key role of accounting in a Socialist economy – they do not require the exercise of high-level skills, given central prescription of accounting methods. Therefore, the accounting role in a Socialist economy tends to be a low status one, with the planning role exercised by the 'chief economist', whose background is often technical.

THE ACCOUNTING PROFESSION

At the time of the Russian Revolution an accounting profession had hardly begun to emerge in Russia. A journal on accounting *Schetovodstvo*, was published from 1888 to 1904 but only achieved a circulation of some 500 copies (Bailey 1977; 1982). Some element of accounting education appears to have been taught in business courses. In 1916 Price Waterhouse and WB Peat and Co opened an office jointly in the then Petrograd, but staff fled at the time of the Revolution 'leaving the firm's books and petty cash behind' (Bailey 1982, p. 25).

In the immediate aftermath of the revolution, during the period 1918–21, the accounting function in Russia disappeared completely. Indeed, there was even an attempt during that period to dispense with the use of money. Thereafter a range of accounting controls were introduced, and those who had gained experience of teaching accounting in pre-revolutionary times were encouraged to publish, drawing on developments in accounting thought in other countries. The most influential theorists to be translated were German, notably Schmalenbach. It appears that these Russian academics found the more theoretical approach of the German writers particularly attractive. Bailey (1982) reports of the leading Russian academic, A.M. Galagan, that he took a dim view of the English accounting tradition:

R.T.C. LIBRARY, LETTERKENNY

In the opinion of A.M. Galagan, with the growth of industry in England, all thought of developing an accounting theory (*schetovedenie*) had been repudiated so that nearly all of the published books on accounting were but expressions of accounting practice (*schetovodstvo*) (p. 27).

From 1923 to 1930 the journal *Schetovodstvo* was revived, while in 1926 a Soviet delegation took part in the International Congress of Accountants in Amsterdam. However, the links to Western practice were broken in 1931 when a special court was convened to denounce A.M. Galagan for 'harmful bourgeois accounting theories and practices' (Bailey 1982, p. 31).

From 1930 to 1960, in a rigorously centrally planned economy, there was no role for skilled accountancy at the level of the individual enterprise. Bailey (1975) quotes an assessment of the level of skill required by the enterprise bookkeeper:

Accounting as a classification and measurement system can be operated, understood and used by folks at the high school level.

Within each enterprise a chief bookkeeper is responsible for record keeping, financial reporting, and internal audit. Berry (1984) points out that the appointment of the chief bookkeeper is the responsibility of the superior unit that oversees the enterprise; any conflict between the director and the chief bookkeeper within an enterprise is settled by the director of the superior unit; and the chief bookkeeper's service organization is strictly separate from that of other service organizations within the firm. The chief bookkeeper of an enterprise reports both to the director of that enterprise and to the chief bookkeeper of the superior unit. Thus the chief bookkeeper tends to be seen as an instrument of control by the supervising unit rather than as a member of the management team. This may well have been a necessary control mechanism.

Crombie (1992) reports an example of how a corrupt bookkeeper, in collaboration with the enterprise management team, was able to profit from abuses of the system:

The books, kept in roubles, not in production units, and subdivided into 105 separate accounts, never read any differently than the books of any other Socialist enterprise (p. 11).

From the time of the Economic Reform Plan of 1965, which rehabilitated the profit criterion, there has been an awareness of the need to improve accounting skills. Bailey (1977) reports the holding of a national accounting conference in 1975 as a step towards this end. Similarly, in 1978 a leading specialist called for *perestroika* (reconstruction) of the accounting profession – a word that has since become internationally known in another context (Bailey 1988, pp. 154–5). Since 1989, Russia has had an Association of Accountants. However, in the new economic environment, a rapid training programme is needed to update Russian accounting skills. Cheney (1990) reports that Western accounting firms setting up in Russia have found it necessary to invest heavily in training locally recruited personnel.

Some other Eastern European countries have a stronger tradition of professional accounting. In Poland, a 'well-paid accounting and auditing profession developed' (Jaruga 1992, p. 977) with an Association of Accountants founded in 1907. In 1956 an Institute of State Authorized Accountants was formed. Jaruga (1976) reports on how membership of this body built up. The Ministry of Finance conferred membership on the basis of State examinations and work experience. Qualified members continued to work in the State enterprises in their normal accounting employment. However they would receive paid leave, averaging one month each year, to perform audit assignments. In addition to their normal pay they would receive prescribed fees for this work. At the end of 1975 there were 6,662 of these qualified accountants. Thus Poland is moving into a free market economy with the nucleus of a trained and experienced audit and accounting profession. Nevertheless, Dixon and Laidlaw (1992) observe of Poland:

> The future is one of considerable uncertainty reinforced by the problem of a lack of skills to cope with the demands of accountancy for a market economy (p. 22).

JOINT VENTURES

The operation of joint ventures, both between East European partners and with Western partners, has created some interesting accounting challenges.

Kortan (1976) discusses joint ventures between members of the Council for Mutual Economic Aid, the association for economic cooperation between Eastern European states. He observes that, given that the legal systems of those states are based on uniform State ownership of the means of production, a difficulty arises in a joint venture based on enterprises in two countries. On the one hand, since each participating entity only has the degree of control over assets entrusted to it permitted by the state in which it is based, then ultimate individual ownership of the assets remains with the respective participating states. An alternative view is that some new form of interstate or supranational co-ownership is created. In either case, such a joint venture raises complex issues as to the subject matter to be accounted for. However, allocation of benefits between the partners tends to be in terms of physical output rather than money. Kortan cites the example of a Polish–Hungarian joint venture in a cotton mill, where each partner supplies half the raw material and receives half the output.

Gorski (1974) identifies the problems of organizing a joint venture in Eastern Europe as:

1. The protection of the ownership of foreign assets in Socialist countries;

2. The protection of the influence of foreign partners to make certain decisions in the field of management, production technology, and sales;

3. The procedure to estimate economic results of joint activities; and

4. The provision of possibilities for the transfer of profits to capitalist countries (p. 32).

Hoyt and Maples (1980) consider the problems that US multinationals have had in accounting for joint ventures in Eastern European countries. They identify four distinct features of such a joint venture:

1. The foreign firm is prohibited from owning an interest in productive facilities even by means of a host country intermediary. The firm has instead ownership rights to a share of the output of the joint enterprise plus certain management authority regarding quality control, engineering design, training of the labor force, and, in some cases, marketing networks.

2. Power in an organizational sense flows from the state to the foreign firm through the contract rather than through a body of common law relating to property rights.

3. There is an absence of currency measures for valuation of individual transactions.

4. There is a fundamental difference in the valuation bases used to price each partner's share of investment contributed to the joint enterprise (p. 110).

Hoyt and Maples discuss the problem this poses in applying US accounting principles where 'the concept of a market economy and the rules for valuing assets and enterprises are absent' (p. 113).

CONCLUSION

The countries of Eastern Europe emerge from a period of centrally directed economies with relatively weak accounting professions. Their tradition of rigorous central control over accounting practice, and the strong influence of German theorists in the first half of this century, may well lead them to develop accounting systems along the German or French model rather than the more flexible Anglo-American approach.

REFERENCES

Bailey, D.T. (1975) 'The business of accounting: East and West', *Journal of Management Studies*, Vol. 12, No. 1, pp. 28–44. Reprinted in Bailey (1988) (see below).

Bailey, D.T. (1977) 'The accounting profession in Russia', *Accountancy*, March, pp. 70–3.

Bailey, D.T. (1982) 'Accounting in Russia: the European connection', *International Journal of Accounting*, Fall, pp. 1–36.

Bailey, D.T. (1988) *Accounting in Socialist Countries*, Routledge.

Berry, M. (1984) 'Accounting in Socialist countries' in Holzer, H.P. (ed.) *International Accounting*, pp. 409–52, Harper and Row.

Brzezin, W. and Jaruga, A. (1988) 'Accounting evolution in a planned economy' in Bailey (1988) (see above) pp. 41–58.

Cheney, G.A. (1990) 'Western accounting arrives in Eastern Europe', *Journal of Accountancy*, September, pp. 40–3.

Crombie, R. (1992) 'Out of control', *Accountancy Age*, September, pp. 8–12.

Dixon, R. and Laidlaw, J. (1992) 'Accounting developments in Poland', *Management Accounting*, November, pp. 20–2.

Gorelik, G. (1973) 'Notes on the development and problems of Soviet Union accounting', *International Journal of Accounting*, Vol. 9, No. 1, pp. 135–48.

Gorski, J. (1974) 'The Council for Mutual Economic Assistance (CMEA): its role in the economic integration of Socialist countries, *International Journal of Accounting*, Vol. 10, No. 1, pp. 19–32.

Hoyt, R.E. and Maples, L.D. (1980) 'Accounting for joint ventures with the Soviet Bloc and China', *International Journal of Accounting*, Vol. 16, No. 1, pp. 105–24.

Jaruga, A.A. (1976) 'Recent developments of the auditing profession in Poland', *International Journal of Accounting*, Vol. 12, No. 1, pp. 101–9.

Jaruga, A.A. (1992) 'Poland' in Alexander, D. and Archer, S. (eds) *The European Accounting Guide*, pp. 975–90, Academic Press.

Kortan, J. (1976) 'International economic organizations and joint enterprises in Socialist countries – principles of operation and management', *International Journal of Accounting*, Vol. 12, No. 1, pp. 147–65.

Kupzhasar, N. (1974) 'Computer applications in Soviet accounting', *International Journal of Accounting*, Vol. 10, No. 1, pp. 33–43.

Satubaldin, S. (1976) 'Methods of analyzing profits of industrial enterprises in the USSR', *International Journal of Accounting*, Vol. 12, No. 1, pp. 91–9.

Tatur, S. (1959) 'The organization of accounting in the Soviet Union', *Accountant's Magazine*, May, pp. 379–80.

Turk, I. (1976) 'Recent professional statements of accounting principles and ethics in Yugoslavia', *International Journal of Accounting*, Vol. 12, No. 1, pp. 111–20.

CHAPTER 18

International Analysis of Accounts

INTRODUCTION **As we have seen, a major argument behind the call for international harmonization of accounting practices has been to facilitate the work of the financial analyst. In this chapter we explore some of the problems.**

THE DEMAND FOR INTERNATIONAL COMPARISONS

A demand for international accounting comparisons may come from any user of accounts with a direct interest in a company based in another country or an interest in comparing a company in their own country with a competitor which happens to be based in another country. Investors, in particular, may wish to hold a portfolio of shares which spreads across a number of countries because:

1. A diversified portfolio of shares reduces risk. That means that by holding shares in a number of companies you are less likely to lose as a result of one company's misfortune. Broadly speaking, the greater number of shares in a market the more opportunity there is to diversify and thereby reduce risk. Solnik (1974) identified opportunities to diversify away the following percentages of risk in national markets:

US	73%
UK	65%
France	67%
Germany	56%
Netherlands	76%
Switzerland	56%

By contrast, an international portfolio would diversify away 88 per cent of risk. Thus international investment would reduce risk for an investor from any country, including the USA, and would be particularly useful for investors from countries with relatively small domestic opportunities to diversify. One reason for this is that stock markets in different countries do not necessarily move in the same direction. For example, share prices may tend to fall in New York at the same time as they rise in Paris (Levy and Sarnat 1970).

2. Apart from investing directly in shares of foreign companies there are two

ways in which a shareholder can seek to achieve international diversification:

(a) Invest in a mutual fund with an international portfolio. Eiteman et al. (1992) cite a study by Proffitt and Seitz (1983) that shows that over the period 1974–82 such funds consistently outperformed the US stock market.

(b) Invest in a multinational spread across a range of countries. This strategy seems less effective. Jacquillat and Solnik (1978) found that the share price of multinational companies moved in a very similar way to purely domestic companies.

3. Some foreign stock markets may be more profitable than domestic stock markets. From a US perspective, Choi and Mueller (1984) offer a list of foreign markets where during the 1970s security returns outperformed those in the USA (pp. 296–7). Some of the world's newer stock markets may offer opportunities to apply profitably techniques of analysis that are in common use, and are therefore less profitable, in more established markets. Ang and Pohlman (1978), while finding indications of market efficiency in Far Eastern markets, saw some possible opportunities for such applications.

4. Investors may be attracted to a foreign country because certain types of investment opportunity are not available domestically. For example, in a country where public utilities are nationalized an investor may choose to invest in privately owned public utilities in other countries. Similarly, certain countries offer investors special opportunities, e.g. the exploitation of mineral resources in Australia.

THE USEFULNESS OF ACCOUNTS

Studies in a number of countries suggest that investors do find published accounts a useful source of information. However, the relative importance of accounts, and the extent to which different parts of the accounts are found useful, vary.

For example:

1. Arnold et al. (1984) compared the approaches of investment analysts in the USA and the UK. They found that US analysts consider previous accounts over a longer period (5.7 years) than UK analysts (4.6 years); that 80.6 per cent of US analysts 'almost always' or 'usually' compute financial ratios compared to 65.4 per cent of UK analysts; that 43.5 per cent of US analysts 'almost always' or 'usually' estimate the net present value of future cash flows compared to 15.9 per cent of UK analysts; that UK analysts rank the chairmens' statement as the sixth most important information source compared with a ranking of thirteenth in the USA, while conversely US analysts rank trade journals as their seventh most important source compared with a ranking of fourteenth in the UK.

2. Belkaoui et al. (1977) compared Canadian, US, and European financial analysts. They contrasted a 'European approach to investment decision making' which 'has been more debt orientated with analysis concentrated on the balance sheet' compared to 'the typical North American approach' which 'is more oriented towards equity investment, the income statement and corporate earning power' (pp. 20–1). They listed 29 types of information item and found that while Canadian and US analysts disagreed on the value of six items, North American and European analysts disagreed on the value of 17 items.

3. A study of users of accounts in New Zealand, the UK, and the USA is reported by Chang and Most (1981) and Chang et al. (1983). They found a number of differences between user priorities. For example, out of 12 parts of the accounts the 5–10-year summary was ranked third in New Zealand, seventh in the USA, and tenth in the UK.

4. Choi and Czechowicz (1983) compared the ways in which US-based multinationals and non-US-based multinationals analyse the performance of their foreign subsidiaries. As an example:

   US-based multinationals tend to emphasize the importance of cash flows to the parent, whereas non-US multinationals express a preference for cash flows to the foreign subsidiary, indicating a more local perspective (p. 16).

Given the range of different priorities identified by these studies, accounts designed to meet user demand in one country are unlikely to meet a different type of demand in another.

ACCESS TO AND TIMING OF ACCOUNTS

In some countries, such as Liechtenstein, filed company accounts are not publicly available. By contrast, in the UK all company accounts are publicly available from the Registrar of Companies. In some countries only the accounts of companies above a certain size have to be filed. In the USA, where company law varies state by state, the availability of small company accounts depends on the state of incorporation. Similarly, many, but not all, countries have services offering summaries of large country accounts in card index or computerized form.

The time allowed for publishing accounts also varies between countries. For example, for listed companies the time limits are 60 days in Korea, 90 days in the USA, and 7 months in the UK.

LANGUAGE AND TERMINOLOGY

Accounting terminology offers a good example of how the USA and the UK are two countries divided by a common language. European Spanish and South American Spanish offer a similar contrast. Examples include:

USA	UK	
USA	*UK*	
Inventory	Stock	
Stock	Investments	
Sales	Turnover	
Receivables	Debtors	
Payables	Creditors	

Spain	South America	
Spain	*South America*	
Beneficio	Utilidad	(Income)
Contable	Contador	(Accountant)
Existencias	Inventorios	(Stock)
Amortización	Depreciación	(Depreciation)
Gasto	Egreso	(Cost)

Nobes and Maeda (1990) point out that Japanese accounts, where they include an English translation, normally use US rather than UK terminology.

Choi and Mueller (1984) report on a survey of company accounts where an English language version is offered. Of leading companies in each country the proportion not offering English language versions for countries covered in this text were:

Belgium	10%	–	50%
Denmark	Less	than	10%
France	More	than	50%
Germany	10%	–	50%
Italy	10%	–	50%
Ireland	Less	than	10%
Netherlands	Less	than	10%
Spain	More	than	50%
Sweden	Less	than	10%
UK	Less	than	10%

(adapted from Choi and Mueller – 1984 p. 301)

Archer and McLeay (1989) report on a review of the published accounts of 42 large European companies reporting in more than one language; none of the companies was British. All the companies prepared an English language translation; the next most common language (other than that of the home country) was French (12 companies). Other non-domestic languages offered were German, Spanish, Italian, and Portuguese. In some cases companies took steps to make clear the language of the definitive version. Thus the Volkswagen annual report is quoted:

> This version of our annual report is a translation from the German original. The German text is definitive (p. 84).

This sensitivity by companies to the potential commitment implied in publishing accounting data for non-domestic users can be found in other contexts. As an example, Montedison reports in Italian lire but also gives a reconciliation between the profit figure in the accounts and profit on a US basis. The 1990 report observes that this is reported at a translation rate of 1262 lire to the US dollar and that: 'This convenience translation should not be construed as representation that the Italian lire amounts could be converted at that rate'.

Where an analyst is considering the accounts of a company from another country where a translation is not published, possible approaches are:

1. Translation of the accounts personally, using an accounting lexicon.

2. Employment of translators.

3. Employment of an investment advisory service that uses its own translators.

CURRENCY PROBLEMS

When a set of accounts are presented in a foreign currency, this presents no problems in the application of ratio analysis. If the reader is not familiar with the reporting currency, there may be a problem in lacking an awareness of the order of magnitude that the figures represent.

Sometimes a set of accounts will offer a translation of figures into more than one currency. This can be confusing when a number of accounting periods are compared, each translated at a different exchange rate. This can be illustrated if we take the 1991 accounts of the Royal Dutch Shell and consider the annual change in turnover as shown in Table 18.1 by the five-year summary in both UK pounds and US dollars, translated at exchange rates fluctuating over the five years between £1 : $1.43, and £1 : $1.94.

Table 18.1

Royal Dutch Shell – Change in Sale Proceeds Net of Related Taxes

	Measured in:	
	£ UK	*$ US*
1991	– 2.2%	–3.6%
1990	+ 13.9%	+ 24.7%
1989	+ 18.6%	+ 9.0%
1988	–7.9%	+ 0.1%
1987	+ 8.1%	+ 20.9%

FORMAT AND DISCLOSURE DIFFERENCES

National practices in the format used to present accounts need to be understood by the analyst.

For example, in the UK assets are shown starting with the least liquid going to the most liquid, while in the USA the reverse is the case. In the UK, the period within which an item must be realized, if it is to be classified as current, is normally up to one year, in Germany up to four years.

National formats may also reveal additional data. For example, in Denmark a number of companies distinguish between fixed and variable costs on the face of the accounts. In Sweden, large companies commonly use a format that first shows profit computed in line with best international practice, then lists adjustments required to bring the accounts into line with Sweden's tax-based accounting rules.

The levels and nature of disclosure also vary enormously between countries and, within countries, between different types and size of enterprise. The UK is unusual in requiring audited accounts from companies of all sizes.

ACCOUNTING CONVENTIONS

In Chapter 1 above we have considered the evidence that different countries operate different accounting rules; in Chapter 2 we have seen the range of organizations that are striving to narrow those differences; in Chapter 3 we have considered the specific types of difference, and in subsequent chapters we have considered the specific accounting rules in European countries.

This range of different approaches to accounting presents a fundamental obstacle to the analyst trying to compare the accounts of companies from different countries. The analyst's task has two elements:

1. To identify comparable elements in the accounts. Within Europe the Fourth Directive has been tolerably successful in procuring similar formats.

2. To recompute the figures in accounts in different countries on to a comparable basis. The list of topics reviewed in Chapter 3 might be regarded as a checklist of items to consider for adjustment on to a consistent and meaningful basis for comparison.

CULTURAL DIFFERENCES

Cultural differences mean that the same accounting rules applied in different countries may produce very different results. As an example, Choi et al. (1983) made a comparative study of accounting ratios for companies in the USA, Japan and Korea. The US companies appeared to earn a higher rate of return on capital and to have a lower level of gearing. These differences were reduced when adjustments to common accounting policies were made, but remained material. The question then arose as to whether the higher rate of return on capital indicated more successful performance, and the lower gearing level indicated a safer financial position, for the US companies. A wide range of cultural factors suggested that this was not a reasonable conclusion because of a wide range of cultural differences between the three countries. Examples include:

1. Investors in Japanese companies are often trade contacts such as suppliers and customers. They are looking for growth in trading, so as to boost their own trading opportunities, rather than high profits.
2. At the end of World War II, Japan's huge conglomerates, the *Zaibatsu*, were broken up into separate businesses. However, new enterprise groupings formed around the banks, and the *Keiretsu* have strong personal ties. Borrowings from a fellow *Keiretsu* group member are shown as external debt, but in practice have the same character as the loans from a fellow group company which in the US would be cancelled out on consolidation.
3. In Korea, the Government assumes a major role in corporate finance. Thus a company with high borrowings is one which has received loans as a result of government direction. This sign of Government favour should be read, therefore, as an indicator of strength rather than weakness.

Sarathy and Chatterjee (1984) use published accounts to compare the financial structures of Japanese and US companies. They identify 'short-term borrowings that are in truth long-term debt in that they are constantly rolled over' (p. 78), and 'parent companies' exercising 'de facto control' over related companies 'though nothing is stipulated in writing'.

Suzuki and Wright (1985) looked at accounting indicators that suggested imminent corporate bankruptcy. They found a range of non-financial factors that explained the difference between companies that were and were not forced into liquidation. They concluded: 'Other measures, reflecting the firm's social importance and the strength of its main-bank relationship, seem at least as important as accounting information in determining which of the financially troubled companies will actually go bankrupt' (p. 109).

CONCLUSION

Accounting differences are an important problem for the international financial analyst. In addition, different cultural environments also require subtle interpretation.

REFERENCES

Ang, J.S. and Pohlman, R.A. (1978) 'A note on the price behaviour of Far Eastern stocks', *Journal of International Business Studies*, Spring/Summer, pp. 103–7.

Archer, S. and McLeay, S. (1989). 'Financial reporting by interlisted European countries: issues in transnational disclosure' in Hopwood, A.G. *International Pressures for Accounting Change*, pp. 73–115, Prentice Hall.

Arnold, J., Moizer, P. and Noreen, E. (1984) 'Investment, appraisal methods of financial analysts: a comparative study of US and UK practices', *International Journal of Accounting*, Spring, pp. 1–18.

Belkaoui, A., Kahl, A. and Peyrard, J. (1977) 'Information needs of financial analysts: an international comparison', *International Journal of Accounting*, Fall, pp. 19–27.

Chang, L.S. and Most, K.S. (1981) 'An international comparison of investor uses of financial statements', *International Journal of Accounting*, Fall, pp. 43–60.

Chang, L.S., Most, K.S. and Brain, C.W. (1983) 'The utility of annual reports: an international study', *Journal of International Business Studies*, Spring/Summer, pp. 63–84.

Choi, F.D.S. and Mueller, G.G. (1984) *International Accounting*, Prentice Hall.

Choi, F.D.S. and Czechowicz, J.J. (1983) 'Assessing foreign subsidiary performance: a multinational comparison', *Management International Review*, **23**, 4, pp. 14–25.

Choi, F.D.S., Hino, H., Min, S.K., Nam, S.O., Ujie, J. and Stonehill, S.I. (1983) 'Analysing foreign financial statements: the use and misuse of international ratio analysis', *Journal of International Business Studies*, Spring/Summer, pp. 113–31.

Eiteman, D.K., Stonehill, A.I. and Moffett, M.H. (1992) *Multinational Business Finance*, Addison Wesley.

Jacquillat, B. and Solnik, B.H. (1978) 'Multinationals are poor tools for diversification', *Journal of Portfolio Management*, Winter, pp. 8–12.

Levy, H. and Sarnat, M. (1970) 'International diversification of investment portfolios', *American Economic Review*, September, pp. 668–75.

Nobes, C. and Maeda, S. (1990) 'Japanese accounts: interpreters needed', *Accountancy*, September, pp. 82–4.

Proffitt, D. and Seitz, N. (1983) 'The performance of internationally diversified mutual funds', *Journal of the Midwest Finance Association*, December.

Sarathy, R. and Chatterjee, S. (1984) 'The divergence of Japanese and US corporate financial structure', *Journal of International Business Studies*, Winter, pp. 75–89.

Solnik, B.H. (1974) 'Why not diversify internationally rather than domestically', *Financial Analysts Journal*, July–August, pp. 48–54.

Suzuki, S. and Wright, R.W. (1985) 'Financial structure and bankruptcy risk in Japanese companies', *Journal of International Business Studies*, Spring, pp. 97–110.

AUTHOR INDEX

SUBJECT INDEX